Tide Players

Tide Players

The Movers and Shakers of a Rising China

Jianying Zha

THE NEW PRESS

NEW YORK
LONDON

Requests for permission to reproduce selections from this book should be mailed to:
Permissions Department, The New Press, 38 Greene Street, New York, NY 10013.

Published in the United States by The New Press, New York, 2011
Distributed by Perseus Distribution

Earlier and shorter versions of the chapters "The Turtles," "Enemy of the
State," and "Servant of the State" were first published in the *New Yorker*.

LIBRARY OF CONGRESS CATALOGING-IN-PUBLICATION DATA
Zha Jianying.
Tide players : the movers and shakers of a rising China / Jianying Zha.
p. cm.
ISBN 978-1-59558-620-9 (hardcover : alk. paper)
1. China—History—2002—Biography. 2. Businesspeople—China—Biography.
3. Intellectuals—China—Biography. 4. Social change—China.
5. China—Social conditions—2000– . 6. China—Economic conditions—2000– .
7. China—Intellectual life—1976– . I. Title.
DS779.48.Z42 2011
951.06092'2—dc22   2010042314

The New Press was established in 1990 as a not-for-profit alternative to the
large, commercial publishing houses currently dominating the book publishing
industry. The New Press operates in the public interest rather than for private
gain, and is committed to publishing, in innovative ways, works of educational,
cultural, and community value that are often deemed insufficiently profitable.

www.thenewpress.com

Composition by dix!
This book was set in Adobe Caslon

Printed in the United States of America

2   4   6   8   10   9   7   5   3   1

To Siri

Tide players surf the currents,
The red flags they hold up do not even get wet.
弄潮儿向涛头立，
手把红旗旗不湿。

   —Pan Lang (?–1009), *Jiu Quan Zi* (酒泉子)

There is a tide in the affairs of men.
Which, taken at the flood, leads on to fortune;
Omitted, all the voyage of their life
Is bound in shallows and in miseries.

   —William Shakespeare, *Julius Caesar*

As life is action and passion, it is required of a man
that he should share the passion and action of his
time at peril of being judged not to have lived.

   —Oliver Wendell Holmes Jr.,
   "Memorial Day Address"
   (1884)

CONTENTS

Tide Players

Introduction

Explaining China to Americans has always been a tricky business for me. Born and raised in Beijing, I have ended up, to my complete surprise, living between the United States and China for most of my adult life. But I will never forget the very first questions I had to answer about China, in 1981.

I had just arrived in Columbia, South Carolina. I was twenty-one, I had never been on an airplane before, and I spoke bad, broken English. China had started its reform and open-door policies, but there were not yet many Chinese students in the United States. And no TOEFL (Test of English as a Foreign Language) yet in China. So it was a small miracle that I, a student in the *Chinese* Department of Peking University, actually obtained a scholarship to study in the *English* Department of the University of South Carolina. Only much later did I realize that this was due largely to the fact that the English Department of USC had never in its history received an application from mainland China—meaning not Taiwan, not Hong Kong, but Big Red China! Evidently the curiosity and the temptation of offering this brave young applicant an opportunity was simply too great to resist. And I remember how much Dr. Ross Roy, chairman of the English department, enjoyed walking me around the campus and introducing me to absolutely everyone we ran into:

1

"This is Miss Zha," he would start, pausing dramatically before dropping the bomb, "She is from Beijing, China!"

It was in those first bewildering, exciting days of my new American life that Larry Bagwell, a fellow English Department student and a charming, bighearted, tall Southern boy who became my first American buddy, started asking me to explain China. It was a beautiful autumn afternoon, and we were sitting on the lawn drinking Coke after class. "Jane," Larry said, using the new American name he had given me, at my request, to overcome the impossibility of being called Jianying, "is it true the Chinese eat fried grasshoppers dipped in chocolate sauce as a delicacy?"

"What?" I blinked, almost choking on my Coke. I knew the word "chocolate," but "grasshoppers"?

If this was half pulling my leg, then Larry's next questions were certainly more serious: "Does China have TV shows, you know, like soaps and sitcoms? Actually, do Chinese have home television?" Before I could answer, he added apologetically, "We just don't know anything about China, you see, and some folks here think y'all don't even have electricity out there!"

This conversation is carved into my memory as a moment of great relief. I realized that I was not the only one so clueless about another big country—about another people and their culture. And it didn't matter that I thought "soaps" referred to a stack of cleaning squares. I knew what "electricity" and "chocolate" meant in English, which was a darn good start! I knew I would be fine in America.

What I didn't know then, of course, was how much and how fast my homeland would change! Nor could I predict that, merely fourteen years after Larry so casually tossed the bizarre, alien word "soaps" to me, I would myself write a book in English and publish it in America under the title *China Pop: How Soap Operas, Tabloids, and Bestsellers Are Transforming a Culture.*

In 2008, Larry finally made it to the grasshopper country. He and his daughter boarded that long transatlantic flight and "did" China. He sent me breathless letters about their bike trip through the Zhejiang countryside, the epiphany they experienced inside the meditation cave of the Tang monk poet Han Shan, the crazy shopping they did in Shanghai. "We are having a swell time here," Larry wrote, "and the Chinese we meet everywhere have been wonderful to us: your folks are such a warm and generous people." I was delighted, and wrote back, "I never had the opportunity to reciprocate your hospitality to me back then, but it looks like my folks are helping me to repay some of that old debt."

I belong to the generation of Chinese who grew up during the Cultural Revolution. My childhood was punctuated with memorable events such as the terrifying night ransacking of our home, witnessing neighbors being beaten to death or jumping to their deaths from the rooftop, my father's years of absence and receiving monthly letters from the labor camp, attending schools with daily political lectures and few books to read. I finished high school in 1977, and even though Mao Zedong had died the previous year and the Cultural Revolution had ended, we were still sent to do farmwork in a village outside Beijing. Everything was in flux as the Communist Party leadership scrambled to reverse Mao's policies and put the country on a different track, including reinstating the university entrance exam, which had been suspended for over a decade. That autumn I made a trip back to the city to take the exam, and, months later, as I was plowing the field with villagers, the news came that I was accepted into Peking University!

I will never forget spring 1978, my first euphoric days at Beida, as Peking University is called. At eighteen, I was the youngest in my class, but many of my older classmates had spent a decade or more in factories or on farms. None of us had dreamt of this day—studying at China's number-one university! To the individuals who remember the Red Guard and those who became the first beneficiaries of reform—disillusioned yet idealistic—the class of 1977 became a symbol and a legend in China. It was a generation burned by radical politics and loss of youth, yet fired up with a sense of mission for the country's future. Many from that class have moved on to leadership positions in politics, business, academia, culture, and media. Many are near the apex of their careers and influence. They form an elite part of the new establishment in today's China.

I have taken a slightly different path from that of my peers. My Beida classmates considered me a bit insane for going to South Carolina—"the Guizhou of America," as one of them put it—and missing out on the fabulous job offers waiting on our graduation day. But, whether it was a genetic connection to my grandfather, who had left his Hubei hometown in the early part of the last century to study in France, or just a wild curiosity about the outside world and a crazy thirst for adventure, I just had to leave. South Carolina proved to be an enchanting, idyllic first chapter of my American education; it was there that I discovered the charms of Flannery O'Connor and Elvis Presley, camping trips in the Smoky Mountains with guitar and marijuana, and horseback riding on a Southern farm. After transferring to Columbia University, I fell in love with New York, the city that would become my second home. By 1986, however, just as I was growing restless and ambivalent about the prospect of becoming an academic professional, I began to hear the calls from my homeland. Chinese visitors to New York and excited letters from my Beida classmates described a scene of great cultural and intellectual ferment; barriers were being broken down and new ideas and experiments were being put to the test. China sounded like a romantic place buoyed on bright hopes and full of possibilities. I had always wanted to be a writer and to be involved with my country's change and progress. So in 1987, right after passing my doctoral orals, I left for China.

The next two years were truly exhilarating and memorable. I rejoined my college classmates, made a lot of new intellectual and artist friends, wrote and published novellas and short stories, participated in critical discussions on culture and politics, and helped launch and edit independent journals. Amid all the excitement, my dissertation research comparing the Chinese literature of the Cultural Revolution to the American literature of the Vietnam War got shelved. By spring 1989, I was working as an assistant at the *New York Times*'s Beijing bureau while adapting one of my novellas into a movie script at the request of Zhang Nuanxin, a leading Chinese film director.

Then, Tiananmen happened. In May 1989 I quit my *Times* office job to march with friends in prodemocracy demonstrations, and I signed whatever petitions or manifestos came my way. Almost all of my Chinese friends were actively involved in the protest movement. I was standing at the southeast corner of Tiananmen Square on the night of the massacre, watching with a crowd of local citizens while an armed personnel carrier (APC) burned brightly in the night sky below the Tiananmen rostrum. We left only after the People's Liberation Army (PLA) soldiers opened fire and a rain of bullets felled a dozen or so people among the loudly cursing and retreating crowd. Ten days after the bloody dawn that scorched my memory, I retreated to America.

The trauma of Tiananmen, the shock of abandoning a thriving Chinese writing career, and the sudden realization that I must now make a permanent home in the United States, where I'd have to try my hand in English if I didn't want to give up writing completely, led to a period of depression and confusion. Through luck, perseverance, and the therapeutic sharing of reflections with a small group of exile friends, I gradually recovered. I was also extremely fortunate to be able to attend the forums at the Center for Psychosocial Studies in Chicago directed by Benjamin Lee, who was later to become my husband. The high-caliber discussions gave me a taste of the vigor of American intellectual life. The encouragement and friendship of two distinguished writers I met there, the journalist Jane Kramer and the novelist Lore Segal, inspired me to view writing in English not just as a forced challenge but also as an exciting adventure that would give me a new pair of eyes and wings. So, in the 1990s, between jobs, married life, and research trips to China, I produced my first English-language book (*China Pop*), wrote a monthly column for a Hong Kong magazine, and recorded essays for the Voice of America. After Ben went to teach at Rice University and our daughter Siri was born, we succumbed to suburban Houston. But I never forgot China.

In 2003, I received a Guggenheim Fellowship award, Ben was going on sabbatical leave, and Siri was turning seven in Houston, Texas, where our great plan of raising a bilingual, bicultural child was not happening. It was therefore with a good deal of excitement and anticipation that we packed up and moved to Beijing in August 2003.

Well, it turned out that seven-year-olds are far nimbler adapters of language and culture than grown-ups, even though in this case the grown-up in question was a home-returning native! Within a year, Siri went from speaking no Mandarin and crying "Chinese school is prison!" and "I was born to have recess!" to being at the top of her class and chitchatting in Beijing slang with our neighbors and her new friends. Meanwhile, I was still thrashing and groping. I had planned to write another book about China, but this new Beijing that was my home city, this new China that was my homeland, had again changed so much since I last lived there that I felt at once amazed, excited, intrigued, and clueless. What's behind all these high-rises looming on the city's horizon? How can new ones pop up every week? What's on the minds of all these people rushing about with seemingly endless energy? Are they happy, excited, full of hopes and dreams, or upset, tired, and dazed? I, for one, wasn't even sure sometimes if I was in a spell or in the clouds. But I was determined to find my way back into Chinese life, and I didn't want to write about it like a foreign outsider.

I made every effort to engage in an authentic way with Chinese cultural life. While renewing old friendships and making new contacts, I also worked as a special feature writer and advisor for the Beijing lifestyle magazine *Le*. To feel the local pulse and vibe, I ran around the city with *Le*'s young reporters covering fresh and sometimes idiosyncratic subjects and characters. To get a sense of the new Chinese urban-middle-class experience, I did what every local homeowner did: I supervised the renovation of my apartment in Beijing. What really thrust me back into the Chinese public eye, however, was a book I produced in Chinese, *The Eighties* (八十年代). Written as conversations with a dozen of China's leading creative minds, it was a cultural retrospective on the 1980s, the momentous decade that paved the way to Tiananmen. Many of the twelve individuals I interviewed for the book—artists, scholars, and intellectual gurus—were my old friends. Half of them had gone abroad and then returned, like me; for me and perhaps for them as well, the book closed a personal loop on a tragic, important era.

When the book came out in 2006, the maelstrom of media coverage and passionate reader response took me by total surprise. *The Eighties* ended up at the top of the sales charts in many bookstores, stirring up a wave of nostalgia and curiosity among young people about an idealistic era they hardly knew existed. A good deal of public discussion about the country's memory gaps followed; critics argued that, as China rose as an economic powerhouse, the need to come to terms with the past and forge a cultural renaissance was becoming urgent. The interest in historical memory also spawned more books and television programs probing neglected and repressed areas of the country's recent past. In 2010, *The Eighties* was voted one of the most influential books of the previous decade in China. In any case, public attention pulled me into the media circuit, and I was frequently invited to comment on all kinds of topics of public interest in the Chinese press and on television.

By then, I had drafted a portion of this book and also had taken a job as the China representative for an American research institute that sent me on regular trips to India and the United States and demanded increasingly more time and energy. I knew I was getting overextended. I was also aware of the danger of losing one's head in the limelight of the public's gaze. Yet the chance to join a community of kindred spirits to push for meaningful change and to build a more democratic, humane China was too enticing to ignore. The work also offered me an insider's perspective on Chinese media and censorship politics. Working on *The Eighties*, I was upset and argued with the Sanlian Press editors who deleted sections of the manuscript and took out an entire chapter before they printed the book, and I was not totally consoled by the uncut edition printed in Hong Kong but banned from the Mainland. Only gradually, after working with various state media and becoming a regular guest on a popular television talk show on current affairs, did I come to understand and appreciate those Chinese journalists and media professionals who are such seasoned veterans in the art of dodging censorship and playing guerrilla wars with the language police in their tenacious efforts to push the boundaries for freer speech.

Of course, I also learned more about the dark side, the ever-present shadows of Big Brother and the price of living with compromises in order to retain one's option to speak. I could never forget the week after Boris Yeltsin died, and we recorded a talk show episode discussing Yeltsin's legacy in Russia's democratization. Before we even left the studio, the episode was killed by the censors, and everyone chain-smoked in the makeup room, angry and despondent. We had to redo the episode, talking about our love for Russian literature instead. Experiences like that, however, did not destroy our resolve to keep pushing, with patience and moderation, toward a better tomorrow. I was ecstatic to be no longer just an observer; I had found my way back into Chinese life.

Some of this experience and insight has helped me in writing this book—in rendering a cleared-eyed yet compassionate portrait of characters situated in all the subtle complexities of this fast-changing China. As I delved deeper into the Chinese mind-set and psychic space, and as I compiled a large amount of data and materials for this book, I also contemplated ways of devising a meaningful narrative form to depict a society and a people living in a space entangled in its own past burdens and future aspirations.

I understand, of course, that you don't sink your teeth in a cow to get your choice cut of beef, and China is way too big a cow for anyone to tackle in full. I know my limits and my strengths. The rural life, the small-town stories, the migrants working in huge manufacturing plants—these are crucial and essential topics, and are being covered by many excellent writers. Continued poverty in parts of interior rural China, surging labor unrest in coastal factories, the injustice of the legal system, rampant corruption among local officials, ethnic tension, and environmental destruction are urgent major matters deserving our special, sustained attention.

But what I happen to know well is the big city, the great metropolis where great fortunes are made, where great political and intellectual battles are waged, and where great cultural industries and media machines operate. The metropolis is the headquarters and home terrain of a country's elite, the mecca that draws bright, ambitious talents everywhere to come to try their luck and gain their glory. In this age of urbanization and globalization—and at this historical moment in China's reemergence as a rising great power in the new millennium—the metropolis is the heart of aggregated convergence, a center stage for passionate human striving and fantastic social drama. Beijing, in particular, demonstrates the attitudes of those running the country and debating its future.

I am a Beijinger. Of all the big cities I have lived in thus far—Beijing, New York, Nanjing, Chicago, Houston, Hong Kong, Fort Lauderdale—I have loved Beijing and New York the most. But if there is one city that is in my blood and soul, it is and always will be Beijing. The site of so much history and memory and the home of high culture, state pomp, bohemian enclaves, northern vernacular, noble plans, fantastic gossip, and tragicomedies large and small, Beijing is, beyond a doubt, China's greatest metropolis. The Beijing I knew as a child has been transformed: the broad, stately avenues; the beautiful imperial parks; and the Soviet-style monuments still remain, but the long flows of bicycles, the huge crowds dressed in blue and gray, and the Mao statues have all but vanished. Today's Beijing is a great urban jungle: cutting-edge architectural landmarks; tacky, plush shopping plazas; large gated communities; shrinking old *hutong* neighborhoods; traffic jams and subway commuters; youngsters dressed in hip international fashion; old ladies bargaining at the farmer's market.

In the summer of 2005, when Paul Goldberger, architectural critic for the *New Yorker* and dean of the Parsons School for Design, made his first visit to Beijing, I accompanied him and showed him around. He looked about very intently for several days, and then one day told me that Beijing reminded him of Houston. It broke my heart. Of all the cities I have lived in, I have to admit Houston is my least favorite. Has three decades of ceaseless dismantling and massive, breakneck construction turned Beijing, a majestic symbol of Eastern imperial splendor and then of socialist utopia, into a . . . Houston? I was so upset I held a silent, intense grudge against Paul for days afterward. But how could I argue with him? With expert eyes, Paul had summed up something about this new Beijing that had also irritated me when I moved back. I had heard much worse verdicts from my Beijing friends!

Nevertheless, I knew then as I know now that Beijing is as great a city as it has always been, because what makes it great is not merely its constructed environment but—more important—its inhabitants, the millions of individuals who give Beijing its distinctive character and unique flair. So I told Paul, after getting over my jolted mood, that he must visit Beijing again and get to know its *people* a little. I thought to myself, *Oh, if you only knew the language and the people, you would understand how little Beijing resembles Houston beyond its physical environment, and why it will never become Houston, not in a thousand years!*

But Paul's remark, in a way, helped me identify and crystallize a central narrative principle that I came to believe in and stuck to in this book: focus on the Chinese to explain China. And if Beijing is at the center of my canvas, then I should train the spotlight on a select group of actors and players whose life stories and contours of thinking and action would help the reader understand the mental and spiritual journeys of a people moving in a rapidly changing physical landscape and unprecedented social transformation.

Through their struggles and epiphanies, their gains and losses, the reader can, I hope, feel the heart and soul of a city and the spirit of a nation.

My growing involvement in Chinese public life, my Chinese books, and the demands of my research institute job may explain the uneven pace of this book's production. But in the end, I hope I have gathered here a collection of useful stories and portraits of individuals whose life journeys have educated and inspired me. At the forefront of the tide of reform, they might be called the movers and shakers of a rising China. To me, they are certainly living proof of an ancient culture's amazing source of energy, intelligence, and unending drive to achieve dignity and glory. The six chapters are divided into two groups. The first group focuses on entrepreneurs. These are various rags-to-riches tales with Chinese characteristics: an unlikely couple who teamed up to become China's leading real estate moguls; a gifted chameleon who transformed himself from Mao's favorite "barefoot doctor" during the Cultural Revolution into a publishing maverick by deftly playing China's commercializing book market; a tycoon of a chain of home-electronics stores who wants revenge for his mother, a "counterrevolutionary criminal" executed in the most brutal manner.

The second group of chapters centers on intellectuals. Here are professors in China's number-one university locked in a deadly debate about education reform; my brother, a dissident jailed for nine years for co-founding the China Democracy Party; and finally, a famous, prolific writer who served as the cultural minister but also kept people divided as to whether he is an apologist for the Chinese Communist Party or a great author that might one day win a Nobel Prize in literature.

Tracking these lives and these stories has been a fascinating learning experience for me. I can only hope that they might also help deepen the reader's understanding of my home culture and shed some light on the complicated, dynamic, and fluid transformation currently driving the Chinese nation and the Chinese people.

Part I

The Entrepreneurs

A Good Tycoon

On a cold December evening, I met Zhang Dazhong at his brightly lit, spacious office in Beijing. Sitting in a black swivel chair behind a T-shaped worktable and against the hypnotic backdrop of a giant fish tank in which eighteen large, beautiful, red fish swam, Zhang cheerfully told me about his recent losses in the stock market. "I was making money at first. I bought some shares one day, and within a week I raked in a bundle. That made me very uncomfortable. Too quick! Too easy! It can't be right! Then, I made some bets, and I began to lose. After that I felt much better: I paid my tuition. I'm learning a few things about the stock market," he grinned. "All those fancy terms, they used to give me a headache. Now I can understand them. But I'm in no hurry."

A year earlier, it could have been argued (and many did in the Chinese media) that it was precisely this "no hurry" conservatism that had caused Zhang Dazhong, at the age of fifty-nine, to be forced out of the business of electric-appliance sales he had pioneered in China. Now, however—given China's year-long steep fall into a bear market, the black clouds of a worldwide financial crisis, and economic downturn—the measured prudence characteristic of Zhang's career appears in a different light.

Zhang Dazhong is a household name in Beijing, known to

millions through Dazhong Dianqi (Dazhong Electric Appliance), a chain he founded that featured his first name and carried television sets, audio systems, air conditioners, refrigerators, microwave ovens, and so on. It was the biggest in the city. But in December 2007, Zhang surprised the business community by selling all of his sixty-two stores to Huang Guangyu, the thirty-eight-year-old owner of Gome Dianqi, thus enabling Gome to claim the number-one spot among national chains. The merger had attracted a great deal of media attention because it involved a war among four electronics giants and a nasty dispute full of intrigue and betrayal. In the end, though, Zhang obtained a good deal, receiving a cash payment of 3.6 billion yuan (over $500 million) for Gome's takeover of Dazhong, which would continue to do business under the Dazhong name. Leaving the field a cash billionaire, Zhang immediately registered a new company, Dazhong Investment, and repositioned himself as a venture-capitalist-cum-investment-financier. Some of his loyal senior staff followed him. In 2008, Zhang paid 0.56 billion yuan ($80 million) in taxes, the biggest individual tax payment in the history of the People's Republic of China. According to newspaper reports, he paid more taxes than the total sum of individual taxes in the entire Qinghai province.

In the business community, however, many viewed Zhang's decision to sell Dazhong as an acknowledgment of defeat. The dominant take among analysts was that Zhang's age and northern conservative approach to business had narrowed his vision and prevented him from seeing the future, whereas Huang, a young Cantonese, not only saw the coming tide of big national chains, standardization, and the power of capital market, but also had the energy, audacity, and skill to play that tide.

Zhang likes to cite a Chinese proverb: "If you don't have a diamond bit, don't take on a porcelain job." He was also fond of saying, "Do as much business as your money allows you." Huang's motto was a simple zinger: "Commerce has no borders." And he has lived up to it in his actions. Taking Dazhong into Gome's fold was but one step in his rapid expansion. Huang's ambition was far greater than running China's Best Buy. He was building a corporate empire, from home electronic sales (HES) to real estate, from regional to national to beyond China's borders. As for the grand gesture of handing Zhang a sack of gold while showing him the door (the equivalent of dropping Zhang from the sky with a golden parachute), it was supposedly trademark Huang style. In China's business media, Huang had been accorded a rock star's flashy fame: his humble beginnings, his family's Catholic background, his penchant for gold ties, all had an exoticness even in a country full of rags-to-riches tales.

Huang also had the reputation of being a mystery genius. Reporters closely studied his business strategies and sometimes described the young tycoon's moves in kung fu lingo, as though they were observing the movements of a cool black-belt master. They admired Huang's risk-taking temperament and gutsy decisions. They noted his liaisons with high rollers such as Bear Stearns and Goldman Sachs, his shrewdness in debt financing, and his growing interest in the capital markets, and marveled at his deft play with various financial instruments (for example, Huang frequently repackaged his various companies by shuffling holdings and reinfusing capital in order to drive up their stock prices), even though few understood them fully. As a matter of fact, the less they could figure Huang out and pin him down, the more fascinating and intriguing he seemed.

Zhang Dazhong, on the other hand, seemed a less-than-dazzling figure: genial and avuncular, he built his business by the sweat of his brow; he remained low-key and avoided the spotlight, and by all accounts lived a simple, ordinary life. He appeared to be quite straightforward. How much can you say about a guy like that?

Then, one bright morning in November 2008, Zhang, like millions of others, opened the paper and read the headline: Huang Guangyu had been arrested for allegedly manipulating stocks, money laundering, and bribing government officials. Like the reaction following the Madoff scandal in the United States, the news reverberated like ominous thunder in the already darkened sky of

economic crisis. Huang was, after all, the wealthiest private entrepreneur in China. On the Hu Run List of the Richest People
in China, Huang was number one in 2008, worth 43 billion yuan
($6.3 billion). He had occupied that top spot twice before. Zhang
Dazhong, at an estimated worth of 3.8 billion yuan (about $540 mil-
lion), was only number 269 in 2007. But now, with the economy
in recession and Huang behind bars, and the official investigation
of the case shrouded in secrecy and rumors, the picture suddenly
changed.

So did perspectives on the two men. Adoration of Huang—
perhaps also tinged with envy—soon turned to condemnation.
Gibes and stabs began to appear on the Internet. The portrait of an
utter scoundrel emerged. Online postings revealed that in his teens
Huang was not only dirt-poor (as a kid he had collected garbage to
scrape by) but also a wild hooligan. He and his brother (a real-estate
developer) were often involved in ruthless exploitation, bribery,
gang violence, and other shady deals; as for scruples or conscience,
neither had any. Recalling the Gome-Dazhong merger, people now
marveled at Zhang's incredible luck and fortune: imagine trying
to sell Dazhong now! What uncanny, perfect timing! How wise
and prescient! Within one year the Chinese stock market's value
had shrunk by 70 percent. Zhang had received the last portion of
Gome's cash payment just two weeks before Huang's arrest! According to a friend of mine, even Beijing cab drivers were gossiping
about Zhang's vindication. "I was sitting in a cab and the radio had
on some news about Huang," he told me, "and the driver said they
are all happy for Zhang Dazhong."

Zhang himself demonstrated no desire to punch the fallen man
while he was down. As usual, he made no public comments about
Huang's disgrace. In our conversation, he shrugged off speculation
that the arrest signaled the central government's intention to reign
in the "Guangdong Gang"—the princeling (children of Party leaders) businessmen and politicians who dominate the rich southern
province where Huang comes from. If he was sympathetic to the

local media's talk about Huang's insatiable greed and love for fancy financial manipulations as the cause of his downfall, he clearly did not want to gloat over it. "He [Huang] is very hardworking and very shrewd," Zhang told me. "I don't want to pass judgment. He was fiercely competitive, and that was a big inspiration and push for me."

Zhang Dazhong is a short, compact man with the soft, pale skin of a gentleman scholar, a scrubbed, glowing complexion that comes from regular exercise and good health. At sixty, he is trim, younger-looking than his age, with alert eyes and a quick, assured gait. In conversation he speaks an informal, colloquial Beijing lingo, lapsing occasionally into earthy expletives. His sartorial style is on the conservative side without being stuffy: on most days he is dressed in "business casual," with a button-down shirt in a solid primary color, dark slacks, good leather shoes, and, on cold days, a blue or gray sweater. His manner is friendly and easygoing yet at the same time careful and vigilant. In a group he tends to listen more than talk, with the self-effacing attentiveness of someone who is accustomed to constantly sizing things up, watching, and absorbing information. This billionaire is definitely not full of himself. Nor is he taking his success and fortune for granted.

"I don't think I'm that much smarter than a lot of the guys out there," he said to me recently in his office, smoking and sipping tea in turns as the hour drew late. Earlier on he had told me about his first encounter with *Benchi*, or Mercedes-Benz. Somewhere in the late 1970s, Beijing had held an exhibition of German-manufactured products, and Zhang had gone to see it. At the time he had a job selling pork at a village grocer on Beijing's outskirts, earning 30 yuan ($5) a month, and after nearly a decade of working he owned a bike and nothing else. He had no apartment, no savings, no girlfriend. At the exhibition, a particular picture caught his eye. "It was a *Benchi* [奔驰]," Zhang recalled. "I looked at it for a long time, thinking: what a beautiful car! Of course I never dreamed of driving my own *Benchi* one day." Today Zhang owns two Mercedes. "If China hadn't shifted to the reform and open-door policies, someone like me, coming from a family like mine, would never have a chance. If you write up my story, you've got to put this in: considering where I was thirty years ago, it's like a trip from hell to heaven."

The journey had started in 1979 when Zhang decided to embark on a mission that back then appeared even more impossible than possessing a *Benchi*: he wanted the Chinese government to change its verdict on his mother.

Wang Peiying, a kindergarten teacher, had publicly criticized Mao Zedong before and during the Cultural Revolution. Detained, denounced, yet refusing to retract her views, she was put in a mental ward and received forced "medical treatment" for two and half years. Later she was taken back to her work unit and locked up in a "cowshed" (detainment center for "counterrevolutionaries"). Besides being subjected to forced labor, she was regularly interrogated, beaten, and humiliated. Her stubborn defiance earned her the label of *zui da er ji* (罪大恶极, "great crime, extremely evil"). On January 27, 1970, at an organized *Pi-dou* (attack and strike) rally in Beijing's Worker's Stadium, before a packed crowd of 100,000, she and sixteen other "counterrevolutionaries" were sentenced to death. They were to be executed immediately. Still defiant, she struggled with the guards on the way to the execution site. They strangled her to death with a rope inside the convoy truck.

Wang and her husband, a midlevel official working for the Ministry of Railways, had seven children: six boys in a row and then a girl. Zhang Dazhong was the third boy. When Dazhong was twelve, their father died of liver failure, leaving Wang to raise the children alone. The family struggled financially. Zhang recalls crying silently on the balcony when they had to let a beloved old nanny go since they couldn't afford her anymore. He learned how to mend his own clothes, which were always covered with patches. For the summertime, each of the Zhang children had just one pair of pants, which they washed every night so they could dry in time to be worn the next morning. To make ends meet, Wang regularly sold things for cash: antique pieces passed down from her parents, her husband's old winter coat. But poverty was nothing compared to what happened after Wang openly criticized Mao. They became a "black sheep" family. Zhang still recoils at the memory of his emotional confusion, of his weekly visits to the mental hospital and the sight of his mother, drugged out, pale, yet unfaltering. The case cast a deep shadow on the children's lives. The stigma of having a mother who was an executed counterrevolutionary meant that none of them could get a decent job or go to a university; their marital prospects suffered since most people would not want to forge such an alliance. Zhang's siblings accepted their lot. Several settled in dreary jobs in the provinces, abandoning hope of moving back to Beijing.

Zhang, too, felt trapped in his job at the village grocery store. "It was a depressing time," he told me. "I could see no direction." Trying not to be idle, he bought a lot of secondhand books and read at random. One day, a line from a book struck Zhang with the force of revelation: "The degree of one's misfortune is determined by one's understanding of it." "I can't remember the title or the author, but this sentence suddenly lifted the lid on me," Zhang told me. "I decided to be an optimist. I was already at the bottom, so be it!" He got up at six every morning and jogged ten kilometers along the country road, wearing shorts even in the dead of the winter. "I'd feel exhilarated all day. I was always cheerful. And if people asked me about my family, I'd tell them: my father was a Communist Party official!"

In 1976, Mao died and the Cultural Revolution ended. Two years later Deng Xiaoping was reinstated, and he started steering China on a path of reform and openness. Still, people moved gingerly in the early thaw. Zhang was the only one among his siblings to grasp the implications of these changes. He wrote letters to Deng Xiaoping and other top Party officials, asking them to reconsider his mother's case: "I didn't tell my brothers; they'd think I was a troublemaker!" To win sympathy, he wrote about his parents' early work for the Communist Party when it was still an outlawed organization and operated underground. He also conceded that his mother suffered mental illness when she criticized Mao. Months passed. Finally, a call came from the Public Security Bureau: he was asked to go to an office at the Banbuqiao Prison. There, he was asked some questions and then sent home to wait. Three months passed without news. He renewed his mailing campaign. "Every week I sent a batch of letters to all the offices. There were so many wronged cases, and so many were seeking redress. I knew only the persistent ones might have a chance."

It finally happened. In January 1980, the Beijing municipal court revised the verdict on Wang Peiying: she was not a counterrevolutionary since she made her anti-Mao remarks while suffering from a mental disease. It was only a partial rehabilitation but still a huge breakthrough. A month later, the seven siblings received their compensation from the government: 7,000 yuan.

Zhang's heart was heavy when he got his share of 1,000 yuan. "Deep down I sensed that my mother was an extraordinary woman, and this is her blood money," he told me. "I was not going to spend it buying a TV set or furniture like my siblings did. I felt I must do something with it that is worthy of her life. In fact, all through the years of my expanding business, this feeling drove me ahead like an invisible whip over me."

In the end, he divided the money into two parts. He had just started dating a young woman introduced to him by a friend, and when they decided to marry, Zhang spent 500 yuan on their wedding and honeymoon trip. "I used the remaining 500 yuan as the start-up fund for my business."

Later that year, Zhang made his first attempt. He bought alkaline soda, clear paint, silver powder, brushes, and cloth wipes; packed them into an old army bag; and went out to the street on a Sunday, hawking with a signboard: CLEAN AND PAINT GAS STOVE FOR 0.8 YUAN. He was a pleasant-looking young man dressed in clean clothes, and people opened their doors to let him into their kitchens. After working many hours on that hot August day, he made the following calculations: he had cleaned and painted ten stoves, collected eight yuan, and, after the cost of tools, cleared a profit of two yuan, not taking into account his labor. "It was my first and last of day of doing *that*," Zhang grinned at the memory.

His next venture was making lamps. Turning his own kitchen into a workshop, and using an assortment of materials acquired from various places—flat pans, weaving spindles, wires, and bulbs— Zhang cobbled together several floor lamps and took his creations to a local farmers' market. He was pleased to find buyers, at six yuan a lamp. A couple of department stores also placed orders: stores were so poorly stocked back then that they lacked even such crudely man- ufactured goods. With the help of his brothers, Zhang made sixty lamps in the same fashion and sold them all. He cleared a profit of 160 yuan. It was a big confidence boost: he had received the market's first confirmation of his entrepreneurial potential.

But the lamp project didn't last long. Sales slowed down and Zhang realized that such a low-craft product had only limited ap peal. Searching for other opportunities, he learned from a friend about an overstock of electronic parts at a research institute. Zhang had always been good at making things with his hands—in his idle years he used to cut furniture for friends and assemble transistor radios—and he knew he could make an audio amplifier from these parts. So he bought some parts cheaply, made an amplifier on the family dining table, and took it to a store. Receiving a positive re- sponse, he immediately bought more parts and made more ampli- fiers. This time it was a real hit: within a month, the store sold a hundred amplifiers that had taken Zhang a month to make. Orders poured in. Demand grew so high that soon Zhang couldn't do it in his spare time. This was the moment he had long awaited. In December 1982, against all his relatives' warnings that he shouldn't toss away the "iron rice bowl," he quit his grocer job. "I decide to resign because this work does not fit my ideal," he wrote in his letter of resignation. His monthly salary then was 41.5 yuan (about $8).

Free at last, Zhang registered his own company, Zhang's Electronic Processing Shop. He and his wife then lived in a thirty-square-meter, two-room apartment. Again, he turned their home into a workshop, moving the bed into the kitchen and the kitchen out into the hallway. He hired workers, training them and paying them piecemeal. Mostly young peasants from the villages outside the city, they were pleased to find a job that paid seventy to eighty yuan a month and worked hard. Zhang himself worked the hardest: he supervised everything, biked across the city to purchase the best and the cheapest parts and tools, and read all the available professional audio journals. He was happy. He had found a direction and was taking his life into his own hands.

By the end of 1983, over fifty stores in Beijing were selling Zhang's amplifiers. His monthly profit reached 2,000 yuan, and it would triple in the next four years.

To widen the scope of his business, Zhang began making and installing audio speakers. He rented a warehouse on the outskirts of Beijing. Rent was cheap, and the over-2,000-square-meter space was fine for manufacturing purposes, but the surroundings were less than ideal: it was right next to a pig farm. Every time clients came to pick up an order, a cloud of flies would descend on their cars.

In time, Zhang saw that manufacturing was not as good a business in Beijing as sales: the profit margin was low and the cash-flow cycle was long. He decided to focus on selling electronic parts and small items. In 1986, he opened his first store in Lingjing Lane, a central location. It was a hole in the wall, but sales were brisk since it carried hot items like pocket-sized calculators, which Zhang bought cheap from Guangdong. Zhang sold these for just 8.8 yuan, and customers lined up. Before long he had about 50,000 yuan saved up in the bank. In the 1980s, the Chinese called their first new rich *wan yuan hu*, "the ten-thousand-yuan household." Given the average income level at the time, it was really like calling someone a millionaire. Zhang seemed to have joined their rank in the blink of an eye.

One day in late 1986, a call came from the municipal Bureau of Industry and Commerce: Zhang was asked to "come have a sitting down." He got nervous. The bureau possessed the authority to close any business at will. Sure enough, he was told that he had "violated rules" by opening two stores under the same name. Chinese laws at the time dictated that no private business operation could have a branch: "chain store" had too strong a "capitalist" ring. Apologizing, Zhang shut down the offending store right away.

Luckily, government policy changed a year later. Branch companies were now permitted. "You can't imagine how mixed I felt when I heard this news," Zhang said.

He immediately set about expanding. In the early 1990s, karaoke became popular in Chinese cities, especially among businessmen and the newly affluent. Zhang cashed in on the trend, shipping whole containers of karaoke machines by freight train from the south. They sold well and the money was good. By 1993, he had a hundred employees and over ten million yuan in annual sales. But he felt restless and ready for something new. While researching the market, he noticed that all the audio stores in Beijing were either small or tiny, ranging only from a dozen square meters to fewer than a hundred square meters, and none of them carried everything a customer would need. A new vision came to Zhang: people would welcome a big store that carried all the brands and all the parts in one place. That would make shopping much easier and more convenient!

Excited by this idea, Zhang decided to "go big." After a round of careful investigation, he settled on a location: a large Westside shopping center on Yuquan Road. He rented a 4,000-square-meter space and stocked it with all the available brands, local as well as international. He named the store Dazhong Dianqi (Dazhong Electronics); it was the first one to carry that name. It was a giant leap, and a bold bet. But Zhang was in for a cruel shock. After the store opened in July 1993, few customers showed up. Sales remained sluggish for the rest of the year. The well-lit, well-stocked store stood quietly, attracting little business. The daily cash flow was not even enough to pay for the sales team and electricity. It was the worst setback Zhang had suffered. His anxiety was such that for weeks he could not sleep; he lay awake night after night, trying to figure a way out of the disaster. He thought about closing the store. "If it reached a point where the loss became unbearable, I'd have to eat it and go back to my little downtown store," Zhang recalled the experience with a laugh. "But then I imagined the expression on the faces of all those little bosses sitting in their little stores. To lose face like that, it's even more unbearable!" He decided to persevere.

Luckily, through advertisements and customers, word about the big store on Yuquan Road gradually spread; sales picked up after six months. The store became known as China's first audio superstore, and Zhang rented more space and diversified supplies. In addition to audio products, the store soon carried TV sets, air conditioners, refrigerators, and the like. The new formula proved successful. Zhang and his crew were also getting savvier in marketing their goods: their ads grew more ingenious and popular, as did their special sales and floor displays. Steadily, the Yuquan store built a reputation as a one-stop shopping destination that boasted variety, reliability, low price, and good service. Within a few years the store space stretched to over 10,000 square meters, carrying over 20,000 types of goods. Zhang knew with satisfaction that he was no longer just a "little boss" selling audio parts.

The upgrading was important in another sense as well: Zhang now had a good formula, a brand name, sufficient capital, and an experienced crew. He was in a position to create a chain, and he moved to do just that. His business entered a period of explosive growth. In 2000, there were just six stores in Beijing carrying the sign of Dazhong Dianqi. In 2003, their number climbed to thirty-two, representing 50 percent of Beijing's market share. In 2004, the number of stores jumped to sixty-eight, covering metropolitan Beijing, all its surrounding counties, and a few in three nearby cities. The biggest of them, opened in 2002 near the CCTV tower just off the third ring road, took up a whole building of 20,000 square meters and boasted an equally large parking lot outside. Today, with annual sales of over one billion yuan since 2004, it is still the largest and most profitable electronic-appliance store in China. By the end of 2005, Dazhong's annual sales were reaching ten billion yuan, the top dog by far in Beijing. With a good tax record and a great reputation among customers and employees alike, Zhang was considered a model entrepreneur. He became a deputy to the People's Congress and served on several government committees.

Perhaps Zhang was too absorbed in his own rapid expansion to notice certain changes that were taking place elsewhere. While he was plowing deeply into the Beijing market, three other chains— Yongle in Shanghai, Suning in Nanjing, and Gome in Beijing—were also moving aggressively. Each had established its brand name locally and then looked for new markets, conquering them rapidly to form interregional chains. Gome's Huang Guangyu led the trend. Originally from a small rice-farming village near Shantou on the southeast coast of Guangdong, Huang first traded goods in Inner Mongolia, then set up his first market stall in Beijing when he was just eighteen. In 1999, after consolidating his local stores into the Gome chain, he started opening stores in other cities. This expansion was followed by that of the Suning and Yongle chains. At that time, the three chains' national market shares were not yet very high—a combined total of 3 percent in 2000. But the race heated up very quickly. Soon they were waging price wars in all major cities, setting up shop on each other's turfs, pushing into new regions, and crushing smaller stores along the way. Within five years their combined market shares had risen to 13 percent. By 2005, all three were listed on the Hong Kong—or Shenzhen—stock exchange. Gome emerged as the fastest growing of the three, with 400 stores and 40 billion yuan in annual sales. Suning claimed second place, with 37 billion yuan in sales and fewer than 300 stores. Yongle was half the size of Gome: 200 stores, 20 billion yuan in sales. But Huang, nicknamed "price butcher" among retailers, had more leveraging capital than all his rivals because he had also become a player in the real estate business.

Number four was Dazhong. Danger hovered around Zhang as the three giants inched steadily toward him. But while they raced to put flags on new territories, Zhang actually scaled back in order to strengthen his dominance in the capital markets. Perhaps because nearly all of Dazhong's staff was from the Beijing area, the few stores he opened in other cities had not done very well. So, it was not until 2005 that the mantra of "be big or be dead" (不做大, 勿宁死) finally hit him, and Zhang made cautious plans to go national. He dispatched a dozen delegations to various provinces to check out possibilities. The investigation, however, revealed a grim picture: while Dazhong maintained a solid lead in Beijing, it was dwarfed nationally by the three giants, who had already taken up position everywhere. Zhang realized with a sinking heart that he was encircled!

Looking back on how things led to Dazhong's eventual decision to sell, the Hu Kai incident seemed to be an early signal. Hu Kai was the younger brother of Hu Rong, one of Zhang's high school classmates. Like the Zhang family during the Mao decades, the Hu family was tossed to the bottom of society after their engineer/professor parents were labeled "rightists." Hu Kai worked a string of lowly dead-end jobs in the provinces and returned to Beijing in the 1980s with no college degree and no career prospects. Hu Rong came to Zhang's office, asking him to give her brother a chance. Zhang took Hu Kai in, starting him off as a buyer. Hu worked hard and soon showed his talents. Zhang groomed and promoted him steadily. Hu became an office manager, a division director, and finally the company's CEO. When Dazhong entered its period of explosive growth, Hu played a central role. A gifted negotiator and meticulous organizer, Hu could clinch a deal, renovate a space, and open a new store—all within a week. And he had Zhang's complete confidence. One day in 2004, after finishing three rounds of negotiations, Hu felt an uncomfortable tightness in his chest and went home to rest. He died of a heart attack the next morning. He was fifty-three.

Hu Kai's death hit Zhang hard. "We had a perfect understanding between us about business," Zhang told me in his office recently. "We'd trade a few words in the morning, and I could leave the day-to-day operation to him and not worry at all. It was smooth." After

Hu died, Zhang was compelled to oversee everything himself. By then, he had been in business for over twenty years, his company had about 20,000 employees, and the scale of the enterprise cried out for a new management style and new blood. Yet, as in many private companies in China, certain calcified cultural habits were not easy to shake off. According to some of Dazhong's senior deputies, the company had always relied on Zhang's business instincts and initiative: the big boss points, they follow. But the situation had changed since 2002: it was as if they had boarded a fast train and realized only in the escalating speed how unprepared and under-staffed they were. The decision-making process was too casual and impromptu. The mechanism of checks and balances was lacking. The company sorely needed more skilled managers.

And then there was the issue of Zhang's career burn-out. For many years his workweek consisted of three elements: Monday–Wednesday, ordering stock; Thursday, advertising; Friday, boosting company morale; Saturday, sales reporting and accounting. "Same routine, year after year," he admitted to me. "I was getting tired of it."

Hu Kai's unexpected death reminded him of his own mortality and age. "People said he died of exhaustion," Zhang told me. He himself was no longer a young man. Was he ready for more cut-throat competition down the road? For many Chinese businessmen, a typical solution would be passing the baton to a son. But Zhang's son, an only child, showed no interest in taking over the business. Zhang had sent him to Australia for a college education, and after graduation had put him to work at one of his superstores, starting with unloading trucks and stocking the shelves. "But he's not an ambitious type," Zhang said to me. "He's not greedy at all about money." Zhang's wife, Lou Hongguang, a thin, graceful woman with meek eyes, was trained as a graphic designer but later was per-suaded by her husband to work as his company's accountant. After an employee embezzled some money, Zhang wanted a family mem-ber to be in charge of the books and taxes. But Lou is a shy person with no appetite for business. "I guess our son takes after me in temperament," she told me with an air of apology. (Lou owns a minor percentage of the company but no longer works for it. These days she's a stay-at-home spouse and plays cards with friends.)

At one point Zhang thought he might solve the problem by hiring more educated, highly qualified young people to build what he called "China's first-class business team." But this would take time. And things were happening too fast for Zhang's normally cautious approach. Gome and Suning simply showed up in his neighborhood one day. Lining the third ring road at about 500 meters apart, the three retail chains now stood shoulder to shoulder, eyeing one another warily.

Thus, it was big news in April 2006 when Yongle and Dazhong announced their signing of a "strategic cooperation agreement" in preparation for merging. Playing on puns made out of the four big chains' names, the press excitedly billed the agreement as Happy (Yongle) and China (Dazhong) forging an alliance to fight off the American (Gome) and Soviet Union (Suning) hegemony. This was somewhat true, though after the two companies completed their merger acquisition process, Zhang would become a minority shareholder in the new Yongle-Dazhong corporation. According to the agreement between Zhang and Chen Xiao, Yongle's founding chairman, Yongle got the priority rights to purchase Dazhong's stock shares in a year; the price would be calculated in a set formula dependent on Dazhong's sales performance during that year. To prove their mutual sincerity, Chen paid Zhang a cash deposit of 150 million yuan as a guarantee, while Zhang agreed to pay twice that amount to Chen if he broke the contract. This was essentially like a gentlemen's agreement, and all was set for a smooth, cooperative merger. Zhang needed only to make sure of one thing: to keep up his store sales over the next twelve months. He knew this was something he could accomplish; after all, his stores still had a 40 percent cut of the Beijing market, the equivalent to Gome and Suning combined.

What he didn't know, however, was that Gome was making its move on the Shanghai market, and that Chen was also being courted by Huang. Three months later came the stunning news: Yongle had agreed to be bought by Gome! This meant, of course, not only an instant collapse of the Happy China alliance, but also a stronger America (Gome) against a disadvantaged Soviet Union (Suning). Dazhong was left out in the cold.

Zhang's initial response was to take the high road. He gave a press conference and sent Chen an open message that boiled down to two words: Congratulations! Goodbye! He would return Chen's 150-million-yuan deposit, forget about their previous agreement, and move on. To his utter surprise, Chen said no: Zhang could keep the deposit because their agreement was still on, except now Dazhong was legally bound to join Yongle and become a member of the growing Gome family!

This enraged Zhang. "Look, a good woman does not marry two men," he claimed, citing a Chinese proverb to explain. "It's like I'm engaged to marry someone who betrays me and marries another man, then insists on taking me along as the dowry!" This was adding insult to injury—totally unacceptable. Zhang announced that he was immediately, unilaterally, terminating the Dazhong-Yongle agreement and keeping the deposit. Chen then announced that Zhang had broken their agreement and demanded 300 million as penalty. In the following year and a half, their dispute would escalate and drag out into a nasty legal battle, and the story would grow more complex as new characters entered the scene. While the reporters were having a field day covering all the juicy gossip and every twist and turn, Zhang lowered his head and remained silent, declining all requests for an interview. For some, he had become an object of pity, even mockery. For others, he was a nice guy who finished last and was about to get run over in the coming stampede. Only in hindsight, after all the dust had settled, would people come to realize that, in his last year in the retail electronics field, Zhang had moved beautifully, like a masterful poker player.

• • •

Liu Ge, a lawyer and senior partner at Beijing's Junhe law firm, had just finished his annual physical checkup on a September day in 2006 and was drinking a cup of coffee in the Lido Hotel's lobby when his mobile phone rang. He was surprised to hear Zhang Dazhong's voice on the other end. They had only met once, about five years earlier, when Liu, whose wife worked for Motorola at the time, helped make an introduction between a Motorola deputy and Zhang. Liu had given Zhang his card but had not heard from him since. On the phone, Zhang explained that he was filing a suit against Yongle at the Arbitrators' Tribunal, an organization under the China International Trade and Economic Commission (CITEC), which was to settle their dispute. Would Liu mind taking a look at the litigation document his lawyer had drafted? Later Liu discovered that, before calling him, Zhang had already shopped around town and gone through a string of lawyers.

Junhe is a top law firm, one of the biggest in China. With over two hundred lawyers, its offices take up two entire floors in the China Resource Building (Huarun), which, looming over the Jianguomen Bridge, has been noted for its resemblance to Manhattan's Chrysler Building. The founder of Junhe (the name comes from a phrase from Confucius's *Analects*) and nearly all its partners share a common career pattern: Peking University (Beida) law school graduate, further training and a degree from a U.S. law school, working experience at a U.S. law firm, returning to China to join Junhe. Liu, too, had traveled this route. A commanding figure, with his six-foot-one-inch frame clothed in an impeccable suit and tie, he was the former captain of Beida's volleyball team, worked for seven years in a Chicago law firm, and plays golf. When he needs a break from his corner office at Huarun, he rides the elevator up eight floors to the American Club, housed on the twenty-eighth floor with a spectacular panoramic view of Beijing's urban sprawl. Like many of his Junhe colleagues, Liu often takes his clients and friends up here to dine. This is where he likes to relax with a cigar.

Liu promised he would look at the document. "I told Dazhong if it reads all right he should stick to that lawyer because we are very expensive," Liu said. "But after reading the document I had to tell him it was no good. Its entire argument was built on one point: the opponent is not playing fair. You can't win a case like this with a moral argument." A few days later, Zhang brought a 50,000 yuan ($7,000) check for a consultation meeting at Junhe and listened to Liu present his line of arguments and strategies. "All strictly based on laws and interpretations," Liu said to me, rattling off legal terms and contract clauses. "But the core theory I employed was a fairly new company theory by an American author. The theory unveils how some companies exploit their corporation status to avoid fulfilling their responsibilities, and it shows how to expose this in court." Liu gave the American theory a local spin, expounding it in Chinese political catchphrases. Zhang dismissed the other lawyer and formally hired Liu. Analyzing the case together, they concluded that Huang was behind it all along, plotting to shoot two birds with one stone even before the Yongle-Dazhong pact. They were not going to let him get away with it.

Chen hired a lawyer who also had some U.S. legal background. Like Huang, Chen was not a novice in dealing with foreigners. While Huang listened to men from Goldman Sachs for advice and had set up an investment fund with Bear Sterns, Chen counted J.P. Morgan and Chase Manhattan Bank among his investors— both had bought shares of Yongle stocks. But with Liu onboard, Zhang knew he had found their match. The litigation continued over the next fifteen months. The Arbitrators' Tribunal held three separate court sessions on their case. For more than a year the lawyers argued on; neither side backed down, and no settlement was reached. Zhang himself went to court once with Liu, while Chen sat on the opposite side with his lawyer. "He sat there mute after I spoke," Zhang told me recently. As time dragged on, Zhang and Liu became confident that their victory was in sight.

Only much later, after it was all over, would Zhang talk about why he wanted a clear sell. Besides personal considerations, and the fact that it was too late for the Dazhong chain to go national, his views about the future of retail business in China were not so rosy. "I thought the space for expansion was becoming very limited," he told me. "Most folks have bought their TV set and their audio system; the first big wave of home purchasing and furnishing is over. Upgrading is a slower cycle. I don't want to wait to sell when the business is in a pinched situation." And after his experience with Yongle, selling for stock options and staying involved as a minority shareholder in a field with a shrinking horizon no longer looked appealing. He wanted a clear, clean way out, with plenty of capital to do something new. "Look, I've been in *shiye* [实业, industry and commerce] for over twenty years; time to move on." So selling for cash was Zhang's sole objective now. The crucial thing, of course, was getting *a lot of cash*.

Despite his seemingly trapped and precarious situation, Zhang was fully aware of his advantage. He was, as Liu put it, "the last piece of fat meat in Beijing everyone was drooling over." Or, in the words of a newspaper report: "De Dazhong zhe de Beijing" [得大中者得北京, He who gets Dazhong, gets Beijing]. By then Dazhong was the only large Chinese retail chain not listed on the stock exchange. While this had previously placed Zhang at a disadvantage when he pondered about national expansion, it now made the company more attractive to buyers. Gome and Suning pretended to be cool, but Zhang knew they were both acutely interested. Other suitors were showing up too. Best Buy, which was looking for an entry into China, approached Zhang. Through Liu's introduction, a major British retail chain also entered the negotiation scene. Zhang let it be known that he was looking for a buyer, but he kept all the talks secret.

Finally, in April 2007, Suning and Dazhong acknowledged that they were in communication about "development and collaboration." Rumors started flying right away. In May, a "leak" from Dazhong revealed that Suning had made a purchase offer at three billion yuan. Though unconfirmed, the news must have kept Huang up at night.

As Gome's biggest rival, Suning had its own grand ambitions. Indeed, thanks to the hotness of the A shares on the Chinese stock market then, Suning's market value had just surpassed Gome's and the company called its stock "the number one IPO among Chinese electronics chains." If Suning gets Dazhong now, a reporter wrote, it would be like "stabbing at Gome's heart—Beijing." This would be intolerable to Huang. And since things were not going his way in court, Huang's hope of using Yongle to ensnare Dazhong and block out other potential buyers was diminishing.

Then "Spy Gate" happened. A Dazhong employee gave Gome certain top-secret company information about sales and fled. Word circulated that "the spy" had been planted by Gome. This was in late May 2007. Dazhong's management scheduled a press conference, saying it would release some "shocking news" and file a suit. The entire local business media showed up and waited in front of a large signboard that read PUNISH ILLEGAL ACTS. BE HONEST IN BUSINESS. But after a thirty-minute delay, a Dazhong public relations director emerged to cancel the event. Pressed by the reporters, the director revealed that due to a private exchange between Zhang and Huang, Zhang decided at the last moment to call off the press conference and drop the "spy" suit. But what did Huang and Zhang talk about? Was Spy Gate a card Zhang was using to play with Huang? The episode only added mystery to the story.

Ultimately, the biggest card in Zhang's hand was his company's sales report. Buoyed by the growing economy and the booming housing market, electronic goods were selling briskly. During the first week of October 2007, during the Chinese national holiday and a big shopping week, Dazhong's stores were so packed that the sales staff worked in twenty-four-hour shifts. Gome's and Suning's stores were doing well too. But when the week ended, Dazhong's sixty-two stores easily surpassed the combined sales of the others' eighty stores by more than 10 percent. On October 1 alone, Dazhong stores broke an all-time record by raking in 350 million yuan. Huang called Zhang to offer his congratulations. Suning's head did the same. Both companies openly courted Zhang. It was a matter of who could pay more cash more quickly.

The negotiations entered their final stage in December. As Suning was getting close to clinching the deal at three billion, Huang moved with more urgency. "He sent his guys to watch us every day," Zhang told me. "They hung around my office building day and night, trying to see whether Suning's people had started to move in." Finally, Zhang offered Huang a forty-eight-hour "ultimatum." "I told him if he agreed to pay 3.6 billion [yuan] in cash, plus a penalty of 20 million [yuan] in cash for Yongle's breaking the contract, then we'd have a deal. Otherwise, I'm signing with Suning." Two days later Huang conceded to the terms. The next day Suning withdrew its bidding for Dazhong. On December 14, Gome announced its purchase of Dazhong. A few weeks later, the Arbitration Tribunal announced its verdict: Dazhong had won the case; Yongle would have to pay Dazhong a penalty of twenty million yuan for breaking its contract.

Huang paid the twenty million yuan. But six months later Zhang returned it! "What Chen Xiao did was unethical," he explained to me. "That's why I sued Yongle. But it was never about money. I just wanted to set things right."

There is something else Zhang would like to set right: the story about his mother. After selling his stores, he had more time on his hands, and his mind often went back to her. He pondered a great deal over the meaning of her life and death. She was, he realized, at the root of everything he had done. Her simple teaching to him when he was a boy, "*Zuo ren yao you gu qi*" (做人要有骨气, Be a human being with a backbone and a spirit), is carved into his mind. She had set a fierce example for her son. Where did she get the courage to openly challenge Mao at a time when he was treated like a deity and ruled in absolute power? If, in 1980, the only way to remove the stigma of her "counterrevolutionary" status was to depict her as a "mental case," he finds it unacceptable now. "It's a stain on her image. She was not mad; the age she lived in was mad. Everyone knows that. I want a real rehabilitation," Zhang told me.

To this end he has hired a lawyer who helps him prepare for an appeal, once again, to reverse the verdict. Zhang is collecting all the data related to his mother from the court, the public security bureau, the work-unit files, the old neighbors, and family friends. Every time I go to his office or speak with him on the phone, he eagerly shows me some newly acquired material on the case or informs me of a detail he has just learned about her. During my first long interview with him, he spent half the time talking about her. An enlarged black-and-white photo of her dating back to the 1950s stood on his desk. She was a beautiful woman, elegant in a simple black coat with a gauze scarf tied around her neck, but her eyes betrayed a melancholy. "I was too young to understand her when she was alive," Zhang told me repeatedly. "I'm trying now." He urged me, time and again, not to focus on his story but hers. "My story is not that different from most other private entrepreneurs in China. But my mother's is truly worth telling. Someone like her should be known and remembered." I asked him whether this is the deepest wound in him. A silence fell; he looked very pale. Then he quickly nodded and reached for a cigarette. Once, during a visit to the United States, Zhang saw a bronze statue on the street depicting a young hero in his final moment, tied up in ropes and suffering. Suddenly, hot tears streamed down his cheeks because it reminded him of his own mother. "I'm going to commission an artist to make a statue of my mother," Zhang told me.

Lately, however, Zhang admits that he is running into a "rubber wall." Nobody has issued a clear-cut rejection, but the authorities he and his lawyer contacted have found various means to put their request on hold. The government, Zhang concludes, is not yet ready to reopen the closet and stare at the skeletons of the past. "They are worried about too many families making demands like this." He tells me about another similar case: a Shanghai musician named Liu Wenzhong who was executed during the Cultural Revolution because of his criticism of Mao. "When he was 'rehabilitated,' they also said he had a mental disease." This April, Zhang had a private discussion about his mother's case with the head of the Beijing High Court. Before they parted, the official said, "Dazhong, tell me how you would handle this case?"

It's clear to me that, personal desire aside, Zhang is very cautious about political action and has no intention of doing anything radical. He tells me: "First, I don't have a bone to pick with the current leadership. Second, I can actually understand why they don't want to handle these cases right now. How fast can China change politically? Too fast is no good either. Say we have a democracy like India's now, then we may not have stability and efficiency. On the whole I'm pretty comfortable with the present pace of change."

Zhang's preference for gradual improvement over radical change reflects not only his own prudence but also a growing consensus among China's elite. There is a general feeling that the dark side of the country's recent history must be faced and that the nation needs to democratize, but few expect it to happen soon. This has to do not only with a sobering sense of realism after Tiananmen but also with the increased satisfaction due to economic prosperity and the fact that personal freedom has expanded greatly in the past two decades. And if businessmen as a species are usually pragmatic and politically conservative, then businessmen in China have even more reason to be cautious, as their very existence depends on the policies and goodwill of a regime that did not begin its rule by being nice to the propertied class.

In his recent works, Wu Xiaobo, a noted expert on the history of Chinese entrepreneurs and the author of many books on the subject, depicted the complex, precarious relationship between the state and the merchant class from the imperial times to the present era. In Wu's view, Chinese merchants, no matter how rich and successful, have always treaded on dangerous ground with the country's political authorities, who have a long history of exploiting and controlling them. "In the past one hundred years or so," Wu said, "many Chinese entrepreneurs were patriotic and passionate about building a strong and modern China. They had sometimes played an important role in pushing for social progress. In certain critical moments of history, many entrepreneurs had shown an idealism that was more rational and real than that of many intellectuals and politicians. But their efforts have not been fairly evaluated, and often they had to deal with a hostile state and public prejudices." However, according to Wu, in the past thirty years, the situation has improved greatly.

Perhaps because of this, Zhang's support of the present Chinese leadership struck me as quite genuine. Leng Tiesong, one of Zhang's childhood friends, told me a story about how Zhang was "bullied" by an official from the city's Bureau of Industry and Commerce (BIC). According to Leng, the official had penalized a businessman, confiscated some of his construction materials, and then forced Zhang to buy them. "It was junk Dazhong had no use for, but he had to swallow things like this," Leng concluded. "It's not easy to be a private entrepreneur in China." But later, when I asked Zhang about the incident, he shrugged it off and said that Leng doesn't know the full story. "I get along very well with those BIC officials. You may say I'm a bit of a diplomat, but a relationship is always give and take. Nobody forced me. He asked if I'd buy those materials at a low price and I said sure, since I've got warehouse space and the stuff comes in handy sometimes." Zhang admitted that back in the 1980s the government and the whole society used to look down on *ge ti hu* (个体户, people doing business on their own). "But that changed after 1992. Official policies toward private business have been improving. On the whole the government treats us pretty well."

Li Shaohua, founding chairman of a private company that offers real estate management services, shares this view of an improved, benign relationship between the state and private business. Li and Zhang had met in 1993 at a business meeting, and the two have become friends over the years. Both served several terms as vice president of *ge xie* (个协, Beijing Association of Private Entrepreneurs), an organization that helps manage relations between the government and private businesses. Launched with a dozen members in the early 1990s, *ge xie* now boasts over one thousand members. "After 1995 the government started paying more attention to us because our ranks swelled so quickly. Dazhong was among the first to be invited to BIC meetings. The government usually favors good men with a solid business, not those commodity-trading and property-flipping types with a showy cell phone."

At first Li thought of Zhang as "just a simple, plain-looking guy who worked really hard and didn't talk much at the meetings." "Until last year, every time I visited Dazhong I'd see him dressed in a blue work vest, looking just like a *da gong zai* [打工仔, a guy who works for a living]. He didn't even drink good tea, not to mention good wine." He was referring to Zhang's recently developed interest in wine and tea. "Now he talks a lot more at meetings and gives his opinions," Li said, chuckling.

Li has come to admire Zhang greatly. "I know a lot of rich people, and frankly a lot of them suck as human beings," he rolled his eyes darkly. "I won't name names here. But Dazhong is a rare specimen. In Chinese we call an educated merchant with culture *ru shang* [儒商, Confucian merchant]. I'd call Dazhong *de shang* [德商, a virtuous merchant]," Li said. He went on, citing his friend's many virtues: decency, honesty, perseverance, calmness, and a self-assured, principled mind that doesn't shift with the winds but dares to challenge itself. These, in Li's opinion, are the personal attributes that have made Zhang so successful in business. But what makes him also a beloved man among friends and popular among his employees, Li said, is his true sensitivity and generosity. "He sent a *hong bao* [红包, cash gift in a red envelope] when he heard from his driver that my driver was getting married—to *my* driver! Once I had to cancel a meeting with Dazhong because my father-in-law died. Then, at the crematorium, we were surprised to see him and his wife: they rushed over to offer their condolences to us. My wife was so touched." Li said he finally realized what the difference was between Zhang and his other rich friends: "All of us know how to make money, but Dazhong is the one who really knows how to spend money. No wonder he is rewarded with this bounty of affection—why, he is living in paradise now!"

Indeed, nearly everyone I interviewed mentioned Zhang's generosity and deep sense of gratitude. Hu Rong, Zhang's former schoolmate, described him with an ancient Chinese proverb: *Di shui zhi en, yong quan xiang bao* (滴水之恩，涌泉相报—someone who repays a debt of one drop of water with a gushing spring). Zhang would seek out anyone who had showed any kindness to his family when they were down and poor—an old neighbor who said a few encouraging words or invited him for a home meal, a classmate who lent him half a yuan—and shower them with appreciation and gifts. To thank those who helped him in his humble entrepreneurial beginnings, Zhang placed a newspaper ad offering 60,000 yuan to anyone who brought him one of the floor lamps he made and sold for six yuan over twenty years earlier. One customer answered the ad. The lamp he brought back now stands in a corner of Zhang's office. Zhang told me he had once heard a cab driver complaining that all rich people in China are corrupt scoundrels who got started by kissing officials' butts. "Well," he pointed at the lamp, "that's how I got started."

Many of Zhang's former schoolmates are retired and living on pensions now, and they appreciate the annual school reunion Zhang has hosted for over thirty years. "When he was poor, he used to invite us all to his home, where he and his wife cooked all the food," Hu Rong told me. "As he grew rich, the restaurants he booked for our reunions got better and better. It's the event all of us look forward to every year." In 2008 Zhang also sponsored a group of them on a sightseeing trip to Japan, paying all their expenses, including those for gift shopping. He often helped their children find jobs at his company; if nothing was suitable, he'd help them with money.

Zhang is also a popular boss. Right after he made the deal with Gome, Zhang celebrated by distributing *hong bao* to all his employees. Shortly after Gome's takeover, Zhang set up a fund, available to all former Dazhong employees, from which they could claim a small monthly subsidy for the rest of their lives in recognition of their contribution to Dazhong's growth. Hong Chun, a former Dazhong store manager in charge of air-conditioner sales, now works for Gome but gets 600 yuan annually from the Dazhong fund. "We all feel nostalgic about the old days," Hong told me. Gome and Dazhong have different company cultures, he said. Gome management is standardized and procedure-based, with its ERP (Enterprise Resource Planning) accounting system and its frequent staff meetings, memos, and regulations. This is better for bookkeeping and overall managerial control, but Dazhong operated in a more personal style, more like a family business. Unlike Huang, whom Hong has never met, Zhang used to show up in the store regularly, wearing the same blue work uniform as his employees, and he liked to stroll around to get a sense of the sales scene. Once, having watched a salesman talking on and on with a hesitant customer, Zhang intervened. "I'll give you a 200-yuan discount if you buy this system," Zhang offered, and the customer bought it right away. "When our salespeople heard that story, everyone tried to follow the boss's example," Hong said.

At lunchtime Zhang would sit down and have a quick bowl of noodles with the sales staff, chatting and laughing. "He has no big-boss airs, but a lot of *ren qing wei* [人情味, a flavor of human warmth]," I have been told by many Dazhong employees. Now, with Gome's stocks reduced to a fourth of its previous value (trading was closed after Huang's arrest), and sluggish sales in 2009, Hong said staff morale was low. "I'm doing my job, but I don't feel the passion and drive I once had working under boss Zhang."

On a balmy April evening recently, I met with Zhang again in his gleaming Westside office. He had just returned from a weeklong driving trip in his BMW jeep with a group of friends to the beautiful mountains of south Anhui, during which he had sent me via cell phone a poem depicting the landscape and the camaraderie shared among good friends. The verse was composed in the classical form and read quite nicely. Zhang laughed upon my inquiry as to whether he was the author: "Oh no, it was written by someone in our group. You must be wondering how my literary level shot up all of a sudden?" He laughed again and leaned back in his chair, exuding the air of a happy man who is living a charmed life after years of hard labor.

These days, Zhang tells me, he spends less than a third of his time on business. After a year of learning the stock market, he has made major investment decisions. He loaned 1 billion yuan (over $140 million) to a state bank that makes commercial loans to clients he considers quite stable and safe. Then he bought 2 billion yuan (over $280 million) worth of stocks and bonds of various companies and enterprises that are more risky. "But I entered at a low point and I'm in it for the long haul," he said. Perhaps as the entire Chinese economy experiences the pains of the downturn and the pressure of transitioning from the old manufacturing and export model to a yet uncertain new phase, Zhang's own long-term plan will also need time to take shape and flourish. For now, while a team of staff keeps monitoring the market and reporting to him, Zhang spends about two-thirds of his time "recharging": traveling and reading. When he is in Beijing, he plays tennis regularly. It's been a hobby of his for over ten years. "My partners say my technique has been improving lately," Zhang smiles. "I used to work 365 days a year, my head full of thoughts about sales all the time. So my mind would wander on the court and the ball would hit me right in the face!"

Besides trips inside China, travels to northern Europe, Canada, and Latin America have also been on Zhang's agenda. He told me about a memoir he had read about an American investor who traveled around the world by motorcycle. "He was also about sixty. Once, in Africa, he ran into some bandits who occupied a gold mine. He got down into the gold mining world pretty deeply and learned it cold. Later on, that experience was crucial in his decision about when to invest in gold mines. I'm not traveling to chase gold, but I believe it would broaden the vision and enrich the mind."

Reading is another activity Zhang takes up with a characteristic seriousness and a methodical approach. (Zhang once showed me a room he sleeps in when he stays late at his office. It's next to the gym where he regularly works out and on the same floor as his office. Everything in the room is kept in perfect order: the ironed, pressed shirts and trousers hanging on different racks; the sturdy sneakers and the well-buffed leather shoes in separate rows; the socks and ties; the books and DVDs. "You can tell a lot about a person from how organized he is in his daily habits," Zhang said.) I browsed through the bookcases, which cover a full wall in Zhang's large office. There are tomes on business and finance. History. Philosophy. Literature. Biographies of great figures from East to West. And on two low tables, books are arranged in tall, neat piles, each with filing cards sticking out from the pages. Zhang has three "reading staff" whose full-time job is reading books on various topics and briefing their boss with written summaries, notes, and quotations. "I can't read all the books from cover to cover, so I rely on these notes," Zhang said, pointing at the book piles. But certain books are deemed so important that he not only reads every page himself but also purchases extra copies to circulate to others.

One such book is *Mao: The Unknown Story* by Jung Chang and Jon Halliday. The 2005 biography offers a devastatingly negative picture of the man whose portrait still hangs on the rostrum in Tiananmen Square today. Officially banned in mainland China, this book gets around in limited ways through the Internet and private hands. It so impressed Zhang that he tracked down the London-based authors to offer his compliments. When Jung Chang visited Beijing in 2007, Zhang took her to dinner and offered his help in any way possible on her future work. After the book's Chinese edition was published in Hong Kong, Zhang bought a thousand copies, which he has been giving to whomever he deems appropriate. Wherever he goes, he always carries several copies in the trunk of his black *Benchi*, just in case. "I don't have the ability to write such a powerful work about Mao," Zhang told me. "The least I can do is to support her in whatever way I can and let more people know about it."

Yin Jinqi, who leads Zhang's reading team, admitted to me that the Mao biography had not been an easy read for her and the other reading staff. Yin is a petite, vivacious young woman with bright eyes, smart manners, and a master's degree in economics and finance. She is a fast reader who could easily finish off a big book a day and still find time to do a few other things. But the Mao biography is tough, she told me, because its content is "very unfamiliar" to young people like her who grew up in post-Mao China. "Boss Zhang got quite upset at us," Yin said. "He demanded that we read it carefully."

We were having this conversation one evening in a car as Yin accompanied Hu Jie, an independent filmmaker whom Zhang had recently hired to make a documentary about his mother. Hu's two earlier documentaries about two woman martyrs—a "rightist" critic jailed and executed, and a high school principal beaten to death by her own Red Guard students—had gained an underground reputation even though they were both banned in China. That afternoon Hu had interviewed and shot some footage of two of Wang's old colleagues; we were now on the way to another house on the eastern outskirts of Beijing to interview a witness who had participated in the mass rally at the Workers' Stadium on the day of Wang's execution. (Pan Shihong, the witness, happens to be a friend of mine, so I decided to go along for the interview.)

That evening, in his comfortable living room, with a camera rolling under bright lights, Pan described in vivid detail the scene at the Workers' Stadium nearly forty years earlier. The rally opened with loudspeakers blaring out revolutionary songs and quotations from Chairman Mao about class struggle, then rounds of slogan shouting. The twelve "counterrevolutionaries," Zhang's mother among them, were brought in. Tied up in ropes and manhandled by three guards, they were forced to kneel in a row on the floor, with their heads pressed down. Denunciations were made, and as each death sentence was announced, the head of the condemned one would be yanked up momentarily to face the crowd. The atmosphere grew frantic, and a cloud of dust flew up as the condemned men and women were pushed and shoved and the ropes on their necks and arms pulled and tightened. Finally, amid the deafening shouting of slogans, they were dragged off to be executed.

As a twenty-two-year-old school teacher back then, Pan was in a vulnerable position because he had relatives abroad (and thus easily could be accused of being a Western spy). Sitting in the crowd, he realized why he was ordered to attend the rally: it served as a warning for someone like him. "I'm sorry to say I shouted slogans against the convicts as well. I was terrified." At that time, nobody had the right to remain silent.

Pan talked about other cases he witnessed: incidents of beating, humiliation, betrayal. Above all, he talked about the pervasive fear in the society.

Later that night, after we got back in the car, everyone was silent for a while. But as the car moved smoothly on the new multilane expressway connecting the suburbs to the city, Yin turned to me and confessed that Pan's account had been absolutely shocking to her. She said none of her friends in her peer group have any real knowledge about this history, and they probably don't want to know about it, either. She said she has become more aware of it only since she started working for Zhang Dazhong.

"I'm still feeling dazed," she said, her voice uncertain and full of a shaky innocence. "It all seems so unfamiliar, so unthinkable. But Mr. Pan seems a kind person, very civil and obliging. So I don't think a nice man like him would lie to us. He couldn't have made all this up, could he?"

Listening to her, I understood why Zhang got frustrated and insisted that his young staff read the Mao biography with care. I understood, too, why Zhang would carry copies in his car trunk. I also thought about a remark Hu Rong had made about Zhang: "He suffered a great deal in the past. But I've never met anyone with greater determination and courage to walk out from that suffering."

A few days before, Zhang had mentioned an article in *Beijing Wanbao*, a local newspaper. It was about a recent incident at a local high school where a student reported to the administration that his teacher was a "counterrevolutionary" because in his lectures the teacher had criticized the government and China's political system. But the newspaper article said that citizens should have the right to free speech and should not be incriminated by what they say. Some Chinese intellectuals were disturbed by the report: to them, the young student's behavior toward his teacher confirmed their pessimism that the poison of the Cultural Revolution has not been expunged, that the ghost of history continues to haunt people despite all the shining achievements China has made in the past thirty years.

But Zhang wants to look at the bright side. "You see," Zhang said to me with an air of satisfaction, "this article is teaching folks about the rule of law. It means our country has developed not just economically. It has progressed politically."

Postscript

On March 27, 2010, Zhang Dazhong convened a public gathering at Beijing's Shangri-la Hotel to commemorate the fortieth anniversary of his mother's execution. About five hundred people, among them many old neighbors and family friends, attended the event. Mao Yushi, a renowned liberal scholar, delivered a moving eulogy about Wang, praising her as a hero and a martyr. Zhang choked up many times during his remarks; he thanked and bowed to all who had shown kindness to the Zhang family in that dark time. Afterward, participants formed long lines to lay flowers before Wang's portrait, and each received a package of materials about her life that included an elegantly printed booklet and a DVD documentary. Zhang also unveiled an oil portrait of Wang he had commissioned. The event went smoothly without any official interference.

On May 18, 2010, Huang Guangyu was sentenced to fourteen years in prison on charges of illegal operation, insider trading, and company bribing. The court also issued a fine of 600 million yuan (about $80 million) and confiscated some 200 million yuan (about $30 million) worth of his property. Meanwhile, the Chinese media reported that Bain Capital had purchased enough stock after Huang's arrest to become Gome's second biggest stockholder.

I have not found a satisfying answer to explain Huang's surprisingly heavy sentence. While gossip goes around dinner tables, the legal process and much of the information surrounding the case remain opaque. But in the course of checking with various local businessmen, I often heard a remark about Huang's personality: he was too ruthless in his dealings. His suppliers hated him because he cut prices so low they could make little profit. He sometimes treated his rivals with brutality. A widely circulated story, for example, tells how Huang handled a "traitor." One of his company managers left Gome and started a competing business, so Huang's men decided to teach him a lesson: they beat him up so badly that he ended up a handicapped man. This man, according to the folklore, became a determined and crucial informant in Huang's investigation and prosecution. The moral of the story seems to be: he who is too greedy and too hard on others will be resented and fall. In popular opinion, Huang had crossed a certain line and was truly a bad tycoon. The fact that the official ties he had cultivated were not quite powerful enough to save him is not discussed but is widely understood.

The Turtles

Zhang Xin likes to talk about her fascination with left-wing British intellectuals during her years at Sussex and Cambridge. Pan Shiyi, her husband, is a believer in Taoism who describes himself as a "feudal" Gansu country boy. When you see them on television and in magazines, they are often dressed in a kind of Shanghai-Tang chic: Pan, with his black-framed techno glasses, might be wearing a silk brocade jacket; Zhang, with a dyed streak of ash-blond hair right above the eyes, might have on a sleeveless linen top with a mandarin collar and butterfly buttons. They look like art dealers or film producers. In fact, they build apartment complexes, office towers, and shopping plazas. At the ages of thirty-nine and forty-one, respectively, Zhang and Pan are the co-CEOs of the Beijing-based firm SOHO China and the most visible real estate developers in the country.

On a cold spring day in 2004, Pan and Zhang hosted a gala to celebrate the opening of their latest project, Jianwai SOHO—twelve white, minimalist high-rises arranged in a tilted phalanx on a prime block of Changan Avenue, Beijing's main boulevard. Despite persistent drizzle, hundreds of luminaries showed up: businessmen and government officials, architects, publishers, artists, fashion editors, actors. A sudden downpour turned the open-air ribbon-cutting ceremony into a brave dash through the rain, spoiling starched clothing and fancy hairdos; at the formal dinner for five hundred guests in a gigantic white tent, some people were shivering in the evening chill. But glamour prevailed, as models sauntered down an improvised catwalk wearing Bulgari jewelry and Valentino couture. Later, a pair of professional dancers from South America performed a tango. The hosts worked the floor separately. They stepped onto the dais together only once. Pan, in a dark Prada suit, thanked the guests in Chinese. Zhang, in sky-blue silk embroidered with yellow dragons, offered appreciative remarks in English for the benefit of the many international guests.

The evening reminded me of a similar occasion, two years earlier, celebrating the completion of Architectural Gallery at the foot of the Great Wall. A pet project of Pan and Zhang's, the gallery featured twelve fanciful houses, each designed by a prominent Asian architect. One, by Shigeru Ban, was a house made of laminated bamboo. Another, designed by Yung Ho Chang, a Beijing architect who was trained in California, was built entirely of packed earth. Each of the twelve houses was priced at a million dollars, which, even for Beijing's newly rich, was a daunting sum to spend on a weekend residence that was more of a designer's conceit than an example of luxury living. The project has since been renamed the Commune by the Great Wall and, partly because of the publicity it generated, has done well as a convention center and tourist attraction.

Jianwai SOHO is far larger in scale: when everything is completed, there will be twenty high-rise towers and four villas, encompassing 700,000 square meters, and its projected sale value is about $1.2 billion. The price per square meter, at about $2,000, is high but not beyond the reach of the intended clientele, who have been drawn by the buildings' style—a contemporary blend of concrete, steel, and glass with interiors of fine-finish woodwork. By the time of the gala, 80 percent of the units had been sold.

The gala wasn't the only promotional event Zhang and Pan had arranged for the complex. Earlier that afternoon, in a conference hall inside one of Jianwai SOHO's buildings, they presided over a forum called "A Dialogue Among Architects: China and the World." Besides Riken Yamamoto, the Japanese architect who designed Jianwai SOHO, the most prominently featured speaker was Patrick Schumacher, the partner of the celebrated Baghdad-born architect Zaha Hadid, who was then designing another project of Pan and Zhang's: an upscale apartment complex on Changan Avenue near Jianwai SOHO. Schumacher showed slides and spoke to a packed hall, with Zhang standing nearby to translate for him. On a screen behind him, a cluster of buildings shimmered, their color somewhere between silver and gold. I have heard the Hadid design described as a "school of fish."

The image that often arises when people speak of Pan and Zhang is that of a pair of turtles. In China, people like Zhang who have spent time in the West are known as *hai gui* (海龟/海归)—a pun on "sea turtle" and "returnee from the sea." As the Chinese economy has become more integrated into the global market, *hai gui* have grown numerous. ("Globalization means going home," one *hai gui* said to me.) By contrast, people like Pan are represented by *tu bie* (土鳖), the local turtles. The *hai gui* are valued for their international perspective; the *tu bie* are the ones who know how to get things done. Pan and Zhang have become the best-known *tu bie-hai gui* team in China. But, as they've learned, the alliance between *tu bie* and *hai gui* isn't always without friction.

China has been called the world's biggest construction site; everywhere you turn in cities like Beijing, there are cranes, scaffolds, steel rebars, skeletons of old buildings, half-finished new ones. Yet the people who are directly responsible for this constant din have largely stayed out of the public eye, and not without reason. Developers are regarded as China's robber barons, men who have taken advantage of the muddled transition to capitalism by means of *guanxi* (connections), bribery, and fraud.

If you bring up the subject of developers at a dinner party, someone will tell you about a "tofu-dreg project"—a building that has started to fall apart after two years—or relate a story of forced eviction where neighborhood residents fall victim to deals made between officials and developers. A television series called *The Winter Solstice* reflects this popular view. It's a portrait of a picturesque old town in central China that is undone by the onslaught of development, and it features a moblike building company: its bosses are greedy, scheming predators, their underlings thuggish killers. A Beijing real estate entrepreneur told me, "Of all the shows I've watched, this comes closest to a realistic portrayal of contemporary reality—though it shows only the tip of the iceberg." Pan Shiyi, who says that he hopes to change the image of his profession, has certainly seen it at its worst.

Pan never planned on a career as a developer. Born in a poor village in the barren northwest province of Gansu, he grew up in the shadow of hunger and political misfortune: his father was labeled a "rightist"; his mother was an invalid. Pan and his siblings often worried about not having enough to eat. It was a considerable achievement when, after getting his college diploma in Langfang, near Beijing, he was assigned to an office job as one of more than forty thousand bureaucrats in the Oil Pipeline Bureau of the Petroleum Ministry. Still, he became convinced that it was a job without a future.

"I resigned because that was an open and exciting time," Pan recalled as we sat in his large but sparely furnished office in SOHO New Town, a complex of high-rise towers he has built on the east side of the capital. The floor-to-ceiling windows offered a bird's-eye view of bustling, traffic-jammed Changan Avenue, a dramatic contrast to hushed and orderly interiors. His large black desk was free of paper; his deputies and secretaries were keeping out of the way. "The words and actions of the nation's leaders, such as Hu Yaobang"—the reformist Communist Party general secretary, whose later disgrace and death triggered the 1989 Tiananmen protests—"wearing a Western suit, made a very big impact on people," he went on. "In that kind of atmosphere, I came to feel that my office job was redundant, useless."

In 1987, Pan quit his job, sold all his belongings, and took the long train ride south to Shenzhen, which had been declared a "special economic zone," exempt from many of the usual rules of state socialism. One of his college professors had started a company there, but when he found the professor, the company had gone bankrupt. Pan found a job at a consulting company helping to move Hong Kong factories across the border to Pearl River Delta. The next two years were gloomy. He hated the hot, muggy climate; couldn't understand the local Cantonese dialect; worked overtime; and felt depressed. Everyone he knew advised him to go back to his government job. Only one friend, who had worked abroad, said to him: "The planned economy is doomed. Persevere. Don't turn back, even if you become a beggar."

In 1989, Pan made his way further south, to the backward island province of Hainan, which had just become a new "special economic zone." It was a "dirty, stinky mess," he recalled, largely without electricity. After sleeping on damp pillows in a moldy seaside establishment, Pan took a morning walk with a friend and discovered that the locals used the beach as a toilet. "A man's taking a shit over there, and here comes a guy trying to sell watches to us. He rolls up a sleeve, and all sorts of watches are strapped around his arm. My friend chooses one, but the watch guy says, 'No sale for you.' My friend says, 'Why not?' The watch guy says, 'Because your wallet has been stolen.' We turn around and the pickpocket is right there, squatting on his heels not far from us. We give chase, he runs. The islanders run much faster than us. And the moment we are out of wind and stop, the pickpocket stops, too, and squats again. That was my first Hainan experience."

Pan eventually became a brick-factory chief in Hainan, had a jeep to drive around, and was happier. But after a huge monsoon hit the island, many went out of business and left. Pan persevered. Finally, in 1992, Deng Xiaoping made his famous "southern tour" and called for faster and more thoroughgoing market reforms. The central government granted further exemptions to develop Hainan, creating a sort of free-enterprise zone that was among the least regulated in the country. Pan and five other young men he met in the south, all educated northerners, decided to form their own company, the Vantone Group, and try their hand at real estate. But they needed money.

Feng Lun, one of the Vantone founders, used to be the deputy chief of a State Council think tank and had government contacts in both Beijing and Hainan. The six men lobbied a state company from Beijing and impressed its boss with their business plan. The boss agreed to lend them five million yuan if they would pay 20 percent in interest and half of future profits. They bought eight villas, at 3,000 yuan (about $350) per square meter. Two months went by, but there were no buyers. Day after day, the young speculators sat in their shabby office, trying to figure a way out.

"We prayed and prayed for something to happen," Pan said. By the third month, buyers began to show up. Pan set the price at 4,100 yuan per square meter and landed his first client: an entrepreneur from Shanxi. The moment another buyer arrived, from Inner Mongolia, Pan pushed the price up to 4,200. Soon, he was selling villas at twice the initial price.

This kind of real estate speculation was a major part of Hainan's legend of wealth creation; a horde of adventurers and speculators were hyping and flipping properties. In the local idiom, the process is called *chao lou*, "stir-fry buildings." Many latter-day "capitalists" were born in a process that Marx-conscious Chinese scholars have called "primitive accumulation."

Feng Lun, who is now the chairman of the Vantone Group, described the Hainan period to me as resembling the gold rush in the American West: weak government controls, vague regulations, a stampede of fortune hunters. "Lots of strange things happened there," he told me as we sat in a cigar chamber at a plush Beijing hotel. A wiry, genial man with rimless glasses, his thinning hair carefully brushed across his scalp, Feng looked more like a scholar than like a business tycoon. "For example, in a business quarrel, you'd be tricked into a night club where you'd be shoved up against a wall in a dark room with a gun pressed in your belly, and you'd be forced to sign a contract. This happened to people in our company. From time to time, someone would just disappear—murdered. Official seals were being faked all the time. But it was a very happy time. Because you suddenly arrived in a completely free zone—no law, no restrictions, no need to care about all that rotten traditional stuff."

Feng told colorful tales of uptight Beijing cadres going to Hainan night clubs—brothels, essentially—where they were ministered to by "little misses," and of their evolution from excruciating awkwardness to debauchery. "When your local hosts asked you to go to a night club, you could not refuse," he told me. "Because that's where people discussed business. You say, 'I'm pure'? Then no business for you." It took Feng, with his State Council background, a while to get used to the absence of order and security. "Then you discovered that life was very free and very crazy, and you enjoyed it very much. Experiences like that would change your view of the world, your norms of right and wrong."

Feng described his education as "totally orthodox," "fundamentalist Marxism." He had joined the Communist Youth League at fifteen, the Communist Party at twenty, and had been a student cadre all the way from grade school to graduate school. "But, in the end, *bah!* I've changed completely."

"And you've become a bad man?" I asked. (Bad man, *huai ren*, was a term jestingly applied to those rule-breaking Hainan adventurers. On another occasion, I'd heard Feng describe himself as "a good man among bad men, but a bad man among good men.")

He laughed. "No, I think I've become a *normal* man."

When Pan talks about Hainan, he stresses the business side of things, and invokes the dot-com era of Silicon Valley: "You are involved in raising market prices, and everyone is investing. You control an angle and make sure you get out in time. Not getting into a big rising market is stupid. But the smart ones don't just drift with the tide. Go up when you can, and, while others are still going, retreat if you think it's time." During a visit to the local planning bureau, Pan noticed two sets of figures. First, Hainan had far more temporary than full-time residents. Second, on a per-capita basis, Hainan, though still a poor island, was building seven times faster than Beijing. This was a case of overbuilding, he concluded. It was time to pull out. Shortly before the Hainan real estate market collapsed, Pan borrowed fifty thousand yuan from the company account and left for Beijing.

Zhang Xin comes from a long line of Chinese immigrant merchants who settled in Burma. In the 1950s, as waves of anti-Chinese sentiment swept across Southeast Asia, her parents decided to move back to their ancestral land. Married in Beijing, they were both assigned jobs as translators at the Bureau of Foreign Languages. But the Cultural Revolution did them in: the two joined rival factions and, Zhang recalled, started fighting viciously. The couple separated in 1970, when Zhang was only five years old. Immediately afterward, her mother took her off to a cadre camp in the Henan countryside.

It was a difficult childhood. Her mother, a feisty, hardworking woman, dropped her off at the homes of various relatives and friends whenever she found her inconvenient. Zhang was transferred seven or eight times in her elementary school years. Even after she and her mother moved back to Beijing in 1972, life was a struggle. "We slept on office desks at first," Zhang recalled. "Every night, we laid out dictionaries on the desk and stretched out on them."

In 1980, when Zhang was fourteen, she followed her mother to Hong Kong, where they lived in a tiny room and had almost no money. For a while, they both worked in a garment factory. Later, Zhang got an assembly-line job at an electronics manufacturing plant.

"They were giant buildings," she said with a grimace. "Over twenty floors high, with hundreds of assembly lines inside, each line a small plant. The workers had no sense of belonging. They switched jobs—maybe just to the plant across the hallway—over the smallest pay raise." Competition was intense but always at a low level; quick hands were all that counted. Zhang yearned to become a clerk in a quiet office.

Two years later, at the age of sixteen, she got a job as a warehouse clerk, fell in love with the math teacher at her night school, and, for a while, was content. But in 1984 a childhood friend visiting Hong Kong "turned my whole world upside down," Zhang recalled. The young man could speak English and attended college. "Gosh, your life here is really no good," he told Zhang. "You should go to America."

She went to England instead. In 1987, having spent a couple of years learning English at an Oxford secretarial school, Zhang received a scholarship that enabled her to attend the University of Sussex. A gathering place for the British intellectual left, the Sussex campus was, in her eyes, full of idealists and eccentrics. She remembers one classmate who never washed his long hair. ("It looked like a shiny mushroom over his head.") But, above all, she was fascinated by her leftist professors. "Many of them took part in the 1960s movements. Their understanding of communism was purely romantic, a metaphysical probing so different from ours."

By then, most Chinese students there had lost their faith in communism, but Zhang wanted to side with the romantic Europeans. "The Chinese talked endlessly about Cultural Revolution sufferings while thinking about how to get their 'eight big pieces' home," she said. (The "eight big pieces" refers to electronic housewares such as televisions, tape recorders, and washing machines, which were scarce in China then.) "I also experienced the life of the Hong Kong assembly lines. Communism was complex for me."

Then came the events at Tiananmen Square. "I stopped going to classes," Zhang recalled. "For a whole semester, I was glued to the television. All the Chinese on campus were like that. As soon as news of the massacre came, we took the night train to London to demonstrate in front of the Chinese embassy. There must have been ten thousand of us there. That was the single most exciting moment in my college life."

Zhang wrote her thesis on privatization in China. "I was very skeptical," she told me. "It was all about the problems privatization would cause." After graduating from Sussex in 1991, Zhang worked on a master's degree in economics at Cambridge. The other Chinese graduate students she met there were an ambitious group of young intellectuals; some of them had been involved in the 1980s reforms back home. When they got together, the future of China was a constant topic, and Zhang felt certain that her own future was in her homeland.

While she was completing her master's degree, Barings PLC sent scouts to Cambridge: their Hong Kong branch needed people to analyze privatization in China. Because Zhang had written her thesis on the topic, she was hired immediately. Going to Hong Kong, she figured, would be the first step toward moving back to China. She didn't know that her Barings unit was about to be acquired by Goldman Sachs. By the summer of 1993, she found herself on Wall Street.

As Zhang Xin was starting off as a young Wall Street analyst, Pan was embarking on a new business adventure in Beijing. One day, while he was having lunch with some local officials, he heard that the municipal government had just issued a document allowing the experimental creation of shareholding companies. Frantic preparations followed. Pan went to every official contact that the Vantone partners had in Beijing to shore up their support. He lobbied several state enterprises and enlisted them as co-founders of a new shareholding company. Finally, six months later, Beijing Vantone Industry, Ltd., was registered. The partners decided to put down 800 million yuan ($100 million) as the company's capital. In Chinese, the word for "eight" rhymes with the word for "prosper."

But this was largely money on paper. Under the new regulations, the company had two months in which to raise the funds by floating shares. Pan placed a full-page ad in a Chinese financial newspaper. It caught the eye of the vice chairman of the State Stocks Security Committee, who alerted various officials. Pan was ordered to appear before a joint hearing at the System Reform Commission.

Facing a roomful of officials, each holding a copy of the Vantone ad, Pan recalls sweat beading on his face: would he be found in violation of some rule? "Young man, relax," one official said, and asked Pan about his company's new stockholder's certificate. Pan told the official that the company had printed on the certificate all the policy guidelines from the System Reform Commission. The official nodded approvingly: the Beijingers do things by the rules, better than those in Hainan. He took out a stock certificate made in Hainan: "Look, this is just a receipt they bought on the streets!" As it turned out, the experiment on shareholding companies had started a new national craze, and since China had no existing company laws, the officials had to make up the rules along the way. They were conducting hearings in an effort to find their bearings.

Pan remembers listening to a moody song called "Like Wind, Like Fog, Like Rain" on the drive home; he says that it captured his state of mind exactly. He wasn't at all sure how to play the Beijing market. But he wasn't inclined to hold back, either.

The company's next project, Vantone New World Plaza, was a giant office-and-retail complex in the heart of Beijing. Pan attributes its success to the simple fact that advertising was a novelty in China. Vantone spent 10 million yuan on a marketing campaign—an astronomical figure then—and was able to take out big ads in major papers, such as the overseas edition of *People's Daily*, Shanghai's *Wenhui Daily*, and Hong Kong's *Dagong Daily*. Prices for the Vantone New World Plaza soared to $6,000 per square meter, an unprecedented figure in Beijing. All the units sold while contractors were still breaking ground. Eventually, the company more than tripled its investment.

• • •

Zhang Xin made good money on Wall Street—a six-figure salary with various perks and benefits—but she detested the ethos of the place. "On Wall Street, all values seemed upside down," she said. "People spoke crassly, treated others badly, looked down on the poor, and adored the rich. They'd do anything to get promoted. Whoever made the most profit was a hero, and everyone was fighting everyone else." It reminded her of the Hong Kong assembly line. "The difference is, in Hong Kong the competition turns people into shortsighted mice, whereas on Wall Street it turns them into wolves and tigers."

"And then there were these so called 'off-sites,' " she went on. "It was just another form of brainwashing and thought-copying, much like those Communist Party study groups." In a company off-site, employees and their families would be flown to beautiful places like Paris and London to eat, shop, and trade snobby notes about clothing brands and children's schooling. Wives would end up demanding their husbands make more money.

Zhang did a lot of traveling. "I lived out of a suitcase, traveling to three cities per week, running around without knowing why I was doing all this," she recalled. "I never had to use my judgment. The work had nothing to do with what I studied at school. In fact, I don't see why they need all those highly educated people. It's a waste of talent."

In 1994, she left Goldman Sachs to become an investment banker at the Travelers Group, where the work was less stressful but the travel remained intense. She yearned to move back to China. A Cambridge classmate suggested that she check out an "interesting" Chinese company called Vantone.

On a flight to China, weary and bored, Zhang took out the prospectus that her classmate had mailed to her. It was Vantone's mission statement. The title read like a manifesto—"Break through brambles and thorns, to the future we strive together"—and the text continued in the same exalted language. "It got me so excited!" she recalled. "The way these young intellectuals wanted to contribute to their country, their grand ideas about building enterprises—suddenly I found kindred spirits in all my romantic longings." It was May 1994. As soon as her plane landed in Beijing, she arranged a meeting with the Vantone partners.

Four days after Pan and Zhang were introduced, he proposed. "He's extremely sensitive to opportunities," Zhang said, smiling.

From the beginning, though, their relationship was to be a business partnership as well as a personal one. Pan had some vague ideas about attracting foreign capital, but he didn't know how to go about it. Zhang wanted to find a role for herself in China, but she didn't know where to begin. She found everything about Vantone, including its muddle-headed, overreaching business style, endearing. When she was taken to a construction site on that first visit, she was awed. "I had never seen a huge open pit like that in my life," she said. "It was gigantic, and suddenly a sensation flooded my veins: China, a great expanse of land and horizon. It was grand. And then I went on a trip with the guys, sailing down the Yangtze. They'd hold their board meetings on the boat, and I'd join them at mealtimes. It felt so different from Wall Street."

Zhang and Pan were married in October 1994. A year later, Pan decided to leave Vantone, and Zhang left Wall Street. She and Pan started their own company. They called it Hongshi. (It was renamed SOHO China in 2002.)

"Feng Lun must hate me," Zhang told me when I mentioned having met with the chairman of Vantone.

"Because you're the Yoko Ono who broke up the band?"

Zhang laughed, but that was her point. Still, Pan's old partners have flourished as well. At one of the busiest intersections in Beijing, Pan and Feng each beam from two giant billboards, their portraits about fifty yards apart.

"East meets West" and "Local unites with foreign" was how the Beijing media touted the alliance. But tensions between *hai gui* and *tu bie* arose almost immediately. On their honeymoon trip to the Great Barrier Reef, they had a heated argument. Pan was enraged by his bride's neo-Marxist ideas: how ignorant, how callous toward Chinese suffering she was! Zhang, for her part, was shocked by Pan's lack of idealism. The relationship grew even stormier when they began working together in their own company. Zhang now says that 1996 and 1997 were the hardest years of her life: she and her husband fought daily.

In some ways, it was a clash between East and West. Zhang might have felt like an outsider on Wall Street, but in the world of Chinese business she was seen as so Westernized that she was practically a foreigner. She wanted regular staff meetings where everyone was informed about company issues and could contribute suggestions, because, she insisted, democracy was the way to manage and solve problems. But Pan's experiences had convinced him that the way to run a company was to follow his own instincts: no questions, no explanations, no overlapping voices. "A country needs democracy, but a business needs autocracy, or it'll go down the tubes," he told his staff.

Relations between Zhang and her husband's old employees, who had followed him from Vantone, were also delicate. These men viewed Pan's "foreign wife" with suspicion and jealousy, and Zhang found little sympathy for her ideas about quality and detail. Every time she rejected something that was done by her staff—and in the beginning she found 99 percent of the work "not up to the standard"—she'd get the same response: "You don't understand the Chinese situation." The Chinese situation, evidently, required a kind of "make-do" mentality. Gradually, Zhang began to doubt her experiments in workplace democracy. It seemed to result in people talking rather than working, and, she discovered, once the sense of hierarchy was weakened, it was hard to order people around. She began to feel defeated.

To Beijingers, the names Pan Shiyi and Zhang Xin are linked to one large apartment-office complex, SOHO New Town. This was Hongshi's first major project, and it hadn't looked promising. The land belonged to a large liquor factory, and the stench was detectable from a great distance. Pan and Zhang went to survey the site on a rainy day, and, plodding through the mud and holding her nose, Zhang decided that it was too unpleasant to build on.

Pan had a different view. The land was on a major avenue in the fast-growing Chaoyang district, near an area with a concentration of foreign embassies, international hotels, and shopping plazas. Traditionally, Beijing had developed along the north-south axis, but a recent trend suggested a rapid expansion toward the east side. New subway lines and highways were due to open in two years; plans to clean up the foul-smelling river nearby were under way. The zoning restrictions were less exacting than they were in the city center, so it would be possible to build much higher. Pan was also betting on a policy breakthrough: so far, the government had not permitted personal mortgages on housing, but he figured that it would do so within a few years, by which time construction would be finished. Personal bank loans meant that more people would be able to afford his upscale apartments. In short, instinct told him that location and timing, the two crucial factors in real estate, were both on their side.

At that time, most Chinese developers were chasing quick money, and a project was often bought and sold many times before a single brick was laid. Contemptuous of this trend, Zhang intended to go international: she wanted to attract major foreign investors and build something grand, like Hong Kong's Pacific Place. Pan was skeptical: he thought that would involve too many moving pieces and too much time. But he gave in, trusting his wife's expertise in raising foreign capital. So Zhang set to work, turning down small investors in order to focus on major backers. After nearly two years of negotiations, GIC, a Singapore government company that manages the country's foreign reserves, finally agreed to bankroll the project.

Then, in July 1997, the Asian financial crisis struck, and the deal was suspended. Pan was furious, telling Zhang that if they had worked with small investors they would have finished building long ago. "You and your Wall Street strategies," he roared. "It's like discussing warfare on paper!" Zhang packed her suitcase and flew west to see her old friends. Pan went to Japan to cool down. Both assumed the marriage was over.

In England, Zhang stayed at a friend's country house. Despite the beauty and tranquility of the place—trees, horses, a pond—she felt restless: life in the West had lost its allure. If she didn't return to China now, she decided, she never would. And if she was to be with Pan, they had to figure out another way to work together.

She called him, and they had a long talk. "I will step down," she offered. "You do it yourself." And, she said, she wanted to have a child. This was, Zhang says, the most "rational" decision she had ever made in her life. "It was as though I gave myself a hard shove on the back."

She returned to Beijing and was soon pregnant with the first of her two sons. Pan took full command of the business. Working with small investors, he signed up contracts building by building. Meanwhile, the couple commissioned Yung Ho Chang, the architect who would later design the packed-earth house for the Commune by the Great Wall, to build a country house for them on the city's outskirts.

Zhang shuttled back and forth to supervise the work being done on the house, meeting and talking regularly with Chang. For him, architecture was the family business; his father had designed the National Museum of Revolutionary History on Tiananmen Square. But the son was American-trained and had an eclectic, postmodern sensibility, with particular emphasis on the cultural dimensions of architecture. Stimulated by their conversations, Zhang delved into piles of architecture books.

"It was like taking a seminar," Zhang told me. And she was delighted with the house, which she and Pan decided to call Mountain Whispers: tall steel columns, stone walls, large windows—cavernous yet flooded with light. It was to be the family's weekend retreat. Her experience with Chang also awakened her to the possibilities of architecture. She looked back at all the buildings she had seen in Hong Kong, Europe, and America. Hong Kong, a city of dense population and high-rise apartment towers, was an especially useful reference: behind that ultramodern cityscape, every inch of space had been carefully calculated. Could this be achieved in Beijing?

Pan Shiyi was too smart a businessman not to make full use of Zhang. So, before the SOHO New Town construction began, he worked out a division of labor: he would take charge of financial affairs (contract negotiations, fund-raising, sales, government relations), and she would handle decisions on architectural design, project management, and foreign relations. This time, Zhang proved to be well suited to the job. "She is moody, romantic, but a very shrewd businesswoman," Hung Huang, a *hai gui* friend of Zhang's and the publisher of several trendy Beijing lifestyle magazines, said. "It's a potent combination."

For SOHO New Town, Zhang sought out young local designers and urged them to be bold. This resulted in a series of features for which the complex eventually became famous. The apartments had large living rooms but small bedrooms and no balconies—the opposite of traditional Beijing apartments. They had floor-to-ceiling windows, which traditionalists considered unsafe, and fine-finish woodwork, rather than the usual unfinished "white box" surfaces. Instead of the traditional gray, the color scheme was vibrant; red, yellow, green, and purple were used on the façade of every tower. At the same time, there were no costly, showy materials like granite and stainless steel. Some apartments had sliding walls, so that they could easily be adapted as office spaces. The concept of "SOHO"— Small Office, Home Office—was adopted with an eye to the growing number of small private companies in Beijing.

And then, to give the place an "artistic" feel, Zhang commissioned Ai Weiwei, a conceptual artist and an eminence in Beijing's avant-garde circles, to organize a group of installations on the grounds. Ai had lived in New York City for years before moving back to Beijing. His reputation as an inveterate troublemaker would have scared off most developers, but Zhang gave him a budget and promised him total freedom. Ai didn't disappoint her. Right on schedule, more than a dozen witty, stylish, and very "modern" sculptures and installations were placed in various public areas inside the towers, helping to attract the young, affluent cosmopolitans Pan and Zhang were targeting.

Then, just before construction was completed and the sales campaign could be properly launched, Deng Zhiren, Pan's sales chief, went to work for another company. Soon, Deng was hiring away much of Hongshi's sales team and bad-mouthing Pan publicly. Pan and Zhang rushed to prepare statements and called for press conferences before more damaging stories could be aired. But suddenly developers, journalists, and even people who had already bought apartments in SOHO New Town were criticizing the project: the high prices, the uncertain quality. One rival developer, Ren Zhiqiang, the president of the Beijing Huayuan Group, called the SOHO New Town project "junk houses that should be bombed." He went on television to complain that the SOHO design had received three points, a very low score, at the Municipal Housing Committee review. "It barely passed it," Ren said indignantly. "But he gets a three-point product sold at a five-point price and makes a ten-point impact."

How to respond to the onslaught? "A hero would draw his sword and commit suicide," Pan said with a sly smile, and his next move certainly looked suicidal. In the midst of the crisis, an elegantly printed volume collecting all criticisms of Pan and the SOHO project arrived at Beijing's bookstands—published by Pan himself. The strategy worked: the more their opponents criticized their project, the more Pan and Zhang were able to defend and explain their ideas, and the more they talked to the press, the more persuasive they seemed. Until now, nobody in the real estate business had seemed as educated and knowledgeable, and certainly nobody was as media-friendly. No other housing project had ever enjoyed as much coverage.

"In this day and age," Pan said, "only a real person, a controversial person, can attract others' attention. Only then will people be concerned about you." Pan cited as his inspiration an American who was even more famous than Donald Trump: Bill Clinton. Clinton's media performance during the Monica Lewinsky scandal impressed him. "When he looked worn out, he still had to go to evening parties, face foreign reporters," Pan noted. "The pressure must have been huge!"

After a long, anxious wait, in late 1999, just as SOHO New Town was nearing completion, the mortgage bill was finally issued. In a way, this was a consequence of the Asian financial crisis, which convinced the Chinese government that it couldn't rely entirely on foreign capital and exports, and that it was necessary to stimulate domestic consumer demand as well. At the sales office, people lined up through the night, and all two thousand units quickly sold. SOHO New Town became an instant landmark. Its modern, minimalist style established a trend, and Pan and Zhang became famous.

"It's an odd but telling phenomenon," a Hong Kong businessman now living in Beijing said to me. "In Hong Kong, business tycoons are the true celebrities. At a glamorous gathering, tycoons get front seats, while movie stars are a bit on the sidelines. But Beijing's celebrities are almost all movie stars and artists. Pan Shiyi and Zhang Xin are practically the only businesspeople." His explanation was simple. "Most superrich people in mainland China cannot publicly explain their fortune," he said. "*Lai lu bu ming*, 'the origin is unclear.' They have to keep a low profile. How can a member of the 'princelings' [the children of Party leaders] preen in the media after using Daddy's influence to rake in millions? Or those who made it to the top through massive corruption and misuse of public funds? Pan Shiyi was poor, a nobody. Sure, they must have some connections, and you could question that first company loan in Hainan. But that's nothing on the corruption scale."

There's no doubt that corruption is endemic in the Chinese real estate business. For example, until recently land sales weren't open;

a bidder wasn't entitled to know what anyone else had bid, and an underbidder could prevail by offering kickbacks to a few relevant officials. In August 2004, though, the government finally established new rules that call for open auctions in Beijing. "With the open-auction law, the government is saying to developers, 'You have made a lot of money from nothing, now you must buy land with real money and compete with others, including foreign companies,'" said Keith Abell, the vice chairman and co-founder of GSC Partners, an investment firm based in New York. Abell has been visiting China regularly since 1979; he also happened to be Zhang's boss at Travelers Group. In the 1990s, when a big American developer came to him wanting to go to China, Abell advised against it: "I told him, 'You are not ready to do the things you must do to build in China—you aren't some guy from Hunan.'" But, he said, the situation in China has improved a lot since then. Others in Beijing real estate are skeptical that the open-auction system will end corruption. Counterstrategies, they pointed out, are already being devised. "Instead of buying the land," one of them explained, "a developer could just buy the factory or the company that's using the land. That way, they could bypass the open auction and cut deals among themselves."

In the real estate community, Pan and Zhang are widely admired, but not because people think they've entirely escaped the usual mire of Chinese land transactions. How can anyone emerge from the mud completely clean? Now that Pan and Zhang are part of the establishment, though, they're intent on rehabilitating the image of their profession; besides, well-funded businesses like theirs stand to benefit from greater transparency and clearer regulation. In both 2002 and 2003, SOHO China ranked first in individual project sales among Chinese real estate companies; in 2004, it paid more taxes than any other real estate company. The firm also bought the first piece of openly auctioned land within Beijing's Central Business District, where it has built another project, called SOHO Shang Du: a 170,000-square-meter office and shopping complex.

SOHO Shang Du is also one of Pan and Zhang's most architec-turally ambitious developments. Designed by the Australian Peter Davidson in a style that has been described as "fractal geometry," its two main towers rise like iceberg shards. In January 2005, the image-conscious couple hosted a tsunami-relief fund-raiser on the Shang Du site, jointly organized by the International Red Cross, and donated a million yuan that day. Other developers later fol-lowed their lead.

Hung Huang, the magazine publisher, sounds almost rapturous when she speaks about China's first generation of self-made mil-lionaires. (According to a recent survey, she told me, there are more millionaires in China now than there are in France.) "China has produced thousands of Horatio Alger stories," she said. "Look at Pan Shiyi and Zhang Xin: a peasant's son, a girl who used to work in a Hong Kong sweatshop. I just love it! Pan Shiyi is the Donald Trump of China. This kind of success story was unthinkable ten years ago."

Not everyone shares this sunny perspective. A Hong Kong-based scholar and critic who writes on architecture and urban culture charges Zhang Xin and Pan Shiyi with being the self-satisfied cre-ators of a new kitsch; in his view, the lifestyles and buildings they promote are nothing but superficial, sterile trend-mongering. "This could be dangerous if people start thinking that's real culture," he said. Pan and Zhang have also been condemned for making the basic necessity of shelter increasingly unaffordable. "Aren't they respon-sible for Beijing's absurdly high housing prices?" the critic asked.

Certainly when Pan's former Vantone partners described him as a "real estate genius" and "the most successful private developer in Beijing," they were referring not to the quality of his buildings but to his knack for selling them at such high prices. In interviews, Pan has been happy to talk about how he had been the only person at the company sales meeting to insist on setting a high price for the Vantone New World Plaza. "They all stared at me as if I was a mad-man," he said. But he got his way, and, in the end, he recalled, the profits were so huge that at a company gathering afterward, "the men's eyes were all glazed, as if they were drunk."

Pan once said, "A businessman should be greedy by nature, but he must also be rational." He has, it would appear, been at once greedier and more rational than his colleagues. That's probably why he has consistently focused on upmarket construction: it's more lucrative as well as more glamorous. (He talked about waiting for the government to open up the secondhand housing market, and he had a vision of a social pyramid: the rich would buy his upscale homes and sell their old homes to those who are less well off.)

"He's someone who can change himself swiftly in a new environment," Feng Lun, Vantone's chairman, said. Similar things might be said of Zhang. But it's also plain that she's the one who has had to change more in order to thrive in China, and this reflects a common pattern in the relations between the cosmopolitans and the locals—between, in turtle terms, the *hai gui* and the *tu bie*. Though well trained, confident, and in demand, *hai gui* usually go through a period of readjustment, because the foreign ideas and manners they picked up from years of living abroad often create tension with the settled Chinese way of doing things. As one of my *hai gui* friends put it, "*Hai gui* will bring in some new ideas, new concepts, but *tu bie* know the rules of the game, and they know how to make it happen, or not happen."

Still, without Zhang, I wonder if it would be possible to distinguish Pan's buildings from those of other developers, like Feng Lun. "In the tide of globalization, it's hopeless to stress a particular regional character," Zhang said to me in one of our conversations. "But I feel that we should at least stop for a minute and think about our own contemporary character, our modern identity. All past dynasties left something special in Beijing: the Great Wall, the Summer Palace. We are so eager to build our big cities, but ten years from now we might be shocked by what we build, and it'll be too late. What we are doing in Beijing is an effort to leave something that we won't be ashamed of."

By now, Pan and Zhang represent both the advantages of a *tu bie-hai gui* partnership and the difficulties. They have two sons, named Rang and Shao, or Concession and Less. The names were Pan's idea: these are ancient virtues in Taoism. Yet there are subtle signs of tension. On an evening that I was to have dinner with Zhang, we were talking in her office when Pan sauntered in from his office at the opposite end of the SOHO tower. We all stood chatting together for a while. Before leaving, Pan said, in a jesting tone, "So, nothing to do with me this evening?"

"Go off," Zhang replied dryly. "Don't think you are so important!"

But he showed up anyway, while we were in their SOHO New Town apartment. "We keep a home for ourselves in every place we build," Zhang told me. The apartment is a duplex, spacious and comfortable, furnished with IKEA-style furniture, track lights, and plants—a typical yuppie home. And dinner was simple: porridge, stuffed pork naan, a couple of pickled dishes, a green leafy vegetable. The three of us chatted for a while, and I brought up the subject of *hai gui*. "You know," Pan said, half teasing, "if you write only about *hai gui*, you'll hurt us *tu bies*' feelings."

Later that evening, I asked Zhang if she had had to make many "accommodations" when she returned to China.

"Yes," she said. "As a matter of fact, for a very long time I was basically shedding the baggage I carried back from abroad. I had to de-educate myself."

She admitted that moving back changed her from a romantic to "a market advocate." But the arrogant new rich in China, she said, made her wonder about her own role. Has her work helped make people more civilized, or just more materialistic? She once wanted to be an intellectual, someone with a sense of social responsibility. But now she is viewed as a rich person, and in China today the rich are assumed to be devoid of social ethics or public spirit.

It was midnight. We had been sitting at a long glass table out on the deck, a large walled-in terrace garden that Zhang calls her "courtyard in the sky." The apartment was dark inside. The boys had gone to bed hours earlier. Pan was nowhere to be seen. The night had grown chilly.

I brought up the issue of land sales, of the pervasiveness of corruption, of "gray areas" in Chinese business and life. I asked her how she felt about all this, having lived in the West for years.

"Each side has its own ways," she said carefully. "Westerners have a simplistic understanding of China: whatever can't be clarified must be *guanxi*. The West doesn't understand that government in China is not as lean and efficient as it is in the West. There are too many governmental bodies: city, county, township, even a neighborhood is a government. It's all a messy tangle. Many things in China are vague. Some of our clients walk in and buy a dozen apartments in one shot. You don't know where they got the money. You just know some Chinese have a lot of it. It's a waste of time to try to clarify everything. I used to argue with Pan about it, because by nature I have a very low level of tolerance for vagueness. I'm not one who can fish in murky water. Pan is totally comfortable with murkiness. That's his normal state. And I've learned to tolerate it."

Postscript

In 2007, Pan and Zhang took their company public and got SOHO China listed on the Hong Kong Stock Exchange. Since 2005, the company has shifted its business focus from building upscale residential housing to developing upscale commercial space, which has a higher profit margin. With a concentration in the Central Business District, in 2009 SOHO China enjoyed the highest contracted sales among real estate development companies in Beijing.

After the 2008 global financial crisis, much of the Chinese government stimulus fund went into real estate. Housing prices in Chinese cities soared despite widespread criticism and warnings of a debt-driven bubble. Pan and Zhang have also talked publicly about the bubble, even as their own business reaped its benefits. In 2010, the government intervened with policy measures meant to put the brakes on the overheated housing market, yet powerful state-owned companies continued to drive up prices by outbidding private developers for land. The new policies, however, would not affect upmarket commercial developers like SOHO China. At the time of this writing, the company had two major projects under construction in Beijing, both designed by Zaha Hadid. Meanwhile, it is poised to expand to Shanghai, having acquired a choice plot of land in the Bund area in June 2010.

Zhang Xin has been ranked on the Forbes list of the world's top ten self-made richest women, with an estimated fortune of $3.8 billion. Besides their numerous houses in China, the family also owns apartments in London and New York, where they spend part of the summer. In recent years Pan and Zhang have found their faith in Bahai. Workshops are offered in their company for employees wishing to study the religion.

Zhang feels pessimistic about China's future these days. After she opened a *weibo*, the Chinese version of a Twitter account, late in 2009, she said she was shocked by how Chinese hated the new rich like her and her husband, and at how much anger and negative sentiment percolated on the Internet. When we met recently, Zhang admitted that she had been disconnected from "the real China" until she opened her *weibo* and read the daily postings. Now she seriously worries that the country is heading toward a major crisis.

In 2005, the SOHO China Foundation was established. The foundation's donations have been modest but slowly increasing: 2 million yuan ($250,000) for the Sichuan earthquake relief effort; 1 million yuan ($125,000) for a migrant training initiative; 10 million yuan ($1.25 million) for building rural school facilities. Its main charity project so far is an aid program in Gansu, Pan's hometown region, where it has funded the construction of thirty-five school toilets and provided teacher training for a student character-building course.

To date, most of the first-generation Chinese millionaires, including Pan and Zhang, have not turned to serious philanthropy. Their support for education and poverty-alleviation causes has been minor in scale. The public image of real estate developers as selfish robber barons persists. After hearing a good deal of sneering comments about Pan and Zhang as a slick, media-savvy, self-enriching couple, I wondered whether and when they might do something significant to prove these criticisms wrong. Do they find stories of great American entrepreneurs-turned-philanthropists such as Rockefeller, Carnegie, and MacArthur inspiring, despite the differences in their social, political, and religious culture? In this age of globalization, China's new rich have been influenced by and have emulated their wealthy Western brothers and sisters in so many ways, but will they someday also follow contemporary examples of iconic figures like Bill Gates and Warren Buffett?

Buffett and Gates have made world headlines for calling on Western tycoons to publicly promise to donate their fortunes either during their lifetimes or in bequests after their deaths. So far, forty people have taken the pledge. At least one Chinese multimillionaire, Chen Guangbiao, a self-made entrepreneur known as China's number-one donor, has said he will heed the two men's call by giving away his entire fortune, an estimated $735 million, to charity upon his death. "I don't want to become a slave to my wealth," Chen told CNN.

On September 30, 2010, Gates and Buffett hosted a much-talked-about dinner in Beijing, inviting fifty of China's richest entrepreneurs to discuss philanthropy in China. Pan Shiyi and Zhang Xin attended, as did Feng Lun, the Vantone chairman. Pan praised the American duo as "setting a fine example for entrepreneurs around the world." Zhang wrote in her *weibo* that "American philanthropy is very mature, especially the Gates [Foundation]. We've only started and have a lot to learn."

But faced with media criticism that China's superrich is too miserly to measure up to Western philanthropic standards, Feng Lun's response has been the most interesting. He reminded the public about the unique history and circumstances of China's entrepreneurial class: in 1956, its entire wealth was nationalized by the young People's Republic, or, as Feng put it, it was "统统裸捐给国家了," a "total, stripped-naked donation to the state," which, ironically, resulted in decades of impoverishment for the entire society. Today, Feng said, Chinese entrepreneurs "should not only have good hearts, but also have good management of good deeds." However, he said, we need not feel morally inferior to the Western tycoons, because "we have started philanthropy earlier than them." He noted that Bill Gates set up his foundation twenty-five years after he started his company, and Buffett got into serious charity only after his company had made money for fifty years. But China's entrepreneurs have typically established their charity foundations within ten to fifteen years of founding their own business companies, even though Chinese law in this area is still quite primitive. At the present, China already has over six hundred private charity foundations, the majority of them by private entrepreneurs. Vantone registered its own foundation in 2008, and Feng himself has also played an active role in SEE, a major environmental foundation funded by over a hundred Chinese entrepreneurs.

Peng Jianmei, director of the China People's Charity Donation Information Center (中民慈善捐助信息中心), expressed a similar view. "Based on our annual account of donation from the business sector," she told reporters, "private companies have given more than state companies, and indigenous companies have given more than foreign companies. There are many large-scale foreign companies in China, such as McDonald's, Nescafe, Carrefour, IBM, and so on, but their donation have not been in proportion with the profit they have made in China. This means that foreigners don't necessarily have stronger ideals about values than Chinese. And Chinese entrepreneurs don't need others to 'persuade' them, because they have been doing so all along." She admitted, however, that America has better laws to protect donations and donors, whereas China is still in the process of drafting its laws on charity. So this is not a problem of the individuals but of the whole society.

Both Gates and Buffett have stated that they did not intend to press the Chinese tycoons but only wanted a dialogue with them. Afterward, the two men pronounced the dinner an unqualified success. "I was amazed last night, really," said Buffett at the press conference the following day, "at how similar the questions and discussions and all that was to the dinners we had in the U.S. The same motivations tend to exist. The mechanism for manifesting those motivations may differ from country to country." According to a Chinese report, Buffett told his guests at dinner that China's philanthropy is growing faster than he had imagined, and will grow faster than the United States' in the future.

The Barefoot Capitalist

My friend Sun Lizhe is in trouble again. One of his protégés betrayed him and squeezed him out of a publishing business that he had spent years turning into a success. It had published many national bestsellers and won an award as "one of the five best new companies in China." As soon as I heard of Lizhe's troubles, I tried to contact him, but he was in America, getting business diplomas from Northwestern and the University of Pennsylvania. Later I discovered that he had enrolled in several other part-time or correspondence degree courses—some in business, some in law—at both American and Chinese universities. Going back to college at his age—fifty-two—seemed bizarre, but, on reflection, it struck me as an action as full of fresh starts and striking transformations as modern China itself.

I had first heard about his publishing venture during a visit to Beijing in the spring of 2001, at a dinner with some people in publishing circles. We were in a new, popular Hangzhou restaurant, a three-story affair with a gleaming white façade, red tile roof, cheerfully gaudy decor (including a large gilt Buddha), and a clientele composed of newly prosperous Chinese. We were discussing publishing trends in China—how the business was getting more commercial, more complicated. Now that China had joined the World

Trade Organization, there was general expectation that government restrictions might gradually loosen up. One important publishing house was making a deal with Bertelsmann, the German publishing conglomerate. Shen Changwen, a veteran Beijing publisher and editor, was talking about the special nature of joint-venture publishing in China. (Commercial firms must cooperate jointly with government agencies.) Shen, a short, colorful figure with close-cropped hair, is greatly respected among publishers as a shrewd politician; he always knows all the gossip, and he mentioned Sun Lizhe as a big mover in the field. Sun, he said, was a *meiguo zibenjia*, "an American capitalist."

"An American capitalist!" I exclaimed. "But don't you know he used to be a barefoot doctor? He was the most famous barefoot doctor in the Cultural Revolution!" An earlier innovation of the Cultural Revolution, "barefoot doctors" were people given rudimentary medical training to work in remote parts of the country, where peasants were still resorting to folkloric remedies. The people at the table stared at me blankly, as if the Cultural Revolution, and Sun Lizhe's part in it, had occurred in another universe. Then they continued talking about the Bertelsmann deal.

Sun Lizhe was a legendary figure in those earlier days. Graduating from one of Beijing's elite high schools, he had answered Chairman Mao's calls for *zhi qing*—another catchphrase of the Cultural Revolution, meaning "educated youth"—to take their knowledge to poor parts of China. Sun volunteered to go to northern Shaanxi and proved to be a born healer, improving his skills so rapidly that he was soon conducting major surgical operations. Sick peasants came from hundreds of miles away to see him. Operating from his crudely equipped clinic inside a mud cave, he treated thousands, working day and night. He and his assistants grew herbs around the clinic to make their own medicines.

As Sun's fame spread, a team of specialists, led by China's most eminent surgeon, was sent to the village. The team watched Sun operating, tested him extensively, and eventually concluded that the self-taught doctor had reached a level of proficiency equivalent to that of someone with a medical school degree and ten years of clinical experience. The news reached the Party Central Committee and so impressed Chairman Mao that, in 1974, he included Sun in a list of five "model educated youths." He was twenty-three.

At the time, the phenomenon of "barefoot doctors" was attracting a good deal of attention both inside and outside China. Sun Lizhe, the most gifted and successful of them, became a celebrity. The newspapers followed his story; television documentaries and a widely seen cinema newsreel were made about him; he was awarded luminous political titles (Party secretary of the production brigade, head of the regional health bureau, member of the provincial Communist youth league committee) and touted as a role model for Chinese youth. I was in my midteens at the time, and, as a high school student in Beijing, was required to study Sun Lizhe's life in my politics class.

Then, in 1976, Mao died, and some of the excesses of the Cultural Revolution were reversed. By the end of 1977, the college entrance exam had been reinstated. Those of us who passed could hardly believe our good fortune to be reading in a university library rather than doing manual labor on a farm.

But the new era wasn't hospitable for everyone. Even though all that Sun Lizhe had done was to treat peasants at his clinic, the many official titles that had been heaped on him identified him as part of the old regime. For an entire year he was taken from village to village and publicly denounced. On open-air platforms he faced huge crowds, among them his former colleagues and admirers, who shouted slogans at him for hours. In the lonely hours inside his mud cave, he began to drink.

Sun Lizhe twice attempted suicide. Then, trying to drink himself into oblivion, he poisoned his liver, which is actually what saved him: he became so weak that the government decided to send him to Beijing for medical treatment. While he was convalescing in the hospital, a romance started with a kind, intelligent, if plain-looking, woman named Wu Beiling. A classmate of mine, she had known Sun for years. Like him, she had been a Beijing *zhi qing* in Shaanxi, and she had evidently fallen in love with him back then, though he had always treated her simply as a comrade. Beiling brought him gifts—homemade food, fresh fruit, books—and stayed by his bed, trying to cheer him up. Along with a few other close friends, she petitioned for Sun's rehabilitation, using family connections to plead his case to senior officials. Within a few months, with the sponsorship of the head of the Beijing Institute of Medicine, who had been so impressed by the young barefoot doctor back in Shaanxi, Sun was allowed to take the 1979 college entrance exam (he scored at the top in his subject) and was admitted into the graduate program at the Beijing Institute of Medicine. His ordeal was over.

I was in my second year at Peking University when Beiling first brought him to our dorm. Tall, good-looking, and very articulate, he impressed us all. He had an excellent command of English—a rarity at the time—and seemed knowledgeable about every conceivable subject. All of us, I think, secretly envied Beiling her famous boyfriend; she was breathless whenever she talked about him, endlessly impressed by his memory, intelligence, and indefatigable energy. I also learned that he used to have a stutter, that his personal hygiene left something to be desired, and that at times he behaved like a little boy. Gradually, through Beiling, Sun lost for me his heroic aura and became like an older brother. I learned to call him Lizhe, as all his friends did.

Whenever I saw him, he was usually with Beiling and other friends who had spent time in Shaanxi. Over hot lamb and cold beer they would reminisce, telling amazing tales of hardship, poverty, and loneliness, but also of naive, passionate idealism. They poked fun at one another, but there was also great tenderness and a shared romanticism about Shaanxi. Shaanxi was their youth.

I noticed something else they had in common: their health had been damaged. These were city kids from comfortable families who plunged into backbreaking labor at the age of seventeen or eighteen. Even though they were still in their twenties, almost all of them had contracted some illness during the Shaanxi years. One man, Shi Tiesheng, who would become a famous fiction writer, was paralyzed from the waist down. He had gone to the same village as Sun, and had been a shepherd in the hills until one day he was stricken by a fever, the cause of which no one could identify, and his legs went numb. He was twenty-one, and he never walked again.

Lizhe was reputed to be a brilliant student at the Beijing Institute of Medicine. But he didn't finish. As China reopened its doors to the outside world, information about the West, though still scarce, began to circulate, and the government was making it easier for people to go abroad. In 1981, Lizhe and Beiling both applied for scholarships to study abroad. They left China separately, but in 1982 they joined each other in Chicago and began a new life.

I didn't see them again until the spring of 1990, when I visited their home in Skokie, Illinois. The neighborhood was classic suburbia—with big cars in driveways and basketball hoops above garage doors—and their house looked just like any other in the neighborhood. The minute the door opened, however, the illusion of Americanness vanished. There stood Lizhe and Beiling, smiling and talking as though they had never left China. There were big couches, multiple television sets, a barbecue in the backyard, but things seemed snatched up and thrown together in a hurry, with no thought for appearance or style. Beiling took me on a tour of the house, and I marveled at its size. What struck me the most, though, were the second-floor guest rooms, a long row of identically furnished rooms, each with a bed, a table, and a TV set. It was like a set of rooms in a functional, no-frills hotel.

Relatives and family friends were constantly dropping in and out. Lizhe's mother helped look after their two kids, a sullen seven-year-old boy and a plump baby girl. The ambience in the house was at once discordant, careless, and harmonious, from the way Beiling shuffled about in what appeared to me like a housedress and her slow, slouchy way of speaking in a colloquial Beijing accent, to Lizhe's jumping up and rushing around, now cutting into the conversation, now issuing orders for refreshments, now shooing the kids out of the room. At dinner, the tables were laden with homestyle Chinese cooking, and Lizhe bustled about serving beer and tea around the table. A group of exiled intellectuals, blithely ignoring the surrounding commotion, carried on an intense political discussion. (This was less than a year after the Tiananmen massacre.) In many respects, the feast was the same as the meals among the Shaanxi *zhi qing* back in Beijing. The role of the Chinese immigrant mixing with other exiles seemed to fit Lizhe as naturally as Maoist hero had years before.

But Beiling seemed distracted and tired, and when she put Sheng Sheng, her seven-year-old son, to bed, I followed her upstairs. Sitting in semidarkness on the bedroom floor while Sheng Sheng dozed off, we talked. Their life over the past decade, it emerged, had been turbulent. To earn income while his medical studies continued, Lizhe volunteered as an experimental subject for Northwestern's medical-school lab and also sold blood. When he started to suffer recurrent asthma attacks, he turned that to his advantage, too, becoming a paid subject in an asthma research project. But the attacks intensified, finally reaching a point where he could no longer enter a lab; the touch of a mouse was enough to trigger a violent bout of wheezing. He abandoned his dream of a medical career and turned to entrepreneurial ventures. Beiling had started a dumpling-making business at home, a project to which Lizhe now brought his usual energy. In the beginning, everything was done by hand, and even Lizhe's parents were enlisted, kneeling on the floor to stuff, fold, and pack dumplings. As demand and profits grew, they ordered dumpling machines from China and turned their house into an assembly line. This lasted two years.

By then, Beiling, too, had quit graduate school. Both she and Lizhe took jobs translating commercial documents from English into Chinese for American companies. This led to their next business: desktop publishing. It started as a home business too, but grew steadily.

Beiling was still swept up by the force of Lizhe's personality. In a large household teeming with in-laws, she was a supportive wife and a dutiful daughter-in-law, but the role weighed heavily on her. She shared her husband's enthusiasm for business, but she wasn't a natural manager, and they had almost no time alone together. Lizhe's mother was a force to be reckoned with, and once, when an argument broke out between her and Beiling, Lizhe sprang to his mother's defense and slapped Beiling. "Lizhe is a big filial son," Beiling said as we headed back downstairs to join the others.

In 1988, a tumor had been found in Beiling's abdomen and was removed. The following year she gave birth to a daughter, Jennifer. In 1990, shortly after my visit, another tumor, the size of an orange, was found and excised. The doctor thought it was benign, but in fact, it was malignant, and the cancer had already spread. Lizhe was furious at the misdiagnosis. "I had suggested to the doctor that he should assume it to be malignant and cut out more," he told me. "I'm a doctor myself, I knew what I was talking about. But the arrogant bastard gave me a contemptuous look and ignored me."

After the operation, Lizhe moved Beiling back to Beijing. I remember visiting her in the hospital there in the spring of 1991. She was pale, feeble, nearly bald from chemotherapy, and depended on morphine to manage the pain. Yet she seemed happier than she had been in Chicago. She was amazingly calm, while Lizhe was haggard and more frantic than ever. He fussed over her constantly, and she let him, with visible pleasure. Their roles were now reversed. In those final months of her life, she became his obsession. Later he told me that he had been racked by remorse for being unable to save her, despite having been a doctor himself, and for not having been more loving to her, especially given how much he owed her. She died that August.

After the funeral he filed a suit against the doctors who had missed Beiling's cancer. He drove through a dozen cities in the

United States visiting hospitals and medical archives in search of the medical information and expert witnesses needed to win the case. His files eventually filled thirty cardboard boxes. "My lawyer was amazed," he recalled. "He never had a client like me." His tenacity paid off; he won settlements of over $2 million for Beiling's two children.

"It was a year of complete madness," Lizhe told me later. "I was sick, broke, and in debt. So, between running upstairs and downstairs attending to Beiling and my father (who was also ill) in the hospital, I set up a little office nearby in a six-square-meter room. I put in a couple of computers and carried on with my typesetting business there. I had to make some money!" That was how business brought him back to China.

Soon after Beiling's death, Lizhe noticed that computerized graphics were not yet used in Chinese publishing, and he shipped high-resolution color-separation scanners from the United States. But the technology quickly spread and he lost his market advantage. Besides, he realized that his local partners were cheating on him. He sold his machines and got out of the business, but he stayed in China. It was 1993, a time when economic reforms were speeding up across the nation. It seemed clear that the great rising commercial tide was carrying society toward a more internationalized, market-oriented future, and, once again, Lizhe sensed opportunity.

With his years of American experience and his command of English, he figured he could bring all kinds of useful American books to China. He immediately invested the money he made from selling his scanners in several businesses, including a number of joint-venture publishing companies that produced books and magazines. The first magazine he put money into was a journal called *Electronics Today*, which published information on computer technology. The journal had impeccable official connections: Lizhe's business partner succeeded in getting President Jiang Zemin to do the calligraphy in the journal's title. Gradually Lizhe entered more joint publishing arrangements, all focused on technology. He began to make regular trips to book fairs in the United States and Europe, searching for promising titles and buying translation rights.

There were ups and downs. Since he had become a U.S. citizen in the 1980s, he could not, by Chinese law, publish in China unless he had a Chinese partner. This meant he was dependent on local partners who were often corrupt, incompetent government officials. Frequently, contracts signed by one official were invalidated by a successor, and people whom Lizhe trusted sometimes disappeared with large bundles of his money.

In 2000, Lizhe joined forces with the CITIC Press. CITIC is a conglomerate with impressive Party connections, but the press had no reputation and little money. Lizhe brought to it his certainty that China was in a great moment of modernization: China used to be a society where the state was big and the individual small. Now, he thought, the reverse was becoming true. And so the books he recommended to the press were all about how to be a modern person—how to handle marriage, divorce, parenting, investing, success. Though technically Lizhe was only a consultant, he threw himself into the CITIC projects, drawing up business plans and title lists. He took CITIC staff to international book fairs and taught them how to scout for foreign books. He bought translation rights with his own money.

Soon after the Beijing publishers' banquet where I first heard of Lizhe's business, Shi Tiesheng, the wheelchair-bound writer, told me that Lizhe was in town and gave me his number. I had not seen him since Beiling's death. I called that evening.

"Guess who I am?"

There was a moment of hesitation before he boomed, "Zha-zha! Are you in Beijing?" He asked me to lunch, and the next day my taxi took me to a new Eastside development of garden residences and pulled over before a pinkish building with a pavilion façade. The receptionist standing behind the lobby desk looked crisp and professional in her purple suit and makeup. She asked who I was visiting.

"Multi-Lingua Publishing International," I read from my notepad.

I went up and rang the doorbell. I heard rapid footsteps, instantly recognizable. The door opened: the man standing before me was an aged version of what I remembered.

"Zha-zha," he exclaimed. "You look exactly the same!"

So I had to lie, too. "And you haven't aged a day!"

Lizhe beamed, the wrinkles around his eyes like a pulled fishnet. "Really?" he said hopefully, ushering me in. "But I've got to lose a little here"—he patted his belly, which pressed against a neatly tucked-in blue dress shirt.

"Oh, it's nothing," I said. That was true: I'd seen far worse among my middle-aged Chinese male friends in recent years—victims of a culture that requires banqueting but no exercise. A few minutes later, as we sipped tea on a couch, I decided that Lizhe really had changed little. He had the same boyish eyes, big laugh, and restless mannerisms.

I looked around. The office must once have been an apartment: besides three or four rooms, there were bathrooms and a full kitchen. A couple of rooms had beds. In every room there were couches, chairs, desks, coffee tables, computers, television sets, and cardboard boxes stuffed with papers and books strewn about on the floor, on a desk, or along the wall. The whole place had the impersonal, makeshift feel that I remembered from my Chicago visit. He told me that he had several other offices in Beijing, some in other cities, and one in Los Angeles. "Take a look around. Let me finish just a few things here and then we'll go to lunch." Before I could answer he vanished to another room. I heard him talking rapidly to one of the two other men in the suite.

At lunch, Lizhe talked proudly of his business accomplishments. In the two years since he had come on board, CITIC Press had begun to create buzz in publishing circles. He told me that he had brought out several thousand books, worth one to two billion yuan in revenue. I remembered something Beiling used to say: "The only size that interests Lizhe is XL." I asked if he would consider more of the intellectually or politically challenging books.

"I don't touch politics for the time being," he said. "And I don't consider books that sell under fifty thousand copies." He cited the bestsellers he had recently brought to China, books like *What Color Is Your Parachute?* and a Jack Welch biography.

"Do you have any other guiding principles besides trends and the market?" I asked. It was strange to hear an icon of my youth, an embodiment of idealism and courage, sounding no different from any other entrepreneur of the current era of so-called "capitalism with Chinese characteristics." The kind of publishing he represents has drawn a good deal of recent criticism from educated Chinese. There have been complaints about the impact of a great flood of imported books, which are often sloppily translated and accompanied by intense promotional campaigns that edge out good Chinese titles.

Lizhe seemed oblivious to such concerns and continued to talk about the demand for his books. "I think the clash between globalization and traditional Chinese culture is causing a psychological crisis in China. For example, people are being divided by the pressures of success and failure—are questioning whether, with all this pragmatism, pure feelings are still worth anything." Still, he said, "I can't think about these issues too deeply. When you face a great tide, the important thing is action. Whatever it is—going to the countryside, to the university, going abroad, returning to China—it doesn't matter. I just always have to play the tide."

"What if the next tide in China is a Nazi state?" I asked abruptly and gave him a dark grin.

Lizhe looked startled. Then he broke into loud laugh. "Of course I won't play *that* kind of tide! I'll play the resistance tide then! Just like in the Cultural Revolution: I didn't play the political card, I played the knowledge card!"

The phrase he used for "play the tide," *nong chao* (弄潮), was an old one. Where there are big waves—like the annual tidal bore at the mouth of the Qiantang River in Hangzhou province—local daredevils, known as *nong chao er* (弄潮儿), have been playing the tides for many centuries. Classical Chinese poets described with amazement the sight of *nong chao er* swirling around in the deadly current, swimming and turning somersaults while they held aloft brightly colored flags. For all the years I've known him, Sun Lizhe has always been playing the tides, sometimes daring and colorful, often nearly drowning in the unpredictable riptide of Chinese history. Operating in a cave in Shaanxi, making dumplings in Chicago, or launching a publishing business in Beijing—for Sun Lizhe, *nong chao* is always the central impulse. He has always been determined to prove his resourcefulness and versatility, moving fast and succeeding in whatever course he has chosen.

A year after Beiling's death, Lizhe had married a young employee named Zhang Jin. She gave birth to a boy and a girl and looked after the children of Lizhe's previous marriage. Lizhe installed his family in two houses in the Los Angeles area. The larger one in Northridge was huge. "My sons could ride bikes in the living room and play golf outside," he told me now. "I once planted thirty apple trees around the house." But Lizhe generally made visits rather than living with the family. "Family life is deadening," he confessed to me—and so his young wife was left with the job of running the household. He also bought a lot of properties in Beijing: eight apartments, two villas, and four office suites. In each place, he kept a room with a bed for himself, but none of them was exactly a home. In 1999, however, while business was slow in China, he spent a lot of time in L.A. with his family. He spent his time day-trading tech stocks, and ended up losing over a million dollars. "That forced me back to concentrating on my China business."

After I moved back to Beijing in 2003, Lizhe and I didn't meet for a while: he was a frequent traveler and hard to reach. But I grew concerned after hearing rumors that he was being forced out of

CITIC. The details, as usual in Chinese business, were hazy, but it seemed that Lizhe had suffered from a series of setbacks. To start with, he had lost a powerful ally within CITIC when an important executive there left to run a state bank. He was replaced by a man named Wang Bin, a protégé of Lizhe's who saw no prospect of further advancement within the joint-venture framework and began maneuvering to squeeze Lizhe out. He had his staff establish direct communication with Lizhe's many international business contacts. After a few months, Wang and his new team were able to cut Lizhe out of the loop altogether.

Wang may have acted with the collusion of his bosses. Thanks to Lizhe, CITIC Press had become prominent, but it was unacceptable to those in charge that the credit should go to someone with a U.S. passport. The press's reputation meant that its executives could now expect great career prospects. And once the management of the parent firm realized that publishing could be a profitable business, they wanted to put it in the hands of their own people.

According to his friends, the ouster hit Lizhe hard. The novelist Shi Tiesheng and his wife told me that Lizhe had been avoiding even old friends like them. "I don't think he can admit defeat," Tiesheng said. "He has always been a winner. He must win."

When I next met Lizhe, in Beijing's plush Oriental Plaza's lobby café, my heart ached at the sight of him: he looked tired and gaunt. But within seconds I was swept up in whirlwind of energy. It turned out that he had stayed up all night studying and had just taken a big exam that morning—for one of his four graduate degree programs. "Exhausting!" he said exuberantly, ordering a coffee and a chocolate cake even though we were going to have lunch soon. While I sipped my grapefruit juice, he wolfed down the cake and talked rapidly, filling me in on his recent business engagements: a meeting with some senior managers of Amazon.com—Lizhe, I learned, owns a Chinese online bookselling service—and his plans to launch a new publishing venue in the States.

At lunch, Lizhe talked about the future. "Where is China

going?" he asked rhetorically, leaning over a plate of smoked suckling pig and beef in black bean sauce. "Three areas will be hot: ethics, law, health care. You are with me? Am I right on this? All right then, that's where I'm going." This is the reason that he is studying law. He is making plans to open hospitals in China, and he is working on yet another joint publishing venture. He has even set his sights on the English-language market; he plans to publish Chinese classics in translation and books about how to conduct business in China. ("The world's interest in China is growing as fast as the Chinese economy keeps growing," he said.) And this time he would register the company in the States, so that his partners would not be able to wrest control from him.

I carefully brought up the subject of the CITIC fallout. "Yes," Lizhe replied coolly. "They want to play me off." He said it had to do with complicated politics among the senior CITIC people. I asked if he was going to sue CITIC. "Yes, and it won't be a small case," he said emphatically. "They think I'm a little guy, but a little earthworm can kick up a big dust storm." I had heard that Lizhe had lost a great deal of money in the previous few years. He now told me he had sold both of his Los Angeles houses to help pay for the CITIC projects. His family would be moving to Chicago. But he assured me that he was fine financially. What mattered the most to him was the nearly four years of time and energy he put into the CITIC projects.

After lunch, I stopped by his apartment, as temporary in feel as every other home of his that I'd seen. Books were everywhere: on shelves, tables, the floor, and in boxes. A cousin was there doing the cleaning. Later she helped pack his luggage—Lizhe hadn't even unpacked his suitcase from his last trip, and he was catching an early flight to Chicago the next morning. We had tea sitting on the balcony, surrounded by more piles of books. Lizhe talked a lot about the delight of learning: how exciting it was to be a student again and to curl up with books night after night, alone in your own room, and have a new world open before your eyes.

Yet I was taken aback by some of the books he had been reading: a history of torture and punishment; a complete set of *Dark Lens*, volumes of prize-winning photographs on war atrocities, famine, and other traumas; several memoirs on the Maoist purges. He explained that he found the accounts of Party politics in the 1950s revealing because they constantly reminded him of his business dealings in China today. "The resemblance is striking," he said. There was the same factionalism, the same sudden, opportunistic power alignments, the same tide playing. "In fact, they are playing exactly the same sort of politics as before," he said.

He'd been reading about older Chinese history too, and asked me if I knew the story of General Yuan Chonghuan. In the late Ming era, Yuan was a celebrated general who won many battles against invaders. But he fell victim to court politics when certain jealous officials saw to it that he lost the emperor's favor. He was executed in the most horrible fashion: the death of a thousand knife cuts. This took several days, since the executioner had to make nine hundred and ninety-nine cuts on his body without letting him die. Ordinary people, believing that General Yuan was a traitor who lost China to enemies, lined up outside the prison house, each demanding a small piece of Yuan's flesh so they could eat it with liquor. I wondered whether Lizhe saw himself, at some level, as a modern-day General Yuan.

Then he told me about an insight he'd had during a class for his MBA Program. "It dawned on me that what they are teaching here is exactly the opposite of what I learned as a doctor. Doctors save people—that's the meaning of life for a doctor. But here they are teaching us how to beat down others, how to defeat them to win the competition, to be the strongest animal. Of course it's all dressed up in pretty language. But the message is brutal: you kill the weaker ones to get ahead."

The youth hero of the Cultural Revolution was determined to ride the wave of Chinese-style capitalism, and this time he figured he could afford no illusions. For the first time, though, I saw something like uncertainty in his face. "It takes time to sort it all out," he said pensively. "But something's got to give one day."

Postscript

Sun Lizhe has continued his publishing business in China, Europe, and the United States. Unlike with CITIC Press, several other partnerships he has formed have proven to be stable as well as profitable. The most successful is Huazhang Books, a joint venture between Lizhe's Chicago-based Multi-Lingua Publishing Company and China Machine Press in Beijing. Through Lizhe's help, Huazhang has established long term working relationships with many leading international publishers, and has brought to Chinese readers a steady string of educational and professional bestsellers. Its publishing of IT, economics, and management books have led to the company being ranked among the top Chinese publishers, and they have led the market for years. Reflecting Lizhe's personal interest in health care and psychology, a more recent division, Huazhang Psychology, has been publishing books in these fields.

Publishing may be Lizhe's bread and butter, but he is also constantly involved in all kinds of other projects, such as consulting for local banks, organizing conferences and giving lectures at universities, and buying and selling real estate. Meanwhile, he continues to take law and business courses everywhere. Tracking him down is difficult because he still travels frequently. When I reconnected with him in the summer of 2010, it took me a while to sort out the various threads of his life and business. I discovered, only gradually, that Lizhe has also returned to his old, true passion in life: helping sick and weak people. "I'm a 网络赤脚医生 [Internet barefoot doctor] these days," he told me one day as I watched him text-messaging a patient. "I've been treating cancer patients."

At first I thought he was joking: how could he do this without a proper hospital, medical staff, and equipment? After some further investigation, however, I realized that Lizhe was not only serious, but that this was actually the work that had the deepest meaning for him. What he has been doing, essentially, is offering medical advice and certain unconventional, alternative treatment (such as the controversial Coley Fluid) to critically ill cancer patients for whom no treatment is available within the present medical establishment. In fact, Lizhe had lost a lucrative job due to this practice. In 2009, while serving as the highly paid executive chairman of a large private Chinese hospital group, Lizhe started masterminding cancer centers within the group and treating cancer patients himself, including providing special, free care for poor people. Among the drugs he used, many were not approved in China; some were even manufactured by Lizhe himself in one of his apartments in Beijing. But who could beat the deal? The drugs were effective and they were free to the patients. This was, however, fundamentally challenging the conventional ideas of running for-profit urban hospitals. In a sense, Lizhe was barefoot doctoring in a modern hospital group! Not surprisingly, after this was discovered, the hospital's board of directors held a meeting and fired him for breaking the rules.

After that, Lizhe decided to practice as an Internet barefoot doctor. His cancer patients now come to him by word of mouth and receive his advice and instruction via the Internet. It is a dangerous gray area on the edge of the system. Lizhe's work begins where conventional hospitals and doctors stop. He listens, analyzes, recommends treatment, and helps secure drugs, all for free. Sometimes he pays for the drug if the patient is poor. He also consoles the patients and their loved ones during the final stage or after the patient passes away, acting as their psychotherapist.

Listening to these stories and reading the touching thank-you messages from the families was a remarkable experience. Admiration aside, it also allowed me to look at Lizhe's many business transactions in a slightly different light. Now I understand, for instance, why Lizhe would put so much energy, time, and some of his own capital in an effort to push for the establishment of a new medical center in Changchun, Jilin Province. There, he has consulted for the regional bank and developed high-level contacts with a large state hospital. He is apparently still striving toward his ultimate goal of setting up a hospital that can provide the kind of medical service often unavailable to critically ill patients in desperate need of help.

Meanwhile, he has been doing whatever is within his own power and means to help sick people. "The source of true happiness in life lies not in self-profiting," Lizhe said to me recently during an international conference he helped to organize on positive psychology and the subject of happiness. "It lies in helping others."

The conference took place at Tsinghua University, Lizhe's alma mater, but his words made me think of a documentary film about his visit to Shaanxi in 2007. A Phoenix television crew followed him on the trip, the first since he left the region twenty-nine years ago. The memory of the young barefoot doctor apparently remained powerful, for the peasants turned out in large throngs to welcome him back with affectionate words and festive banquets to follow. Watching the black-and-white footage of a young Lizhe operating in his cave clinic, the old peasants telling tales about how he saved their lives yet suffered politically, and Lizhe toasting in Shaanxi dialect was all quite moving. It was also revealing. As one of Lizhe's old friends put it: "Lizhe's fundamental belief remained the same all these years: serve the people. This is what he was taught and believed in his youth, back in the Shaanxi countryside. It's still what he believes in today."

What is more remarkable, I think, is that he still practices it.

Part II

The Intellectuals

Beida, Beida!

It must be considered that there is nothing more diffi-cult to carry out, nor more doubtful of success, nor more dangerous to handle, than to initiate a new order of things. For the reformer has enemies in all those who profit by the old order, and only lukewarm defenders in all those who would profit by the new order, this luke-warmness arising partly from fear of their adversar-ies, who have the laws in their favor; and partly from the incredulity of mankind, who do not truly believe in anything new until they have had actual experience of it.

—Niccolo Machiavelli, *The Prince*

1.

My friend Liu Dong is a warm, colorful character. A professor of comparative literature at Peking University, he is a large, bulky man with a large, bulky head and a big, sonorous voice. "If I wasn't a scholar, I'd certainly be an opera singer," he told me. In his youth Liu had trained to be a tenor and had seriously considered a career in singing. Even now, he is prone to showing off his top-of-the-line sound system, his opera CD collection, and his own vocal talents: with any excuse he'll let out a famous aria right in the middle of a conversation, then, with a childlike smile, wait for praise. Of course, thinking and discussing have long overshadowed singing in Liu's life. He's also known as much for his hospitality as for his love of talking: to be his guest usually means to be his listener and debater. Liu is very good at trapping people in marathon discussions.

A discussion that has obsessed Liu lately is "Beida reform," a topic that has gripped not just Liu and his colleagues but a lot of educated Chinese as well. This is partly because Peking University—or Beida, as everyone calls it—is not only the nation's number-one university but also a beloved symbol. An American scholar familiar with Beida's history once said to me: "For the Chinese, Beida is really Harvard, Oxford, and Ecole Normale rolled into one." This is hyperbole, but only if one takes it literally.

As the country's very first "modern" university, Beida has always been tied to the fate of China's modernization. Its faculty in the early twentieth century used to be a list of who's who in China's "New Culture Movement," boasting celebrated scholars like Hu Shi and Qian Mu as well as great writers like Lu Xun and Shen Congwen. Student movements at Beida had a tendency to occur at critical moments, giving rise to watershed events influencing national politics. This tradition's last glow was in 1989, when Beida stood at the center of the Tiananmen protest, producing famous student leaders like Wang Dan. The campus was an early arena for founders of the Chinese Communist Party to spread their message (Li Dazhao taught here; young Mao worked as a library clerk). Yet it also abounds with traces of the West, especially America: the campus with its landmark pagoda overlooking Weiming Lake, was designed by an American architect; the gorgeous garden mansion near the lake belonged to John Leighton Stuart, the famous American missionary educator who had been the president of Yanjing University, which later merged with Beida; and Edgar Snow is buried here. Such a place, inevitably, stands for a great many things and becomes an overloaded symbol.

It's not unusual, therefore, to find someone like Liu Dong, who, though he joined the Beida faculty only in 2000, talks about Beida with intense feeling. His favorite routine with visitors is taking them on a leisurely tour through the beautiful old parts of the Beida campus and telling them that this is the only spot left in China that still has an "aristocratic spirit." After that, he usually brings up John Fairbanks, who was supposed to have said, "I'm not a religious person, but Harvard is my religion."

"Well," Liu would add, "I'm not a religious person, but Beida is my religion."

Beida is my alma mater—I graduated from the Chinese department in the early 1980s before leaving for the United States—and so I once joked to Liu that he had the fervor of a new convert. He smiled and shook his head, then confessed sheepishly that in fact he had always romanticized Beida: fifteen years before he became a Beida professor, he had written a sentimental play about the life of Cai Yuanpei, Beida's legendary president in the 1920s. At the time, Liu was a young assistant professor at Nanjing University and the play was never produced, but Beida remained an idol in his heart. It must have been a dream come true when Beida finally embraced him as one of her own.

The love and idolization Beida commands in the hearts of so many Chinese is probably what made the controversy over the "Beida reform" such a ferocious one. The first time I heard it discussed was at a dinner party in a Beijing artist's loft: within fifteen minutes the conversation turned into an argument, then escalated into a shouting match. With Liu Dong, the subject never failed to unleash a torrent of opinions which, more often than not, would end up in an emotional explication of why, for a unique institution like Beida, the best thing is to "conserve" it, not to "reform" it. "If this makes me a conservative," Liu would say, "so be it."

2.

The so-called "Beida reform" was essentially a proposed plan to reform Beida's faculty hiring and promotion system.

It began in May 2003 during the SARS period. While the city

lived under quarantine and campus life came to a halt, a document the Beida administration had issued to its deans and department chairmen for feedback somehow appeared on the Internet. Though coated in dry, technical language, the changes it proposed were significant. The old system of the "iron rice bowl for all" would be cast away; an American-style "tenure track" system would be adopted, though tenure would be granted only at the rank of full professor. Assistant and associate professors would be given two chances to apply for promotion; then it would be "up or out." Beida would not hire its own graduates, as had been the tradition, but would fill future vacancies through a global "open search," with at least half of the jobs reserved for outside candidates. Outside reviewers would be invited to participate in the promotion/evaluation process. The departments that continually ranked low in their disciplines would be shut down. One item stipulated that Beida faculty should be capable of teaching in English.

There were other measures aimed at micromanaging faculty, all in an effort to establish a more open and competitive system. As though a bomb had been tossed into a still pond, the reaction to the plan was explosive. Beida's Web sites, as well as many other sites, were instantly jammed full of cantankerous comments. Professors from Beida and elsewhere—including many overseas Chinese academics—posted their remarks; many sent in full-length articles. The division of opinion was as sharp as it was revealing. The supporters, many from the sciences and social sciences and with Western training, cheered the plan as a brave step leading to China's long overdue university reform. The critics, many from the humanities and locally educated, called it "shock therapy," a high-handed, misguided act from the arrogant Beida administration—an act that slavishly copied the American system but coldly betrayed the Beida faculty.

Within days, mainstream media smelled blood and rushed in. A flood of coverage followed: newspaper reports, television forums, magazine features. Reporters relentlessly chased Beida officials and professors for interviews, pushing the controversy quickly beyond academic circles. With the city barely recovered from the shock of SARS, Beida reform was already becoming the new hot topic in town. Several years earlier, when Beida designed her new "core courses" using Harvard's curriculum as a reference, some Beida history and philosophy professors had written to *People's Daily* accusing Beida of having a Harvard fixation. That was nothing compared to the opposition this time.

Surprised by the media uproar and stung by the criticism, the Beida administration issued a second draft in June, qualifying and modifying many "offending" clauses in the first draft. The ready compromise disappointed the more radical supporters but failed to stop the critics. More comments poured out. The debate kept going. Six months later, the Beida administration still hadn't issued its third—reportedly final—document, and the dust around "Beida reform" refused to settle. In December, three collections of articles on the subject came out, a fourth book came out in January, and several more were at the printer. In educated circles, the subject was still discussed with heat, sometime venom. Public curiosity hadn't faded either: every time a Beida official faced the media, he was bombarded by questions about the "reform."

Then, in January, CCTV, the largest television network in China, aired in its popular show *Dialogue* an hour-long conversation between Beida president Xu Zhihong and visiting Yale president Richard Levin. Inevitably, the host pressed Xu Zhihong on the question of Beida reform. Xu replied that Beida would carry on with reform, but emphasized that it would be a "step-by-step" process, not "shock therapy." He said that he, as a scientist, never believed in radical changes, and that the experience of China's reform proved that radical changes had no future. Levin ended up endorsing the Beida reform by saying that he'd do the same if he were the Beida president.

Toward the end of the show, Xu spoke of the toughness of being a university president in a time of rapid change, when one must confront so many levels of reality at once. He said he envied the American university presidents, who could rely on a well-established system and even have some leisure time to "go sightseeing with their wives after a conference," whereas a Chinese university president must hurry back to the big pile of work waiting for him at home. "Being a university president in China," Xu said, "is like sitting on top of a volcano."

He wasn't totally exaggerating. As he spoke, Min Weifang, Beida's Party secretary and de facto number-one official, was in the hospital. Doctors suggested that Min stay there for a while to get some badly needed rest. Min had been suffering hearing loss induced by stress and exhaustion.

3.

Volcano. Sickness. It reminds me of how a Beijing intellectual friend of mine once summed up the present state of the Chinese universities: "A mountain of problems, and sick to the bone." He is a pessimist, one of those Cassandras who has been predicting for years the coming collapse of China and each year wonders why on the earth it still hasn't happened. But as extreme as he sounds, it's not a minority opinion. The feeling that Chinese universities, Beida included, are sick with problems and badly in need of "reform" is widespread. Too much political control. Too little intellectual freedom. Overemployment. Underfunding. Growing commercialism. Slipping academic standards. Lack of mobility. Sloth. Inbreeding. Factionalism. Corruption.

But who to blame for these ills? How to fix them? Well, that's where the quarrel begins. Some accuse the Party and the state, others the market and capitalism. Some lament the spineless professors, others attack shortsighted administrators and greedy bureaucrats. Plenty of critics, no consensus.

Meanwhile, the lives of the professors keep getting better. In the early 1990s, my Beijing academic friends owned nothing but their books. Every one of them lived in a small, cramped rental apartment overloaded with books. Now all of them have bought homes—more spacious, freshly renovated apartments—at a subsidized mortgage rate. Many have bought second, even bigger places while renting out smaller ones. Some have bought cars. Back then professors were just making ends meet; now they go to restaurants, take holiday trips, attend all-expenses-paid conferences at scenic spots. The star professors, though still a new breed on the scene, are joining their cosmopolitan cousins, enjoying a lifestyle similar to that of the globe-trotting intellectual elite, visiting Davos, London, Harvard, Berkeley. In the 1990s a young Beida professor's salary was one-tenth that of a Beijing taxi driver's income, and you could tell how low the scholars were in social status by popular phrases like "Those who make the atom bomb earn less than those who sell tealeaf eggs," or expressions like "as poor as a professor." Imagine the intellectual who, just a few years earlier, had been regarded as the leader of the public, the conscience of the society: yesterday he was the priest, today he is kicked down from the altar and has become the church mouse! What a psychological shock! But then, all of that changed again. Now, Chinese professors' incomes are at their highest point since 1980. On the job market, an academic career, with its comfortable income, stability, and respectability, has once again become a very attractive option. All these metamorphoses have occurred within a short span of twenty years!

This, however, has not won universal approval. There is a view that Chinese intellectuals have been "tamed" since 1989, the year of Tiananmen. The state first silenced them with tanks and guns, then "bought" them with material gains (subsidized mortgages, discount housing, fat bonuses for officially commissioned research projects, licenses for "university corporations," opportunities to make money and fame from the foreign and domestic academic market) and turned them into silent, corrupt partners in a march toward prosperity that is as dramatic as it is troubling and inequitable.

So, here is the landscape in 2004, fifteen years after the massacre on Tiananmen Square: there is no political reform, the local

media carefully avoids the same taboos, self-censorship is pervasive, and the dissidents—a small cluster of hardheaded, isolated
individuals—are locked up, kicked out of the country, or kept on
the margins. Beida, with her long tradition of political activism, had
been heavily involved in the Tiananmen protests and had thus been
singled out afterward for punishment and special monitoring. In the
first years after the massacre, the government forced all Beida freshmen to spend their entire first year in military training and indoctrination. That notorious program has long since stopped. However,
Beida's campus gates are still patrolled by security agents every June
4, the date of the massacre, except the patrol has become less notice-
able and so far no "disturbance" has ever occurred.

And the intellectuals? Well, the intellectuals are becoming comfortable, some even affluent. I recently asked the question, "So,
what's happening with the Chinese intellectuals these days?" of two
Beijing intellectual friends and got two answers. One said, "Everyone is making mortgage payments!" Another used a phrase *tu beng
wa jie*, which means "coming apart like dust and tiles."

There is an old Chinese proverb: "He who understands the times
is smart" (识时务者为俊杰). And it is in this sense that the majority of Chinese intellectuals have turned out to be smart rather than
stubborn.

But not everyone looks upon this situation kindly. And once in a
while, a jarring note might disrupt the silence, reminding people of
the compromises they had to make in order to get on with life.

In October 2003, at a Beida conference entitled "Beijing: Urban
Imagination and Cultural Memory," one of the speakers broke the
taboo and told a story about June 4, 1989, the day of the Tiananmen massacre. The conference, jointly sponsored by Beida's Chinese Department and Columbia University's East Asian Studies
Department, had been going along smoothly. Scholars from China,
Europe, and America had been examining the city from a variety of
perspectives. Dozens of papers were delivered—on old architecture,
on traditional literature, on drama during the republican era. It had

all been quite professional, genteel, refined—as a conference should be. Then, toward the end of the second day, Chen Danqing, an artist invited to join a roundtable discussion, rose to speak.

Beijing's urban imagination, Danqing said, has always been dominated by big power: emperors, Mao, and today's city authorities, real estate developers, and big international architects. It is their willpower that decides Beijing's urban landscape, while the ordinary Beijingers' task is to be cooperative in being moved away from the city to the outskirts. And Beijing's cultural memory? Well, it is full of holes or simply frozen. He said he looked carefully over the titles of every paper presented at this conference, and all of them referred back to a "time" before 1949—the precommunist time, the time of the officially permitted "cultural memory." This is like an old man's memory, he said: he remembers only things in the distant past but not the more recent happenings. Finally, he said he'd tell a little tale that might help patch up a bit of the memory cracks. The story was simple: it was about a man, a Beijinger, who fled Tiananmen Square in the early dawn of June 4, 1989. The man ran and ran toward home, and out of sheer horror and madness, he cursed loudly all the way until the sound of gunshots gradually faded behind him. But when he reached the beautiful Houhai park, he suddenly heard a different sound: amid the chirping birds in the trees came sonorous, long, drawn-out singing. The man stopped, listened, and slowly came back to his senses: it was the voices of old Beijingers practicing Peking Opera, the urban sound of a Beijing familiar to him and generations of Beijingers.

While Danqing told the story, the conference hall went dead quiet. When he finished, there was a moment of silence, but then loud applause rose, and it went on and on. The conference sponsor tried to speak several times, but the audience, mostly students (and a few faculty members), went on applauding for a long time.

Afterward, one of the students in the audience posted a long report on Beida's Web site describing Danqing's speech as "shaking up the entire conference." When people increasingly speak in a genteel, indirect style, the student wrote, he was truly impressed by Danqing's courage. "But I also noticed," the student went on, "that among those who expressed their gratitude and respect to Chen Danqing [after Danqing's speech], there were no mainland Chinese scholars. Not one."

I heard about Danqing's Beida speech almost immediately. Friends who happened to be in the audience that day called me afterward, describing it vividly, excitedly. It was obviously an unusual occurrence, something worth retelling. But they also noted that Danqing has a U.S. passport, which gives him protection and in a way explains his "courage." They speculated about whether or not something might happen to Chen Pingyuan, a Chinese department professor who was the conference organizer for Beida. Chen Pingyuan was not protected, like Danqing, and could have been held responsible for this "incident" if someone sent a "little report" to the "higher ups"—to the authorities. After all, this has happened often enough: the actual troublemaker is spared, but those who are supposed to prevent it from happening are punished. In other words, skip the criminal, nail the police. It looks arbitrary but works quite well: it has turned more people into police.

On that day, Chen Pingyuan handled it calmly. After Danqing's speech, he simply said: "Today's speeches are excellent," and wrapped up the day. Later on, he told Danqing that he intended to include his speech in the planned conference volume. Danqing said that he didn't want to cause him any "trouble," but Chen Pingyuan replied that he would do "some prepublishing treatment." That meant, of course, that he, as the volume editor, would cut out whatever lines were unfit to print. Danqing said that would be fine, that he could cut whatever was necessary.

Days went by, then weeks, then months. Nothing happened. No punishment. The excitement of the moment was over. The incident also faded. It didn't seem to have left any traces.

A friend of mine, a magazine editor, made this observation about the incident: "Chen Danqing managed to keep a certain freshness and edge by staying abroad all these years, but he might not understand what the Chinese intellectuals have been through in the years since Tiananmen. So he did his show, and people watched his performance and smiled. Then it's over."

I talked with Danqing later on. He said he "totally understood" what Chinese intellectuals had been through in the 1990s. "It's not that they don't like what I said. I think they don't like themselves— they don't like the circumstances that made them *not* say what I said." He sighed. "All of us are pitiable. We all have to make a living off this bowl of rice."

He continued: "University life nowadays is all about personal interests and careers. Unless you really step inside, become a member of the system, like I did when I got this job—which means that I'm on the university's payroll and depend on the university for housing and so on—you won't understand the real picture." The picture he painted is rather unattractive. The professors generally appear as selfish careerists, hypocritical philistines, or timid weaklings. Unmoved by higher ideals or true intellectual passion, they are petty creatures chiefly motivated by protecting and advancing their own economic and political advantages. Real intellectual or scholarly debates don't exist anymore; what professors really fight over are power and material gains.

"I understand now why my students have a certain contempt for their teachers, because they've watched them behave like cowards and hypocrites." Chen Danqing said. He said he also realized that he would never be fully trusted or allowed to get close to any position of power at the university, since he has been away for so long. "When I had just returned from the United States, a friend asked me what my plans were: to really do something, or just to get by. I said of course to really do something. But now I know I could never make any difference within the system."

Liu Dong would never agree with Chen Danqing's verdict. Even though he himself has stayed within the system, paid a price for it, and been through plenty of ups and downs, he remains convinced that one could, yes, not only make a difference, but also help make history.

In the 1980s Liu used to be one of the active public intellectuals: he was on the editorial boards of two very influential book series that translated and introduced important Western intellectual works to general readers in China. Then, in the wake of the Tiananmen massacre, he was investigated and left jobless and nearly homeless. His wife left him and took their apartment, and for years he moved from one borrowed apartment to another. He was kicked out from these apartments three times. Now he owns three apartments and a car. Remarried, he and his young, pretty wife live in a 269-square-meter (around 3,000 square feet) nicely renovated penthouse apartment with a rooftop garden, an ornamental waterfall, a Japanese-style dining room, a movie-screening room, a giant jacuzzi bathtub, and a huge library.

Once, while we were drinking tea and chatting by the grape trellises on his deck, I said to Liu Dong, "This is probably how professors back in the republican era used to live. Now you are finally living as comfortably as them!" Liu beamed. There was pride and satisfaction on his face.

Later on, Liu said to me: "You know why I made my home such a plush place? It's for my students. I invite them over a lot; sometimes I hold seminars here. Nowadays so many students want to go abroad or go into business when they graduate. I want to show them a scholar can also live well."

But Liu is touchy about the compromises a Chinese scholar has to make to stay within the system. He likes to tell his story about the American general Patton and the Soviet general Zhukov. Once he asked his students which general they admired the most; all the students chose Patton. But Liu told them Zhukov was the more admirable hero because, being Stalin's general, he had to fight both on the war front and back home. Stalin never trusted Zhukov and was on the verge of killing him, even though Zhukov had won the war for the country. Patton, with all his military genius and principles, had a single focus; Zhukov had to overcome tougher, far more complicated circumstances, since he had to fight not only against the country's enemies but also for his own survival!

After telling me this story, Liu told me, almost in the same breath, about a visit he made to an old Chinese academic friend. The friend left China after the Tiananmen massacre, declaring that he would never return as long as the government refused to reverse its stance on the incident. Liu had recently seen him in London, where the friend has been teaching and residing. "I admired his high moral principles and integrity," Liu told me. "He still sticks to his decision. But this means he will probably spend the rest of his life in this self-exile in a foreign country, doing some inconsequential teaching. No influence. If he had stayed in China, how much more he could do! With his knowledge, his ideas, he could do so much work to help change the system!"

Do not leave China, stay close to the homeland, or your work will lose meaning, your life will become weightless, and you will be irrelevant to those who care about and value you until you fade into oblivion in some faraway corner of the earth (which includes New York, London, Paris). This notion, this fear, is so central, so deep, that it justifies a lot of the compromises one has to make in order to stay "in."

Or not get kicked out. Chen Danqing is not afraid of speaking out as he did at the Beida conference. In fact, he views it as the duty that comes with his privileges. "Precisely because I have a U.S. passport, I'm in a position to say things that my colleagues cannot say." Though he was disappointed about the university life, about not being able to "really do things" as a professor, he still feels excited by China's changes. "Even if I quit teaching and go back to my freelance artist life, as long as I live in Beijing, I can walk on Changan Avenue, feel the energy, observe what's happening. That way I *am* a part of this historical moment."

And he can go on painting, writing, and speaking out. He worries about one thing only: "I don't want things to get to the point where they won't allow me to stay in China."

4.

Nobody doubts that China is undergoing an important historical moment. After over two decades of remarkable economic growth, the world is waking up, finally, to the fact that a dominant event of the twenty-first century may be the extraordinary transformation of the world's most populous country. While others are busy analyzing whether this is a threat or a blessing to the international economy and geopolitical balance, the Chinese government has been busy with its own agenda. It wants to cultivate a new image: China is a "peacefully rising" nation who wants to "link tracks" (接轨, *jie gui*) rather than clash with the world. *Jie gui* has become the slogan of the day in China.

Another new slogan is 科教兴国 (*ke jiao xing guo*), "raise the country by science and education."

Peacefully rising. Link tracks. Raising the country by science and education. All of this points to a new image of China. This is our new path. We are not in an arms race—that's proven to be a losing cause. Military is not our focus. Economy is—so we are trading on the world market. Science is—so we are building a manned spaceship. Education is—so we are trying to build world-class universities.

The phrase "building world-class universities" is supposed to have been dreamed up by some Beida officials at a meeting. By now it has become a state policy, an official goal set to be accomplished within a deadline of about twenty-five years. The question is: how?

The central government under Jiang Zemin, in its own blind, condescending manner, seemed to consider funding the crucial factor.

In May 1998, when Beida commemorated her one hundredth anniversary, Jiang showed up on campus at the celebrations. His speech, which lauded Beida above all for its "tradition of patriotism," was much highlighted in the media. The occasion, in the eyes of many critics, was a symbolic moment of China's most celebrated liberal bastion hijacked by big politics, the intellectuals' voices made weak and subservient to the voice of the Party. But it turned out that Jiang Zemin, who had a childlike love of the limelight, came to the campus to perform a double role: Boss and Santa. Calling on Beida to lead other Chinese universities in the drive to "build world-class universities," the general Party secretary also announced that the state would dole out, on top of the routine support, 1.8 billion yuan (about $150 million) in the following three years to help Beida achieve the goal. Considering the paltriness of state support—200 million yuan a year, about one-third of Beida's annual operating expenses—this was a big bag of money.

By now, this fund, known as the "985 Project," is more or less used up. It has helped increase faculty income and add some new buildings and new facilities on campus. But has Beida gotten very close to becoming a "world-class university"? On a campus where few could agree on anything, that's a question to which everyone would have the same answer: "no." And many professors I talked with thought the slogan itself was absurd.

"What's a world-class university?" Liu Dong demanded over our lunch. "Let's pick an obvious one: Harvard. Now, the government gives us this 985 money and asks us to compete with Harvard. But what's Harvard's annual budget? This is like giving an old broken car—say, my little Renault—a tank of gas and ordering it to race with a Rolls-Royce. Isn't that a joke?"

This is a point noted by a lot of observers. Funding is not the solution to Beida's problems. Beida has always been number one in China, but if it wants to become a truly first-rate university by international standards, it needs a deep structural treatment, not merely a cash injection. This is where the current reformists—the Beida reform plan drafters—come in. To them, the key is faculty: since faculty is the heart of a university, it follows naturally that if you design a system that filters out those not up to the standards and keeps only the first-rate scholars, then Beida would be a world-class university.

But the critics cried foul: this is another terrible misdiagnosis!

Yung Ho Chang, a professor of architecture at Beida, explained it to me: "The most corrupt, rotten part of Beida is the administrative sections. Why don't they reform *that* first? Because it's too fat and too powerful, so they turn to the professors, who are weak and powerless!"

Liu Dong put it this way: "Let's say Beida is sick—seriously sick. But here comes a doctor who takes a look at this patient, with all his troubled organs, and decides to take a jab at the heart first! It's ridiculous! Because in fact the heart is the only part that functions relatively well—at least better than the other organs. This sort of surgery might just kill the patient!"

This remark reminded me of a popular expression in the late 1980s. It was about the dilemma China faced then: to reform, or not to reform? And it went: "Not to reform is waiting for death. To reform is looking for death."

Back then, this applied mainly to the big, failing state enterprises such as large factories. And for a while, when political reform looked hopeful, people applied it to the Party. This time, it has shifted to the universities.

5.

To the doctor, the "brute surgeon" who drafted the Beida reform plan, a Chinese university is in many ways like a big, failing state enterprise. And as such, it has a lot of the same problems and needs similar treatment.

Zhang Weiying is a forty-four-year-old economist. He joined the Beida faculty in 1994 after receiving a PhD in economics from Oxford, which put him in the swelling ranks of *hai gui*—海龟, sea turtles, or 海归, returnees from abroad. Since 1997 he has been serving as the vice dean of Beida's Guanghua School of Management. Then, in 2002, he was appointed assistant to the president, and his special duty was to be in charge of all the business companies under Beida's name. Min Weifang, the current number-one leader at Beida, is also a *hai gui* and had been promoted exactly through that route: after receiving a PhD in the economics of education from Stanford, Min had come to Beida and served as an assistant to the president in charge of Beida's companies before becoming vice president and Party secretary.

But then came the Beida reform, and Zhang was appointed the chief drafter of the document. His life suddenly changed.

In the fury of the controversy, Zhang Weiying became the primary target. Two things about him earned the distrust—and often palpable dislike—of the critics (who are mostly scholars in humanities): he is an economist, and he is a *hai gui*. For these critics, Zhang is walking proof of China's warped reform—a Western-trained economist who brings home a wannabe mentality and half-baked formulas he learned from the West and who, instead of solving old problems, makes a mess of things and creates new problems. Like a typical economist, he marches on stridently by the logic of the market and tries to turn the university into an efficient production line, a lean and mean academic market. He is bent on standardizing and downsizing because he sees running the university essentially as a management affair, not a supple and subtle art which requires, among other things, a laissez-faire tolerance and the ability to recognize idiosyncratic geniuses who don't fit a cookie-cutter plan.

This is, partly, a backlash from the intensified management in the Chinese universities. Since the early 1990s, officials introduced all sorts of new measures: ranking disciplines, departments, and professors; selecting "PhD and MA sites"; naming "core journals" for publications; subcontracting research projects; and grading awards. This web of "quantifiable standards" and "digital indexing" was then pegged to money: they were used to evaluate and decide a professor's promotion and pay. So, a professor's promotion or annual bonus depended on, say, the number of papers he published in the officially designated "core journals" and the number of officially approved "research projects" he participated in. An endless stream of forms and reports were imposed on the faculty so their performance was regularly assessed and monitored. Then, in the past few years, there was also a wave of "merging" universities into "superuniversities" and "upgrading" departments into colleges.

The rationale for all this was "reform": to battle sloth, to run universities in a more "scientific" manner, and to divide funds by "objective" standards. But one consequence was a swelling of administrative offices and staff, including "officials with a scholar's hat"—officials who also take on academic titles such as professors and doctorate advisors.

Scholars in the humanities fields are especially bitter. "This is not 'world-class university' but 'world-class bureaucracy'!" wrote Deng Xiaomang, a philosophy professor at Wuhan University. "A university is not a chicken farm," Li Ling, a Beida professor specializing in ancient Chinese language, wrote in a scathing article. Li called it "academic Taylorism." In his article entitled "From Beida to McBeida," Huang Ziping, a former Beida professor of Chinese literature now teaching in Hong Kong, called it "McEducation." Huang noted that Chinese universities have contracted a new disease on top of the old one: before they can get rid of the problem of official control, they are also suffering the problems of the market.

To all of these critics, Zhang Weiying's reform plan is another step in this misguided direction. It is worse in some ways, because in this age of "globalization," *hai gui*, playing the role of the cultural comprador, appear to be gaining more influence in shaping China's future.

Nothing I had heard about Zhang Weiying prepared me for the man I actually met for dinner. I arrived on time to find Zhang already sitting at an upstairs corner table. I recognized him right away: in my folder was a July issue of *Shenghuo Weekly*, with a huge head shot of him on the cover and the boldfaced words, "北大改革" (*Beida Gaige,*

"Beida Reform") printed right bellow his chin. That evening Zhang was dressed in a well-tailored navy blue suit, a white dress shirt, and no tie. He looked younger than his age, with a kind, faintly Buddha-like face and clear, regular features. But his salt-and-pepper hair and wire-rimmed glasses gave him a distinguished, scholarly air. He reminded me of those well-groomed, clean-cut Hong Kong professors until he opened his mouth: he spoke with a northern country accent.

Zhang Weiying comes from Shaanxi, a very poor part of the Chinese countryside. His parents and grandparents were illiterate peasants. As a kid he used to earn cornbread by helping others with their homework. He was always a brilliant student. While still at graduate school, he wrote a paper proposing a "double track" price system to pave the way for gradual economic reform. It became a big hit at a national economists conference and ended up influencing government policy. Zhang was only twenty-five. That article got him a research job at *Tigaisuo* (体改所), the important State Council think tank under the liberal premier Zhao Ziyang. From there on Zhang became a player at the forefront of China's economic reform, quickly establishing himself in the double role of scholar and policy advisor. But, a year spent at Oxford in 1987–88 as a visiting scholar made him realize that he needed deeper training. So, in 1990, a year after Tiananmen, Zhang went to Oxford again on a World Bank scholarship. This time he spent four years there, receiving a PhD in 1995.

At our dinner that evening, Zhang seemed reserved at first. I mentioned that some people got very upset about the Beida reform because they saw it as a *hai gui* plot: that the real agenda was replacing Beida's current *tu bie* (locally trained) faculty with a mostly *hai gui* faculty. "Some *tu bie* scholars feel that your plan gives *hai gui* a certain advantage—global search, outsider review, English skills. It will let more *hai gui* into Beida to grab *tu bies'* rice bowls. This is serious, like a life-and-death class struggle!" I said.

Zhang listened to this with a half-amused, half-frowning

expression. But when I mentioned the one item in Zhang's draft that attracted the most virulent attack—that Beida professors should lecture in English—his face fell. "What I meant," he said flatly, "was simply that a Beida professor should be able to give a talk in English at an international conference. Is that so unreasonable?"

I guess not, in this day and age. But in the heat of the controversy, Zhang's point was exaggerated beyond recognition. It was interpreted as an evidence of the reformers' inferiority complex: only a real colonial subject would worship a foreign language like this! In three widely cited articles, Gan Yang, an influential critic with a New Leftist leaning, charged that Zhang's plan would turn Beida into a "prep school for American universities for the next ten thousand years." It is "a design to mess up Beida and China's higher education," Gan concluded. And he pointed out that this kind of reform would make China's universities "abandon their scholarly independence and become other people's tribal states." By "other people" he clearly meant Americans.

"Their arguments lack logic," Zhang said in a tone of suppressed anger. For emphasis he used the English word for "logic." He had said the same thing when we first spoke on the phone. In a long interview recently published in a newspaper, Zhang pleaded for *gong gong li xing*, the rational, reasonable spirit in a public debate. Obviously this was important for Zhang. You could criticize and disagree, but please take a dispassionate, disinterested position and make your position coherent and clear. Please don't take things out of their context and attack. Please don't get personal.

And I understood why. He had taken some nasty shots: besides the signed articles in print, there were loads of venomous remarks on the Web by pen-named critics—a prevalent phenomenon that was a part of China's new Internet culture. Everything about Zhang was subject to the darkest speculation and questioning: his loyalty to Beida, his commitment to Chinese language and culture, his motives for action, his credentials as an economist. There were even doubts about his Oxford degree—was it real or fake? I got a taste of this in a private discussion with a Beida professor who, though he wasn't an economist, dismissed Zhang's scholarship as "superficial" and "watery." He was convinced that Zhang's true ambition lay in *dang guan* (当官), to be an official. It was to that end that Zhang designed the "reform plan," the professor said. The plan gives the present Beida leadership something to boast about—it's their *zheng ji gong cheng* (政绩工程), their official achievements project—so they can climb to higher positions. It also gives officials a new tool with which to control scholars—by rewarding the obedient and punishing the unruly in the name of the new standards. "He's selling out the intellectuals to climb up," the professor concluded firmly.

Xu Youyu, a well-known political philosopher at the Academy of Social Sciences, also warned me not to be naive. "Beida reform is all about *zheng ji gong cheng*," he said in the tone of someone well-seasoned in Chinese politics. "If you don't see this, you haven't seen through it." Xu liked Gan Yang's articles against the Beida reform—to his own surprise. Just a short few years earlier, the two men were on the opposite sides of a ferocious debate between the "Liberals" and the "New Leftists"; but this time, Xu admitted that Gan was the opposition camp's rightful flag holder. He particularly approved Gan's questioning of Beida reform's legal legitimacy. Gan had written that since Beida is a *state* university, any reform would be illegal unless the *state* passes new laws to sanction it. To a Liberal like Xu, the notion of law is extremely important.

So, basically, Zhang Weiying stands to be a treble traitor: as an official servant, he betrays the intellectuals for his own political ambition; as a comprador for the West, he betrays Chinese culture and Chinese dignity; as a designer of an illegal reform, he betrays the Chinese state.

"He seemed defensive," one of Zhang's old friends noted to me. "I think this controversy must be hurting him."

I told her that the opposition, so far, has been much louder than the support.

"It's very hard to push reform in China," she said finally. "I think he'll be sacrificed in the end."

"Sacrificed? By whom?"

"Who else? By the higher-ups."

6.

After our dinner, Zhang Weiying e-mailed me a number of his articles on university reform. Unlike the author of the cool, technical, official Beida documents, Zhang in these articles was more frank and more thoughtful.

He was also quietly passionate, as a man who was fully aware of the weight of his task and the importance of careful reasoning. The central piece was a long essay entitled "The University's Logic," based on an interview Zhang gave to a Beijing newspaper. Here Zhang offered an incisive, bold analysis of the problems of Chinese higher education. In his view, nearly all the problems could be tracked to two sources: government control and the unsatisfactory quality of the professors. He did not mince his words about either one.

Chinese universities, Zhang wrote, are the product of China's old planned economy. They are in fact special institutions set up by the government. When all the fundamentals of a university—funding, appointment of the president, organizational structure, size of faculty, curriculum, degree programs, enrollment quota, admission, and tuition—are determined and controlled by the government, the university has very little autonomy. It is not a real university. The only competition within such a system is the unhealthy battling— often through personal connections—for government funding and quotas; and because these battles often depend on the skills of the administrators, it makes them overly powerful and results in a swollen bureaucracy. The officials clamor everyday about "world-class university" and "academic prosperity," but they themselves are the roadblocks of academic progress. "If China wants to produce world-class universities," Zhang wrote, "I think the way of government controlling the university must be truly, thoroughly changed, and the university must be allowed to govern [itself]. Otherwise, there is no hope for a first-rate university."

This was sharp and direct. Unfortunately, Zhang admitted, changing this basic paradigm is beyond any Chinese university's power. Commenting on the trends of university reform in Europe and Japan, where the state also plays a heavy role in higher education, Zhang noted that the situation is much worse in China. Unlike in Europe, Chinese universities have almost no tradition of self-governance and therefore few resources with which to confront the government. So, as important and urgent as it is, we can only urge the government to be more liberal.

But Zhang isn't satisfied to be merely a finger-pointing critic. His philosophy is that one should do whatever is within one's power to improve the situation. What the Chinese university can do, he thought, is a kind of partial reform. If we can't alter the university's relationship with the government, we can perhaps try to handle the other problem: the unsatisfactory quality of the professors. China's reform of the big state factories, Zhang pointed out, had also started with small steps, such as introducing the bonus system and encouraging worker mobility. Later it went deeper. At the university, Zhang thought, faculty is the most crucial element, so if we were to design a system that promotes more openness, mobility, and competition on scholarship rather than playing politics, it would help raise the quality level of the faculty. This may not solve the problem of government control, but it would help break down academic tribalism (the powers of older mentors over their students who stay on to teach in the same department). It may not make a world-class university, but it would help put the pressure on incompetent scholars and attract good scholars to join. In short, it may not be perfect, but it would help push things ahead.

The intense reaction to this partial reform, Zhang felt, was a sign that it had indeed touched a nerve. It might even be a *tupokou*, (突破口), a breakthrough point, for deeper reform later.

And finally, Zhang believed this reform would get the higher officials' attention. How can they "ignore the wind and waves and just sit still in their fishing boat!" Zhang said.

Is he a shrewd strategist or a naive dreamer?

7.

A week later I met with Zhang Weiying again in his Beida office. I wanted to see him in his own work environment.

Arriving early on a cold morning, I entered the campus from the south gate. Beida looked very different from the days when I was a student there in the early 1980s. The old part of the campus—the part around Weiming Lake, with the pagoda, the willows and bamboo, the sloppy pine forest, the lovely Chinese courtyard houses and elegant republican-era brick mansions that Liu Dong loves to show off to visitors to prove that the aristocratic spirit is still alive in China—is still there, but it is now surrounded and broken up by the new campus. The new campus consists of modern-style concrete and glass buildings: classrooms, offices, lecture and concert halls, cafeterias, and an expanded library. These are bigger, taller, architecturally mediocre affairs, topped occasionally by a huge tile roof as a nod to tradition. Then, beyond the campus walls, rows of high-rises are visible: these house various business companies Beida built and owned in the 1990s. These new giants, while aesthetically unappealing, stand around with an air of bravado, as though completely confident of their own stature and power in a new era of money and practicality. In 1993, in a gesture of "opening the campus to face the market," the university took down its southern wall. The wall was erected again in 2001, but the "market wind" had already blown in. "Beida's campus soil is no longer pure," an old professor put it to me.

Zhang Weiying's office was on the second floor of the Guanghua School of Management, housed in one of the new contemporary building complexes.

On the lobby wall an introduction of Guanghua's faculty was posted. It showed many *hai gui* with doctorate degrees from Western universities. Later Zhang told me that about half of Guanghua's existing faculty is *hai gui*, many personally recruited by him—"at a much higher salary than mine." This seems to confirm what I had heard before: Zhang Weiying is simply trying to expand to the whole of Beida the "reform" he had already implemented at Guanghua.

Zhang was on the phone when I walked in. Dressed in a dark suit with a purple tie, he was having a typically busy workday: as the vice dean, he had to oversee many of Guanghua's administrative affairs. That morning he was trying to enlist a Beida vice president's attendance at the school's upcoming e-MBA graduation ceremony. "Please help us," I heard him plead. "It's a very important occasion for the students."

There are more than ten vice presidents, but he couldn't find one to attend. He shook his head; again I detected frustration.

His office was spacious but unpretentious; everything in it was functional. Economics books in Chinese or English filled the book cases. The only personal item was a photo of him in his hometown. When I asked about this, Zhang took out a photo album and showed me some more pictures taken during his last visit to Shaanxi. His village is still very poor and you could see it in these pictures: Barren yellow earth. Mud caves for homes. His illiterate parents. His old elementary school principal. A crowd of peasant folks with weather-beaten faces, and Zhang in his polo shirt and spectacles, looking almost like a character from outer space. This peasant's son has come a long way.

I asked him about his work as the assistant to the president. His special charge was Beida's commercial companies, which had been a thorny issue. These companies, founded mostly in the 1990s, were important sources of Beida's "income creation"; annual sales revenue in 2002 reached 20 billion yuan, by far the highest in China among university companies. Yet in Zhang's view, by investing so much energy and resources into profit-seeking business, with its endemic corruption and other managerial problems, Beida has paid a heavy price. The university's image has been tarnished.

"In the last ten years," Zhang told me in a disapproving tone, "there were more media reports about Beida's companies than about Beida's scholars." So he had been working to get Beida to gradually phase out its involvement in so many businesses. He had already shut down twenty to thirty Beida companies. "This made a lot of people unhappy, but for me the number one issue is protecting Beida's reputation. Plus," he smiled, "I have an iron face. Coffee is okay, but I don't go to banquets, and I don't take money. So there is nothing they can do. . . . So many resources are being wasted at Beida. If my plan gets implemented, it will be worth at least half a billion yuan a year."

I don't know how he arrived at this sum, but at that moment he did sound like an economist with a calculator in hand. And I remembered professor Li Qiang's retort to the critics: "They say a university is not a chicken farm, because if it is, then those chickens who don't lay eggs should get the hell out! But I say a university is not a retirement home either!" Li Qiang, a professor of political science with a PhD from London University, was also a member of the reform plan draft team. He didn't like being labeled a *hai gui* because, like Zhang Weiying, he too had grown up in the poor northern countryside. "We know how starved of funding rural schools are. China's educational spending is so pitiful. Yet the state gives so much money to a few famous universities like Beida."

This was no exaggeration. According to a September 2003 United Nations report, China's average educational spending per person is less than—get ready—Uganda's! Education spending takes up merely 2 percent of China's GDP, with 53 percent of it coming from the state budget. But Li said that at Beida, this precious state fund is spent without efficiency. "Why not give some to help the peasants and workers? Weiying and I just want to help save some money!"

Nevertheless, certain "waste of the resources," such as Beida's overemployment, was a messy business to tackle. Besides a swelling bureaucracy, much of it is a socialist legacy, and so the problems are especially severe in the older, bigger departments. The Chinese department, for instance, has always been Beida's flagship department and has more faculty members than, say, Harvard's English department. But it has used up nearly all its quota for full professors, with dozens of associate professors waiting in the wings to be promoted. A wide age gap caused by the hiring freeze during the Cultural Revolution has resulted in too few retirements in the next ten years to accommodate new promotions. But firing people because of a quota problem? This is still unacceptable in China, at least at a university—especially when these untenured younger professors are often better trained and therefore better teachers and scholars than some of the full professors who got there chiefly due to seniority. Also, the Chinese department, along with other humanities departments such as philosophy, history, and religion, has suffered a drastic enrollment decline. Since the late 1990s, about half of the Chinese department freshmen were students "reallocated" to the department after failing to get in their first-choice departments such as economics and law. History and philosophy have done even worse. At some universities, the entire freshman class in history and philosophy are "reallocation" students.

Newer departments such as Guanghua or Beida's China Center for Economic Research (CCER) don't have problems like this. They are leaner and financially more independent. Guanghua's e-MBA program, for instance, charges a U.S. private school rate since it is jointly taught by Guanghua's faculty and visiting American professors, and its students are mostly wealthy Chinese CEOs. CCER also has lucrative joint-venture course offerings and workshops. Initiated by a group of U.S.-trained young economists, it was founded in the early 1990s with Hong Kong, Taiwanese, and American money, and all of its present twenty faculty members have PhDs from abroad. Some hold visiting positions at other universities; many earn extra income from research projects commissioned by private companies, regional governments, and foreign foundations.

Support for Zhang Weiying is strong in these departments.

I talked with three professors at CCER; all enthusiastically endorsed the reform plan. Zhou Qiren, an economist with a PhD from UCLA, told me, "The Beida reform is not about *hai gui* and *tu bie*. It's about how to distribute resources, whether by the market or by the state. So all my arguments point ultimately to the state domination." Zhou admitted that he was inspired by Milton Freedman's "education voucher"—by the idea of turning the choices of higher education to the customers—the parents and children. Bai Lanzhi, an urban planning specialist with a Berkeley PhD, said, "Those humanities scholars don't like the government—*that* I understand. But they don't like the market either. Is there something they *do* like?" Chen Ping, with a PhD from the University of Texas, called Beida "a forest of feudal fiefdoms" and the reform plan "a very small step to change." He told me, "I'd go much further if I were doing it."

Their sentiments are hardly surprising. As Western-trained experts in a field in great demands nowadays, they have a confidence and optimism that have everything to do with their advantage on the current market. Faced with marginalization and dwindling influence, their colleagues in the humanities naturally have very different perspectives.

And then a *hai gui*, a straight-shooting *economist* bent on "efficiency" and "logic," was appointed to design the reform!

"Zhang Weiying is a very nice person," said a Beijing editor who didn't want to be named. "But like a lot of science and engineering people, he may not be very sensitive to politics." She has known Zhang for years but is also friendly with many of the humanities scholars who attacked Zhang's plan. She said that as a neutral observer of the Beida debate, she was intrigued by its subtle psychological undercurrent: some of the prominent critics were already full professors but would like to appear as gallant defenders of their junior colleagues' interests; others were privately sympathetic to the reform but didn't want to publicly support it for fear of offending its opponents—after all, the reformers could lose, and they'd go on living on the same campus with the same colleagues, probably for the rest of their lives. "I don't think Zhang Weiying could grasp such complex psychology. He is a bit *han* [憨]." (The word means something like gauche and thick.)

I told Zhang Weiying that some people thought his ambition was aimed at an official career. Zhang looked insulted and a bit contemptuous. He responded with a Chinese proverb: "That's like a petty person trying to imagine a gentleman's mind. Why would I come to Beida if I wanted an official career?" He explained his involvement in the reform this way: "I'm like the goalie in a soccer game. Because our team has been doing so badly and can't get the ball in [the goal], I feel so anxious I run across the field and try to help. But that's really not my job."

Already he seemed to be missing the simpler life of being just a scholar. He is a popular teacher and enjoys wide respect at Guanghua. And in Chinese economists' circles, Zhang Weiying is a big name. He was the first one in China to teach and edit a textbook on game theory. His books and articles on property rights and the theory of business enterprise and its relation to the government have been well reviewed and influential. He is a leading champion for private enterprise and a fierce critic of government's interference in business. In 2002, he was chosen by CCTV as the "economist of the year," the youngest to win the accolade.

Being an official, he said, doesn't fit his personality. You can't talk freely, and you have to sit through long meetings. "There are so many VPs and other officials at a Beida meeting, by the time it's my turn to speak, the day is over."

He was moved by the Oxford dons. "Their seminars had just a few students but very sharp debates, and they enjoy it so much. *Zi de qi le* (自得其乐), enjoy your own happiness. That's the best thing I learned at Oxford: a scholar's state of mind. It's like the Chinese saying 'getting one soul mate in a lifetime, that's enough.'"

8.

By March 2004 the controversy finally cooled off. On February 14, when school resumed after winter break, Beida's administration issued, quietly, the final document. There was no media fanfare, but the university made it clear that this was not something for feedback, debate, or comments. This was final: the document was the new official *policy*. And policy, of course, was to be obeyed and implemented.

I had sensed this shifting wind months earlier when I heard about a speech by Beida's Party secretary, Min Weifang. He was addressing the midlevel officials—Party heads, deans, and departmental chairmen—at a staff meeting. Of the lessons to be learned from the stormy controversy over the reform, Min said, a primary one was to avoid overexposure. He looked back on an earlier reform Beida did in 1999, which was also an attempt to stir up competition by evaluating all professors into nine grades and awarding bonuses accordingly. There had been a good deal of faculty complaint and grumbling about that, too. But the task was accomplished without any serious hitches because, in Min's view, the midlevel officials had all been well-briefed and prepared. The administration had held a closed staff meeting off-campus and the officials had reached a clear consensus. No one was allowed to take the draft document home— the whole thing was kept secret while the officials got ready for the pressures ahead.

This time, it would have been handled the same way but for the SARS scare; to avoid the risk of a face-to-face meeting, the draft document was sent to the midlevel officials, which led to its being leaked to the Internet. But Min said that from here on, "hyping" must be avoided: to accomplish reform we need to keep a sharp edge and "someone to take the brunt of fire," but in our actual work we should be "low-key, practical, and steadfast."

Dismissing the critics' charges as *wujie* (误解), or misunderstandings, Min reasserted the leadership's resolve to carry on with the reform but told the officials that its fate lay in *their* hands. Min said the administration had been planning to give more power to the heads of colleges and departments. They had studied the first-rate foreign universities, Min said, and discovered that a powerful midlevel management was a common feature at great universities like Harvard, Yale, and Stanford. Beida would now take a step in this direction as well. But more power means more responsibilities. It would be against our reformist intensions, Min said, if you people end up using that power to promote a bunch of low-quality professors.

I think that meeting set the tone. On December 4, I attended a Beida official press conference on the topic of "talent-breeding education." Min and the entire corps of his "midlevel officials" were there. It was an impressive sight. Facing a roomful of reporters, Min was seated at the center of a long table, flanked by a long row of smart-looking men in smart suits and ties, each behind a microphone and a bottle of mineral water—a phalanx of China's new, educated, well-dressed technocrats. And they certainly knew how to handle the media. Min gave the keynote speech. He talked about the importance of human talents if a country was to be competitive in the new age of globalization; he talked about Beida's mission in breeding new talents for China; he reported Beida's strategies and progress in this task—the reforms and experiments being made in admission policy, curriculum, graduate programs, and faculty systems. He quoted Beida's legendary president Cai Yuanpei but also Jiang Zemin and Alan Greenspan. He talked about increased cooperation and exchanges with foreign universities (Stanford, Harvard, Yale, Oxford, etc.), but also about the increased ratio of Party members among students (34 percent of recent graduates had joined the Party). He talked about promoting a "relaxed, lively" campus culture as well as efforts of "making the red flag fly on Beida's Internet Web sites."

I must admit that I found this speech, like Min's address to his midlevel officials, remarkable in its own way. I had heard that Min was arrogant, that he had a penchant for peppering his speech with

English phrases. But here he was, speaking for half an hour without notes, in a curious lingo that mixed Party jargon with New-Age-speak. And it all flowed out smoothly, even with a touch of eloquence. The tone was confident but *not* arrogant. And no English. Here was a man who knew his audience and how to balance things.

Min mentioned the faculty reform plan, but only briefly, and left right after he spoke—he was also attending a weeklong meeting at the State Council. Then the "midlevel officials" spoke one by one, and it was a long time before the reporters were invited to ask questions. Many asked about the faculty reform plan but received only pleasant, short, general replies. The officials were being "low-key, practical, and steadfast."

I had a brief chat with Min before the conference. A media official introduced me as "our Beida graduate, but she has lived in the States for many years and is now writing a new book about China in English." Min shook my hands warmly and immediately chatted about his years in the States. He told me, in English, that his Stanford PhD was in "economics of education." But this amicable exchange ended the moment I mentioned my interest in interviewing him on the Beida reform. It was subtle. I said I understood that he'd be very busy in the next few weeks attending the annual Beida Party Congress, but maybe after that? Min smiled and said: "Okay, just call my secretary. He will help you arrange it."

In the end I didn't get the interview because Min checked into the hospital as soon as the Party Congress ended, but he probably wouldn't have granted another interview on the touchy subject anyway. Then a piece of news about the Party Congress spread. As usual, the congress voted on the new members of Beida's Party Committee. One of the candidates was Zhang Weiying: he received the lowest number votes. Everyone understood that Zhang had taken a fall because of the reform plan.

I recalled a line in Min's address: "Someone must take the brunt of fire" for the reform. Perhaps Zhang's old friend was right after all:

as the point man, the public face of the Beida reform, Zhang was now paying a price. He was being "sacrificed by the higher-ups."

9.

Chen Pingyuan, the professor who had organized the conference on "Beijing: Urban Imagination and Cultural Memory," was one of Beida's best-known humanities scholars and one of the few who were critical of but also sympathetic to the reformers. His colleagues in the Chinese department were overwhelmingly opposed to the reform plan, and they found Chen's attitude "evasive." "You don't know where he really stands," one of them complained to me about Chen's articles on the debate. "I suppose with Pingyuan's stature he wants to be careful not to offend people."

I think it has less to do with stature than with temperament— Chen had always been a "gentle liberal." Neither did I find Chen's articles evasive. Rather, I sensed that his was a rare moderate voice in a cantankerous debate over complex issues where emotions ran so hot that highly intelligent people who were otherwise friendly to one another ended up in radicalized "positions" and "camps."

Chen Pingyuan had a different perspective. He was mindful of Beida's complicated, volatile politics. He told me about a conversation he had years ago with a Beida vice president. At a meeting, Chen had been critical of the administration, accusing it of being too powerful. Afterward, the VP pulled him aside and told him: Beida is full of liberals and conservatives, rightists and leftists; the administration must keep balancing all sides in order to avoid bigger trouble. Chen has since learned to appreciate the toughness of such a job.

To him, reform needs critics but also builders. "Everyone can only perform on a certain set historical stage. I sympathize with the reformers' hopes and ideas, even though I don't agree with their approach." He thought the administration should have involved more humanities professors in drafting the plan; they might have offered more vision and delicacy and helped in winning broader support.

But he endorsed the reformers' general ideas like open search and hiring more *hai gui*. He admitted that inbreeding and overstaffing were a real problem, and that the present system made it nearly impossible to fire anyone no matter how incompetent he was.

"My hope is that the final plan will be the result of compromises. There will be some changes in the area of hiring, promotion, and retaining graduates. And transition should be calm and steady."

The final document appeared to be exactly what Chen had hoped for. The essential features of the original were kept but were phrased in milder language, with room left to adapt to special circumstances. For example, the document announced that Beida would not hire its own graduates from now on, but used the phrase "in principle" to qualify it. It was also quite soft on the existing faculty: associate professors in the humanities would be given fifteen years to get their tenure promotion before they could lose their job. It also said that each department could "supplement certain details in implementation according to their own concrete circumstances."

The reaction was cool, even flat. Zhang Ming, an associate professor in the Chinese department and one of the most intense critics I'd talked with during the controversy, didn't even bother to read the final document. "It's over. Doesn't interest me anymore." He shrugged as we chatted in his new and freshly renovated apartment. "Anyway, whatever *we* say makes no difference."

Yung Ho Chang, the architecture professor, was equally passive. "I haven't read it," he told me weeks after the final document was issued. "It will affect us in the future, but anyway, *our* opinions don't matter." He said he has been too busy with other more pressing matters to think about this. (Chang would leave Beida a year later to head the architecture department at MIT.)

This sudden loss of interest intrigued me. It is becoming a familiar trajectory of many local controversies: a hot debate, a media rush, then it bursts like a bubble and fades off. Before long, public attention moves on to the next "hot" topic, which won't last very long either. Meanwhile, everyone is busy, busy, busy. The Chinese attention span seems to have grown much shorter than it was just a few years ago.

But could it be that the final document has become so moderate that there isn't much left to quarrel about? "I think people got relaxed because basically no one would be fired," Liu Dong said simply.

Chen Pingyuan's wife, Xia Xiaohong, who is also a Chinese department professor, agreed. She had heard that some departmental leaders were already telling their faculty to rest assured: nobody will get fired. "Don't you remember that saying? *Shang you zheng ce, xia you dui ce* (上有政策, 下有对策)—When there is policy from above, there is always a way of handling it on the ground." She said that, like much else in China, these new rules could be managed and fixed as well.

"It all depends on the wording of the document," Xia said. "If it's clear, hard wording, then it will be obeyed. But if it's soft wording, then people will find ways to work around it."

Zhang Weiying himself said in a newspaper interview that this final document is "very conservative": "I don't think there is any other reform plan in China that is more gentle."

Zhang has remained gracious throughout the debate, but when the reporter asked how he felt about his opponents, a note of disappointment escaped him: "I've heard a lot. I am never afraid of debating with others. . . . But sometimes I felt a slight sadness. In such a great university, sometimes we lack basic consensus in a discussion. We lack even a common language. Why does a university exist? People have different understandings. We don't have shared beliefs."

This reminded me of my conversation with Li Qiang, the *hai gui* political scientist on the reform plan draft team. Li was dismayed by the whole debate. He found some critics rhetorically high-flown yet mean-spirited. "They fight with literary style but it's a kind of language violence. How can we have democracy in China if even our university professors lapse into personal attacks so easily in a public debate? I told Weiying maybe we were too Westernized—when we studied in the West we used to think: how nice is democracy! But it doesn't work here. Deng Xiaoping was right: the best way in China is *bu zheng lun* (不争论), no debate. Why? Because our debate here descends to the lowest levels, and the winners are those who are willing to sink to the lowest to get the attention. Certainly a cabdriver good at street shouting matches will win any debate." Li had predicted that the Beida administration would solve the controversy "conservatively" because Beida is "too sensitive a place" to allow any *zhendang* (震荡, shock) to happen. He was right. Nobody, not even the most vigilant critic, called Beida's final document "shock therapy."

In the end, both Li and Zhang seemed wistful for the kind of enlightened, charismatic, and strong leader that was Beida's old president Cai Yuanpei. Oddly enough, their critics share the same nostalgia. Standing in front of Cai's bronze bust on campus, Liu Dong had told me: "He is Beida's God." And like a god, Cai was constantly cited, praised, and eulogized during the debate. Different sides used him for different purposes. Min Weifang and Zhang Weiying liked to recall Cai's international vision: how he, a *hai gui* himself (studied in Germany and visited the States), embraced both Western and Chinese values; how he borrowed and copied many things from German, Japanese, and later American university systems in his days of reforming Beida; how he ruthlessly fired some incompetent professors and invited many *hai gui* to join. The critics, on the other hand, liked to remember how many great humanities scholars Cai had hired (Cai himself had studied art and aesthetics in Germany) and how it was these humanities maestros who coined Beida's golden image.

But perhaps these contradictory views of Cai and the nostalgia for a strong leader like him reflect both the inner tensions within the idea of a modern Chinese university and a sense of helplessness at the present reality. Anyone who knows the history of Chinese universities would have to admit two basic facts: that traditional

Chinese academies (书院, *shuyuan*), mentor-oriented private schools that focused on Chinese classics, were a long-gone tradition, and that the Chinese university as we know it today was a Western import that had arrived on the heels of China's nineteenth-century military defeat. Beida was the very first such "modern" Chinese university, established by imperial decree and with funds from the Qing court, which reluctantly conceded that the Chinese needed some Western learning in order to handle the aggressive foreign barbarians. The desire and drive to learn from the West, therefore, was embedded in the very notion of the Chinese university. Yet stirring in its soul is also the deep yearning to somehow retain Chinese integrity and carry on the Chinese cultural heritage. This is especially powerful among the educated Chinese, since modernization for them has often been viewed as the means to regain Chinese glory. Today, after fifty years of copying the Soviets with disastrous consequences, learning from the West has returned with a new urgency. But so has the yearning for a strong Chinese identity.

Meanwhile, as Zhang Weiying pointed out, Chinese universities had a very weak tradition of self-governance. Whether under the imperial court, the republican/warlord governments, or communist rule, with perhaps a few fleeting, minor exceptions, Chinese universities had never gained true autonomy. Even a legend like Cai Yuanpei was, in reality, far from being a real independent. The government appointed him and sponsored the university. In the ten years of his Beida presidency, Cai threatened to resign nearly every year, and often he was doing so to protest against some government policy or interference. This in itself showed how much the university had depended on the government back then. But at least Cai got away with it. He was not fired; more often than not, he got what he wanted.

Nevertheless, Cai was a special case. He was the first minister of education in China's first republican government. He was a famous revolutionary and famously erudite—in both traditional Chinese and modern Western learning. Like many prominent intellectuals of that era, he was cosmopolitan yet deeply patriotic. And then he had just the right personality: he was charismatic and charming; he was gentle and open and tolerant. Everyone I talked with agreed that there can't be another Cai Yuanpei today. It's just not possible. And even if there *is* someone like Cai, he would not be allowed to have that sort of power—nor would any university president in China today. This is not a question of personality; it's a question of the system. In the mid-1980s, there had been a short period when the liberals in the government talked about separating Party power from the president's power in the university. That's now gone after Tiananmen. Today the official policy is "the university president takes responsibility under the leadership of the Party Committee." Min Weifang *is* Beida's Party secretary. He is also the person behind Zhang Weiying's reform plan. But if Min should concede to any talk of reforming the Party power away from running the university, he would be the first one to lose his job. No wonder Min has been emphasizing the importance of Party leadership in his speeches.

"Ultimately, a real university reform means a real political reform in China," said Zhu Zhenglin, a former Beida graduate who now works for CCTV. "Precisely because of this, it won't be allowed to happen—not yet." His prediction of Beida reform's fate had consisted of four words: *hu tou she wei* (虎头蛇尾, tiger head, snake tail)—start big, end small.

But then again, not everyone is resigned to simply waiting for the future. Like Zhang Weiying, Yang Dongping, a professor of education at the China Politics and Law University, wants to take action. Besides offering his "unreserved support" for Beida reform, Yang has launched "The Twenty-First-Century Education Development Research Institute," a private research and advocacy group with the self-assigned mission of drafting education reform proposals for official review and public discussion. "We would be thorough," Yang told me. "We propose to set up a new financial structure for public education, new education legislatures, civil and intermediate organizations, new evaluation systems, and so on. But the first step is university self-governance. The Education Ministry must let go of its grip on the universities."

Yang considers Beida reform a very important event. The accusation of "Americanization," he said, is narrow-minded and too nationalistic. "The question is: do we accept the institution of the university as the flower of human civilization and therefore a universal good? If we do, then we Chinese should learn and benefit from it."

Yang said that even though the immediate effects of faculty system reform might be limited, Beida reform started the ball rolling and had a great symbolic impact. He thought the public debate was a very good thing, even though it had happened by accident. "Public debate is so rare in our country. And since this happened at a high-profile place like Beida, people are now much more aware of the issues. It's created a momentum for a more general education reform." He also views the creation of the professors' committee in the Beida plan as a significant first step to give faculty more power.

Yang expects other universities to follow Beida's lead. In fact, while media spotlights focused on the Beida controversy, a number of other universities were already making their own moves. In the north, Dongbei Normal University established their "professors' committees." In the south, Zhongshan University and Suzhou University reformed their faculty hiring system. Nearby, Qinghua University had also quietly made its own reform plans. The Party secretary of Wuhan University even re-proposed the 1980s liberal idea in a printed article: "Let the party govern the party, the president govern the university, and the professors govern the scholarship." Professor Yang thinks that these are important, exciting signs.

"Beida reform has tossed a stone into a stagnant pond," he said. "So far, Chinese education reform has lagged behind a lot of other areas, but it's now emerging out of the water."

When I had dinner again with Zhang Weiying, he brought me a copy of his new book in its somber blue jacket—a collection of his essays on university reform. But he said he's been fighting another

"war" lately: Guanghua's old dean is retiring, and there has been a
struggle over the changing of the guard. Issues such as meritocracy
versus cronyism are being put to the test. "I want to prove that principles and fair play can work," Zhang said gravely, hardly touching
his food. "Otherwise there will be another big stir at Beida. I'll take
certain steps and I know a lot of the Guanghua faculty will be with
me." This is just like the Beida reform conflict, he added a moment
later; it's the same kind of battle. That evening he talked with an
obsessive fervor, his salt-and-pepper hair and spectacles shining under the restaurant's soft lamplight. He looked like a tired but determined warrior.

Postscript
In 2010, the Ministry of Education issued a new document, the
"Middle- and Long-Term State Education Reform and Development Plan." It was dutifully reported in the newspapers and posted
on the Internet for feedback, but public interest was low. I pored
over the long document full of dry official jargon and came away
with a headache and a very foggy notion of what would actually be
"reformed." As far as I could tell, the most important item in the bill
was increased funding: the state education fund will reach 4 percent
of GDP by 2012.

This time, not even Zhang Weiying bothered to read the plan.
He wasn't impressed when I told him about the 4 percent GDP
target: "They think money can solve all the problems, but it can't."
He admitted that he was no longer enthusiastic about the Chinese
education reform, and he didn't think the state was serious about it.
As long as the Party and the Education Ministry kept their control of all top-level university appointments, there would be no real
academic autonomy, no real reform. Other administrative changes
might only create unexpected new problems.

But he is an optimist about China's future in general. He had won
the smaller battle at Guanghua Management School and has been
focused on his work there as the dean. As an economist and a consis-

tent advocate for the free market and privatization, Zhang continues to stir controversy but remains an active, outspoken figure in all the important Chinese debates on economic policy and modes of development. He has been reading a lot of history books in recent years. Understanding the past, he told me, has helped him to put the present and the future in perspectives: "When you squat down, you see a lot of bumps; but if you stand up and look around, you will see that the earth is quite flat. Take American history: only a few decades ago black people couldn't vote or share a bus with white people. But today Obama is the president. Every Chinese intellectual carries an idealized world in his head, so he sees disharmony all around him. But I believe China is making progress, slowly but surely, because I am looking at the long-term trajectory, and I can see history's great curves."

Liu Dong shares no such optimism, especially when it comes to present-day Beida. In 2010, Liu left Beida and moved to Tsinghua University, Beida's neighbor and often considered to be its rival. "When I first joined Beida faculty, everyone teased me about my Beida hang-up," he told me. "But I wasn't reluctant to leave. It's becoming more and more like an empty shell of what it once was."

Enemy of the State

Beijing Second Prison is on the outskirts of the city for which it is named, and you can drive past the drab compound without ever noticing it. It's set about a tenth of a mile off the highway, and when I visit I usually have to tell the cabdriver about the exit on the left, because it's easy to miss. The first thing you see, after the turnoff, is a heavy, dun-colored metal gate framed by a white tiled arch, and then the guards standing in front with long-barreled automatic weapons. Electrified wires are stretched taut along the top of the outer wall; it's a maximum-security facility. Inside the waiting room, adjoining the gate, I stow my purse and cell phone in a locker, present my documents, and wait to be called. The guards recognize me but maintain a professional remoteness. This is 2007; I'm visiting my brother, Zha Jianguo, a democracy activist serving a nine-year sentence for "subverting the state."

Jianguo was arrested and tried in the summer of 1999, and I remember with perfect clarity the moment I learned what had happened. I was standing in the kitchen of a friend's country house outside Montreal, drinking a cup of freshly made coffee and glancing at a story on the front page of the local newspaper. It was about a

Note: Most of this chapter was written in 2007.

missile China had just test-launched that was supposed to be able to hit Alaska; in the last paragraph, Jianguo's trial was reported. I was astonished and outraged, and, as his little sister, I was fiercely proud as well: Jianguo's act of subversion was to have helped start an opposition party, the China Democracy Party (CDP). It was the first time in the history of the People's Republic of China that anyone had dared to form and register an independent party. Jianguo and his fellow activists had done so openly, peacefully. Now they were going to prison for it.

My first visits, back in 2000, were particularly arduous. I had to obtain special permits each time, and during our thirty-minute meetings Jianguo and I were flanked by two or three guards, including an officer in charge of "special" prisoners. I was shocked by how changed Jianguo was from when I'd last seen him, two years earlier. It wasn't just his prisoner's crewcut and uniform of coarse cotton, vertical white stripes on gray; his eyes were rheumy and infected, his hands and face were swollen, and his fingernails were purple, evidently from poor circulation and nutrition. We sat on opposite sides of a thick Plexiglas panel and spoke through handsets—they were an incongruous Day-Glo yellow, like a toy phone you'd give a child. Our exchanges, in those days, seemed fraught with urgency and significance. After the first few visits, I also met with the warden, who turned out to be a surprisingly cordial young man. ("You expected a green-faced, long-toothed monster, didn't you?" he said to me, smiling.) We discussed various issues regarding Jianguo's health. Within weeks, he granted my two main requests. Jianguo was taken out of the prison in a van with armed guards to a good city hospital, where he received a medical checkup, and he was moved from a noisy cell with eleven murderers to a less crowded, quieter cell.

Since I moved back to Beijing, the monthly trip to Beijing Second Prison has become a routine. I try to make conversation with the officer at the "book desk," where you can leave reading material for the prisoner you're visiting; he excludes whatever he deems "inappropriate." Anything political is likely to be rejected, although a collection of essays by Václav Havel got through: the officer peered at the head shot of the gloomy foreigner, but didn't know who he was.

The so-called "interview room" is a bland, tidy space, with rows of sky-blue plastic chairs along the Plexiglas divider; you can see a well-tended garden outside, with two heart-shaped flower beds. Farther away, there's a row of buildings, gray concrete boxes, where the inmates live and work. (They're allowed outdoors twice a week for two-hour periods of open-air exercise.) You can even see the unit captain lead the prisoners, in single file, from those buildings to the interview room.

Gradually, I have become just another visiting relative, and, though the phones are monitored, the guards have long ago lost interest in watching my brother and me. Time passes quickly. Jianguo and I often chat like two old friends who haven't seen each other in a while. I start by inquiring after his health and general condition, then report some news about relatives or friends. After that, we might talk about the books he's read recently or discuss something in the news, such as the war in Iraq or Beijing's preparation for the 2008 Olympics. Sometimes we even exchange carefully phrased opinions on China's political situation. Finally, I make a shopping list. Each month, a prisoner is allowed about eighty yuan in spending money (about ten dollars) and a hundred and fifty yuan of extra food if a visiting relative buys it at the prison shop; this is for security reasons, but it also provides a source of income for the prison. Jianguo often asks me to buy a box of cookies. Another prisoner, who is serving a ten-year sentence for being a "Taiwanese spy," has been teaching him English. The man's wife left him, and no one comes to visit. Apparently, he really likes the cookies.

In the first couple of years, I kept asking Jianguo whether he was ever beaten or hurt in any way. "I'm on pretty good terms with all the officers," he would tell me. "They are just following orders, but they all know why I got here, and they've never touched me. My cellmates have fights among themselves but never with me. They all kind of respect me." He told me that the jailers let it drop when

he refused to answer if he was addressed as *fan ren* (犯人, "convict")
So-and-So; he objects to the title because he doesn't believe that he
committed a crime. He has also refused to take part in the manual
work that all prisoners in his unit are supposed to do: packing dis-
posable chopsticks and similar chores.

A family friend told me that Jianguo might be able to leave China
on medical parole, and I asked him many times if he would consider
it. He wouldn't. "I will not leave China unless my freedom of return
is guaranteed," he insisted. I have stopped asking. Jianguo repeatedly mentions the predicament of exiled Chinese dissidents in the
West, who, in the post-Tiananmen era, have lost their political ef-
fectiveness. "Once they leave Chinese soil, their role is very limited,"
Jianguo says. But how politically effective is it to sit in a tiny cell for
nine years—especially when most of your countrymen don't even
know of your existence?

That's something I've never had the heart to bring up. The mainland Chinese press didn't report the 1999 CDP roundup, so few
people in China ever knew what had happened. Outside China,
there was some media coverage at the time, and some protests from
human-rights groups, but the incident was soon eclipsed by the Fa-
lun Gong story. After almost eight years of incarceration, Jianguo is
unrepentant, resolute, and forgotten.

Jianguo is the older of two sons my father had from his first marriage. He was seven when my father divorced his mother and married mine. Although my father had custody of Jianguo, the eight
years that separated us meant that my childhood memories of him
are mostly dim. As was the fashion at the time, he went to a boarding school and came home only on Sundays. He remained a gangly,
reticent figure hovering at the edge of our family life.

Divorce was uncommon in China at the time, and no doubt
it cast a shadow on Jianguo's childhood. My mother recalls that,
when Jianguo slept in the house, she sometimes heard him sobbing
under his quilt. In letters written from prison, he described those

weekends as "visiting someone else's home" and said that he "felt like a Lin Daiyu"—referring to the tragic heroine in the Chinese classic *Dream of the Red Chamber*, who, orphaned at a young age, has to live in her uncle's house and compete with her cousins for love and attention. But his mother, whom I call Aunt Zhong, says that Jianguo was ambitious from a very young age. When she first told him the story of Yue Fei, a legendary general of the Song dynasty who was betrayed and died tragically, Jianguo looked up at her with tears in his eyes and said, "But I'm still too young to be a Yue Fei!" She was startled. "I didn't *expect* him to become a Yue Fei!" she told me.

She probably expected him to become a scholar. After all, the boy was surrounded not by military men but by academics and artists. My father was a philosopher. Aunt Zhong is an opera scholar and librettist from a distinguished intellectual family; her father was a university vice president, her mother a painter who studied with the famous master Qi Baishi. Aunt Zhong's stepfather, Li Jinxi, whose elegant courtyard house Jianguo frequently visited as a boy, was a renowned linguist who used to be Mao Zedong's teacher. But in another letter from prison, Jianguo described those primary-school years as "uneventful," aside from a vivid memory he has of a great summer storm that struck while he walked back to school one Sunday afternoon. In heated language, he recalled how he fought the wind and the downpour all the way, how he was drenched, alone in the deserted streets, but, oh, the awesome beauty of the thunder and lightning and the ecstasy he felt when he finally reached the school gate, the feeling he had of having beaten the monstrous storm all by himself!

Jianguo was also a voracious reader and a brilliant Go player. At the age of fourteen, he was accepted to an elite boarding middle school in Beijing, receiving the top score in his class on the entrance exam. Yet he felt restless. School life was confining, and he disliked the petty authorities he had to contend with. During this period, he began to worship Mao Zedong. He read Mao's biography closely and tried to imitate his example: taking cold showers in winter, reading philosophy, and pondering the big questions of politics and society, which he debated with a group of friends. His first political act was to write a letter to the school administration attacking the rigidity of the curriculum and certain "bourgeois sentiments" it enshrined. This was something that Jianguo is still proud of: even before the Cultural Revolution, he had challenged the system, alone.

My own sheltered childhood ended with the Cultural Revolution. My parents were denounced as "stinking intellectuals" and "counterrevolutionaries." Our house was ransacked. Under the new policy, I went to a nearby school of workers' children, some of whom threw rocks at me and even left human excrement on our balcony. But Jianguo thrived amid the social turmoil, and became a leader of a Red Guard faction at his school. He seldom came home. When he did, he dressed in full Red Guard fashion: the faded green army jacket and cap, the Mao button on the shirt pocket, the bright-red armband. He was tall and broad-shouldered, and, with his manly good looks, he seemed to me larger than life. I was shy and tongue-tied in his presence.

Two years later, in 1968, Jianguo left for Inner Mongolia with a group of other Red Guards. He was answering Chairman Mao's call for the educated city youth to transform China's poor countryside. My parents held a going-away party for him; I remember the din of a houseful of Red Guards talking, laughing, and eating, my mother boiling pot after pot of noodles, my father sitting silently in his study watching the teenagers as though in someone else's house, and Jianguo, seventeen years old, holding court like a young commander on the eve of battle. He invited his friends to take whatever they liked from my father's library; many books were "borrowed," including my mother's favorite novel, *Madame Bovary*, never to be returned.

Aunt Zhong went to the railway station to see him off. When the train started leaving, she waved at her son. "But he acted as if I wasn't there," she told me. "He just kept yelling 'Goodbye, Chairman Mao!' The Cultural Revolution really poisoned his mind."

Millions of urban youngsters went to the countryside in those days, but not all of them were true believers: some felt pressure to show proper "revolutionary enthusiasm," while others went because there were no jobs in the cities. Most of them, shocked by the poverty and backwardness of rural life, became disillusioned. And as the fever of the Cultural Revolution waned, in the mid-1970s, many returned home, getting factory jobs or going to university, which in those days depended not on your exam results but on your connections and political record.

Jianguo wasn't among them. During the seven years he spent on a farm in Inner Mongolia, he had served as the village head and was popular among peasants. He was a good farmhand. He could drink as much *baijiu* (白酒), the hard northern liquor, as the locals could. He had married a former Beijing schoolmate and Red Guard, who stayed on because of him, and they were making a life for themselves in the countryside. The villagers ignored whatever "revolutionary initiatives" Jianguo tried to introduce, but his personality—honest, warm, generous—won him their affection.

In 1976, Mao died, the Cultural Revolution ended, and Jianguo's daughter was born. Jianguo named her Jihong ("Inheriting Red"). The next few years were critical in China: Deng Xiaoping began to steer the country toward reform and greater openness. The university entrance exam, which had been suspended for more than a decade, was reinstated; I was among those who took the exam and went to university, a welcome change from the farmwork to which I'd been consigned. But Jianguo seemed stuck in the earlier era. He framed a large portrait of Mao with black gauze and hung it on a wall of his home; he would sit in front of it for hours, lost in thought. His wife later told me that Jianguo spent two years grieving for Mao.

Jianguo eventually took a job with the county government of his rural outpost, working for the local Party secretary, a Mongolian named Batu, who took a shine to the bright young Beijinger. Then Jianguo criticized one of Batu's policy directives, which he saw as disastrous for the peasants, and even took Batu to task in front of a crowded cadre assembly. Jianguo lost his post and was placed under investigation. Condemned as a "running dog of the Gang of Four," he was locked up in solitary confinement, allowed to read only books by Marx, Lenin, and Mao. Two years later, Batu left the county for a higher position, and Jianguo was released. He was given various low-level posts, and was never promoted.

In 1985, when I was a graduate student in comparative literature at Columbia University, I went to visit him. After an eighteen-hour ride on a hard-seated train from Beijing, I arrived at a dusty little county station. The man waiting for me there looked like all the other local peasants hawking melons and potatoes from the backs of their oxcarts. He was dressed like a peasant, spoke with a local accent, and had even developed a habit of squatting. His torpid movements suggested years of living in a remote backwater where nothing much ever happened.

It was early 1989 when Jianguo's wife finally prevailed on him to move back to Beijing. She was a practical woman, and she wasn't reconciled to a life of rural squalor. She was the one who, driven by poverty, sewed Jianguo's last piece of Red Guard memorabilia, a faded red flag bearing the Guard's logo, into a quilt cover. Now she was determined not to let their daughter grow up a peasant. For Jianguo, however, their return marked a humiliating end of a twenty-year mission. The idea of bringing revolution to the countryside had turned out to be a fantasy. He changed nothing there. It changed him.

Four months after Jianguo's return to Beijing, students started marching on Tiananmen Square. Going to the square each day, listening to the speeches and the songs, watching a new generation of student rebels in action—for Jianguo, it was a profoundly moving experience. Twenty years earlier, the Red Guard's god was Mao. Now the idealistic kids in blue jeans and T-shirts had erected a new statue: the Goddess of Democracy.

I was living in Beijing at the time and visited the square daily. Jianguo said little when we met, though he was evidently in turmoil.

One afternoon, I asked him to join me while I visited a friend who was active in the protests. Outside on the square, my friend greeted me warmly and invited me to come inside the tent where a group of student leaders were meeting, but when Jianguo followed me he frowned and barred him: "No, not you!" I explained that the man was my brother. My friend looked incredulous. Here, in his native city, Jianguo stood out as a country bumpkin. And, in 1989, the democracy activists were members of an urban elite. My friend's snobbery must have driven home the message to Jianguo: *Stand aside. This is not your revolution.*

Soon, it was nobody's revolution. What happened to the Tiananmen protesters on June 4 showed what awaited those who openly challenged the system. After the massacre, all government ministers were required to demonstrate loyalty to the Party by visiting the few hospitalized soldiers—"heroes in suppressing the counterrevolutionary riot." The novelist Wang Meng, who was then the minister of culture, got out of it by claiming ill health and checking into a hospital himself. He was promptly removed from office.

During the spring demonstrations, reporters for the *People's Daily* had held up a famous banner on the street: WE DON'T WANT TO LIE ANYMORE! It was a rare moment of collective courage. Two months later, they were forced to lie again. A journalist at the newspaper described to me how the campaign to purge dissent was conducted there: meetings were held at every section, and everybody had to attend. Each employee was required to give a day-by-day account of his activities during the Tiananmen period, and then to express his attitude toward the official verdict. "Every one of us did this—no one dared to say no," he said, recalling the scene seventeen years later. "Can you imagine how humiliating it was? We were crushed, instantly and completely."

Among journalists and intellectuals, a brief interval of exhilaration had given way to depression and fear. Many withdrew from public life and turned to private pursuits. (A few, like me, moved to the United States or Europe.) Scholars embarked on esoteric research—hence the *Guoxue Re* (国学热), the early 1990s craze for studying the Chinese classics. A friend of mine, the editor of a magazine that had been an influential forum for critical reporting, turned his attention to cuisine and classical music. Meanwhile, Jianguo, whose residual faith in the Communist Party and in Mao had perished on June 4, was adrift, both politically and personally.

The driver of the gypsy cab was a stocky man with a rugged, weather-beaten face who wore a cheap, oily-looking blazer. He was leaning on a Jetta, smoking a cigarette, when I got out of the prison snack shop. On this particular afternoon, I was the last visitor to leave. As soon as he saw me, he took one hard draw on the cigarette and flicked it away.

"Good thing you're still here," I said as I got into the car, "or I'd have had a long walk to the bus stop."

"I was waiting for you," he said simply, and started the engine.

I told him my city address. "Thirty yuan," he said. I agreed, and we were on our way. At the end of the long asphalt road, the car turned right, onto a wider street, passing enormous mounds of construction material. In the distance, a line of silos was silhouetted against the horizon. Though we were just a forty-minute drive from the city, everywhere you looked there were old factories, low piles of rubble, industrial-waste dumps, half-deserted farm villages on the brink of being bulldozed and "developed." The farm I'd been sent to work on when I was in my late teens was just a few miles away.

I was in my usual post-visit mood: tired and unsociable. I closed my eyes and drowsed until a sharp horn woke me. When I opened my eyes, there were cars everywhere: we had gotten off the expressway and entered the maw of downtown traffic. We were hardly moving. It was about four o'clock, the beginning of rush hour.

"You were visiting your brother, weren't you?" the driver asked.

My eyes met the driver's in the rearview mirror. "How did you know?"

"Oh, we know the Second Prison folks pretty well. My father used to work there. Your brother is a Democracy Party guy, right?"

"You know about them?"

"Oh, yes, they want a multiparty system. How many years did he get?"

"Nine. He's halfway through."

"Getting any sentence reduction?"

"Nope, because he doesn't admit to any crime."

The driver spat out the window. "What they did is no crime! But it's useless to sit in a prison. Is he in touch with Wuer Kaixi?"

This gave me a start. Wuer Kaixi was a charismatic student leader at Tiananmen Square who, after years of exile in the United States, now lives in Taiwan. "No! How could he be?"

"But you know some foreigners, don't you? You should tell your brother to get out, and get together with the folks in America and Taiwan. Most important thing is: get some guns! How can you beat the Communist Party? Only by armed struggle!"

"That's an interesting idea," I said, taken aback and trying to hide it. "But then China would be in a war. It would make for bloody chaos."

"That would be great!" the driver said.

I was appalled. "If that happened, don't you worry that the biggest victims would be ordinary people?"

"The ordinary people are the biggest victims already!" the driver replied, his face mottled with fury. "You look at this city—at what kind of life the officials and the rich people have, and what kind of shitty life we have."

During the next ten minutes, while navigating traffic on Chang-an Avenue, the driver told me about himself. He had worked in the same state plant for more than twenty years, first as a machine operator, later as a truck driver. Then, a few years earlier, the plant went bankrupt and shut down. All the workers were let go with only meager severance pay.

"But they must give you partial medical insurance," I said. I was thinking about three high school friends with whom I've stayed in touch over the years: all three women, now in their forties, were state factory workers; all were laid off, but all have since found new jobs and are making more money than before. Two of them even own their homes.

"The insurance is a piece of shit!" the driver replied. "It doesn't cover anything. I'm scared of getting sick. If I'm sick, I'm done for. For twenty years we worked for them, and this is how they got rid of us!" He spat again. "You look at this city, all these fancy buildings and restaurants. All for the rich people! People like us can't afford anything!"

On both sides of Changan Avenue, new skyscrapers and giant billboards stood under a murky sky. When it comes to architecture and design, most of this new Beijing looks like some provincial official's dream of modernization. It's clear that there is a lot of money in Beijing, and a great many people are living better than before. But the gap between the rich and the poor has widened. I wondered whether Jianguo, or someone like him, could be the kind of leader that people like this aggrieved cabdriver were waiting for. Under the banner of social justice, they could vent their rage against China's new order.

Despite the emotions that the Tiananmen massacre had awakened in Jianguo, he had a more pressing matter to deal with that year: he had to make a living. Legally, Jianguo and his wife were "black" persons: they had no residential papers, no apartment, no job. Worse still, they had no marketable skills. So for a period they stayed with relatives and took temporary jobs at an adult-education school that Jianguo's younger brother, Jianyi, had started. Jianguo worked as a janitor, his wife as a bookkeeper.

The school was a success, mainly because it offered prep courses for the Test of English as a Foreign Language (TOEFL). During the chill that followed Tiananmen, studying English became ever more popular, and TOEFL was crucial for applying to foreign schools. Jianyi was growing rich, fast. It was an awkward reversal of roles. The two brothers had very different personalities: next to his serious, ambitious, and hardworking big brother, Jianyi was always viewed as a baby-faced "hooligan": he goofed off at school, chased girls, and squandered his money on dining out and having a good time. But in the new China the free-spending playboy was thriving. At first, he'd wanted Jianguo to help him manage the business, but Jianguo declined; he preferred to have more time to read and think, and being a janitor allowed for that. "He is always interested in saving China, but he can't even save himself!" Jianyi once said to me about Jianguo. I wondered how Jianguo felt about pushing a mop around for his little brother.

Jianguo didn't stay on the job long. In the following decade, he moved frequently, from apartment to apartment, and from job to job, mainly low-level office work. But he seemed to have decided that he'd spent enough time reading and thinking; he was eager to try something bigger. After 1992, when the society was seized by an entrepreneurial fever, Jianguo tried a number of ventures. He got involved in a scheme to buy coal in the north and sell it in the south. He sold motorcycles. He set up a factory producing a new licorice soda. (It tasted like cough syrup.) He ran business-training programs. But he always ended up either quitting the job or closing the shop. I had seen him dressed in a badly cut suit taking a bank official out to dinner, trying to get a loan. This wasn't easy since Chinese banks were notorious at snubbing small private entrepreneurs with no connections, and Jianguo certainly wasn't savvy at the subtle art of greasing. His market instinct was no better. By the summer of 1997, the last time I saw him before he was arrested, he had filed for bankruptcy several times. His personal life was in disarray as well. He had divorced his wife of nearly twenty years and married a young, pretty girl from Inner Mongolia who worked in the soda factory. This second marriage lasted less than a year, collapsing as soon as the business did, and Jianguo ended up moving in with his daughter.

By then, Jihong ("Inheriting Red") had been renamed Huiyi ("Wisdom and Pleasure"). The girl attended a community college and spent her time reading pulp romances and chatting with her girlfriends. But she was devoted to her father. When she graduated in 1998, she got a job as a front-desk receptionist at the upscale Jing-lun Hotel and turned over half her salary to him. It was clear to both of them, by now, that he wasn't cut out for business. Then, in 1998, Jianyi died, of a brain tumor, and Jianguo inherited his Beijing apartment. Finally, Jianguo had a place that he could call his own. With a home, and the help of his daughter, he was free to do what he wanted.

That August, I received a long, wistful letter from Jianguo. Jianyi's death, at the age of forty-four, was obviously a shock. "He's gone, and the sense of life's bitter shortness presses on me more urgently," Jianguo wrote. "Yesterday was my forty-seventh birthday. Will my remaining twenty or thirty years also slip away in the blink of an eye?" Now he looked back on his existence:

> My whole life I have had a strong mind but my fate has not been good. Over the past few decades I have been fighting this fate, clenching my teeth and not crying. I am an idealist. For the ideal of democracy, I quit the Party; for the ideal of freedom, I quit my job, over and again; for the ideal of love, I divorced, over and again. To this day I am, intellectually, professionally, financially and emotionally, a "vagabond." . . . The Chinese market is now in a slump, and the majority of businesses are not doing well. China, too, is floating in wind and storm, not knowing where it is heading. When will there be an opportunity for people like me to rise up with the flagpole of rebellion?

Jianguo hadn't changed, I remember thinking with a vague sense of foreboding. Within the striving, clueless businessman was a rebel waiting for a new cause.

What I did not know was that Jianguo had already found it. A couple of years earlier, he had met a man named Xu Wenli, a former railway electrician and a veteran dissident from the Democracy Wall period. (That was a brief political thaw in the late 1970s, when, on a wall at a busy intersection in the heart of Beijing, people put up posters, essays, poems, and mimeographed articles, attracting huge crowds who read and discussed what had been posted. In late 1979, the government cracked down and cleaned it up.) When a friend introduced Jianguo to Xu Wenli, he had just emerged from a dozen years in prison. The two men had passionate discussions about Chinese politics, but at first they also planned to go into business together. One idea was to start a car-rental company. They did some market surveys and decided on their own business titles: Xu would be the chairman of the board, Jianguo the vice chairman. In the end, the venture didn't work out; a loan that Xu was counting on never materialized.

In early 1998, the atmosphere in China was unusually relaxed— the government was negotiating for membership in the World Trade Organization, President Clinton was coming to visit—and small groups of dissidents in different cities decided to take advantage of the new mood, moving to form an opposition party. They settled on the name China Democracy Party. Xu assumed the title of the chairman of the CDP's Beijing branch, Jianguo that of the vice chairman, the two reclaiming their business titles for a loftier cause. With peculiar daring, or naïveté, the officers of the CDP decided to do everything openly: they tried to register the party at the Civil Affairs Bureau, they posted statements and articles on the Internet, they talked to foreign reporters. For a few months, the government allowed these activities, but, shortly after Clinton's visit, in June, a crackdown began, and a first wave of arrests and trials took place. Xu Wenli, among others, received a thirteen-year sentence. Jianguo remained free but was followed by four security agents every day. He assumed the title of the party's executive chairman and carried on: he called meetings and urged the few CDP members who came to stand firm; he posted new statements on the Internet, expressing his political views and demanding the release of Xu Wenli and his other jailed comrades. When the police finally arrested Jianguo, in June 1999, he had long been ready for them. He had even taken to carrying around a toothbrush.

"Heroic deeds are not appropriate to everyday life," the Czech dissident Ludvik Vaculik wrote in the 1970s. "Heroism is acceptable in exceptional situations, but these must not last too long." Another Czech writer, Jirina Siklova, explained why: "Heroism frightened people, and it provided them with the excuse that they were not fit for it and preferred constructive activity. The point was to preserve the nation, not to sacrifice it." Those words were borne out by the tenor of post-Tiananmen Beijing. Over time, a semblance of normalcy returned. Throughout the 1990s, while new market reforms were launched and people's energies were directed toward the pursuit of wealth, the Party established clear guidelines about which topics could be publicly discussed and which topics could not (such as the infamous "three Ts": Tiananmen, Taiwan, and Tibet). As the economy boomed, the ranks of the educated elite splintered: some plunged into commerce and some—notably the economists and the applied scientists—built careers selling their expertise to the government and to corporations. Artists and scholars scrambled to adapt to the marketplace.

Gradually, a tacit consensus emerged, which was captured in the title of a book published in the late 1990s: *Gaobie Gemi* ("Farewell, Revolution"). The book was written by two of the star intellectuals of the previous decade, Li Zehou, a philosopher and historian, and Liu Zaifu, a literary critic. Both men had been hugely influential figures during the movements that led up to Tiananmen. Both became involved with the Tiananmen demonstrations, and ended up living in the United States. Yet their book was a scathing critique of the radicals and the revolutionaries. Looking back upon the past century of Chinese history, Li and Liu observed that attempts to bring about radical change had always resulted either in disaster or in tyranny. China was too big, its problems too numerous and complex, for any quick fix. Incremental reform, not revolution, was the right approach. In a separate article, Li also laid out four successive phases of development—economic progress, personal freedom, social justice, political democracy—that stood between China and full modernity. In other words, achieving real democracy wasn't a matter of throwing a switch.

These were the arguments of two smart, reasonable Chinese with liberal-democratic sympathies. And they struck a chord with other smart, reasonable Chinese who were equally sympathetic toward liberalism but increasingly uncomfortable with the idea of radical change. Though the book was published in Hong Kong, it gave voice to a subtle reconfiguration in the attitude of Mainland elites during the 1990s.

The new consensus was shaped by a curious combination of trends. Outside China, the exiled prodemocracy movement had foundered, beset by factionalism. Inside China, the tone for public life was Deng Xiaoping's mantra, "no debate"—that is, forget ideological deliberation and focus on economic development. While the technocrats moved to the politburo and pushed market reforms, the ideologues stayed in the propaganda ministry and tried to muffle voices of criticism. Meanwhile, the economy kept growing at breakneck speed. As China integrated into the international marketplace, 400 million Chinese were lifted out of poverty. A new affluent class began to emerge in the cities and coastal areas, where the younger generation, reared on the pop culture of consumerism, shied away from politics. As beneficiaries of the boom, they were generally "pro-China"; nationalist sentiments were growing. But "prodemocracy"? It's unclear whether these young people cared enough to give it much thought.

So when Jianguo and his comrades formed the China Democracy Party in 1998, they not only failed to grasp the limits of the government's tolerance, they failed to take the measure of the national mood. For the most part, they lacked deep roots in any particular community; they weren't well educated or connected to the country's elites; and they had little contact with other liberals and reformers. A few, like Xu Wenli, were marginalized because of their former prison records and their continued refusal to recant or compromise. They had the courage of their convictions, and not much else. Some, like Jianguo, had tried to do something "constructive," and join the entrepreneurial ferment, but got nowhere. They had, in short, lost their way in the new era.

When I first started visiting Jianguo in jail, I could tell, despite his disavowals, how much he cared about the outside world's response to what he'd done and to what had been done to him. So I tried to tell him every piece of "positive news" I could find. His eyes would light up, or he'd assume a look of solemn resolve. My task got harder as the CDP faded from the news. In late 2002, Xu Wenli, the star dissident, was released on medical parole and was flown to the United States on Christmas Eve. Afterward, coverage of the other jailed CDP members largely ceased.

Once, I had a sobering conversation with a woman while waiting for the prison interview. She was visiting her younger brother, who had killed another man in a quarrel and had been sentenced to twenty years. "He was in the restaurant business and the guy owed him money," she explained. "He was young, too rash." She asked me what my brother had done. When I told her, she was flabbergasted. "Organizing a party?" she said, and blinked as though I were speaking in tongues. "I didn't know our country still had political prisoners. I thought everyone here got in trouble because of something to do with money."

Another time I was having dinner with a German friend and his Hong Kong wife, a manager at the Shangri-la Hotel in Beijing. When the German friend inquired about Jianguo's case, his wife turned to me and asked in an innocent tone, "So is your brother a redneck?" For a brief moment her husband, one of the most entrenched bourgeois leftists I've known, looked very uncomfortable in his chair.

The last time I saw the CDP mentioned in a major publication was in March 2002, in a profile in the *New York Times Magazine*. The subject of the article was my friend John Kamm, a former American businessman who became a full-time campaigner for Chinese prisoners of conscience. The article dismissed the CDP as "a toothless group of a few hundred members writing essays mainly for one another." The line made me wince. The CDP men could take pride in their status as "subverters" of a totalitarian state. And they could forgive their countrymen for not rising up with them: they are heroic precisely because most other people are not. But how could they face this verdict—of laughable irrelevance—from the *Times*, a symbol of the freedom and democracy for which they'd sacrificed everything? Toothless men writing for one another: the words were heartless. They were also true. And perhaps it didn't much matter that these men were toothless because their powerful opponent had rendered them so, or that they were writing only for each other because in China a message like theirs was not allowed to spread further. I felt like weeping. But I wasn't sure whether it was because I was sorry for Jianguo or angry at him—for being such a fool. While he sat in his tiny cell, day after day, year after year, the world has moved on.

"You can't say the world has forgotten about him," John Kamm insisted when we spoke in 2007. "I haven't! I care about what happens to your brother!" We were drinking coffee in the lobby café of a Beijing hotel where John was staying during one of his trips to China.

John is, by his own description, "a human-rights salesman." Formerly the chairman of the American Chamber of Commerce in Hong Kong, he had a lucrative business career, with a chauffeured Mercedes, maids, and a condo in a prime location. Then, in the mid-1990s he gave all that up to become an advocate for political prisoners in China. Shuttling frequently between Beijing and Washington, D.C., and meeting with high-ranking officials on both sides, John uses everything in his power—hard data, personal connections, cajoling, name-dropping, bargaining—to make sure that the issue of Chinese political prisoners doesn't go away.

He's a big man with a sonorous voice, earthy humor, and gregarious charm. He's also a devout Catholic with a missionary fervor, and his conversation glistens with biblical cadences. ("Justice will flow down like a river and righteousness a mighty stream.") He has been my main advisor on all questions concerning Jianguo and my prison visits, and if Jianguo has been treated better than some political detainees it's probably because of John's efforts. But he acknowledges that Jianguo's name has fallen off the annual list of political prisoners compiled by various Western governments and watchdog groups. I once asked John what he would do if he were in Jianguo's position. John thought for a moment and told me a story about what had happened in the late 1940s when Bertolt Brecht, then living in the United States, was subpoenaed by the House Un-American Activities Committee. He agreed to testify, assured the committee that he had no sympathy for communism, and was thanked for cooperating. Then he flew to Europe, and ended up in East Berlin, where he doesn't seem to have given a second thought to anything he might have professed on the stand. "If I was arrested, I'd do exactly what Brecht did," John told me. "I'd lie to save my ass. Then I'd have a life!"

I sighed. I consider John, who abandoned his career to devote himself to the plight of strangers in someone else's country, to be an American hero. So, if even a man like him would do what was necessary to stay out of jail, why must my brother be so stubborn? Doesn't it make more sense to chip at a wall, little by little, than to bash your head against it?

The harshest comments I have heard about Jianguo come from his own mother. "It's not bravery," she once told me. "It's arrogance and stupidity. He's had a hero complex from childhood. The problem is, he's not a hero. He is a foot soldier who wants to be a general, but without the talent and the skills of a general."

Aunt Zhong was a beautiful woman when she was young. Purged

as a "rightist" in 1957, she lost her job and labored in a camp for years. She is now a little white-haired woman in her seventies, with a kind smile and swollen, aching legs. She has no illusions about the Communist Party, but thinks that change can occur only slowly. In her view, the CDP was "banging an egg against a rock." She had tried to talk Jianguo out of his involvement in the CDP, by reminding him of his responsibilities to his own family. Jianguo had replied with a classical saying: "*Zhong xiao bu neng liang quan*" (忠孝不能两全)— "One must choose between loyalty and filial devotion." Upset by Jianguo's obstinacy, she did not visit him for two years after his arrest.

Her exasperation is reciprocated. Aunt Zhong and I once went to visit Jianguo together. During the interview, we took turns speaking with him by phone. At one point, Aunt Zhong started talking about how China was too big a country to change quickly, how the situation was gradually improving and many things were getting better. I watched Jianguo's face darken steadily, until he said something and Aunt Zhong handed the phone to me. As soon as I got on, Jianguo said in a voice shaking with emotion, "I don't want to listen to her! She only makes me angry!"

After the visit, I told Aunt Zhong about a conversation I'd had with Han Dongfang, a workers'-union activist who had been jailed after Tiananmen. When we met, Han had been living in Hong Kong for many years, hosting a radio call-in show on Chinese labor problems. His credentials as a dissident were impeccable: during his two years in jail, he was tortured, got violently sick, and nearly died. Refusing to yield, he staged a hunger strike. Unlike many Chinese dissidents, though, Han is decidedly urbane (stylish clothes, fluent English, polite manners) and reflective about his past and his personal weaknesses. He was critical of Chinese dissidents on the whole, including himself. "Please don't get me started on that topic," Han told me. "I don't have anything nice to say about the lot." He believed that many Chinese dissidents were afflicted with an inflated self-regard. "It's a sickness so many of us are not aware of," he said. But, Han said, one should not discuss these things with a dissident in prison. "Because to get through prison you need to mobilize all your strength, to be self-righteous and believe that you are a hero," he said. "You need that kind of mental arrogance to prop up your spirit. You cannot afford self-doubt."

Aunt Zhong listened to what Han had told me and accepted the point. She promised not to discuss politics again with Jianguo. "I just hope he will get through his term and come out in good health," she said, shaking her head. "After that, maybe we can all have a good talk with him. I hope he will change his way of thinking and not get back in jail again."

The political landscape in China has grown more complex since the days of the CDP crackdown. After years of rapid growth, China was by 2007 the fourth-largest economy in the world, poised to surpass Germany and Japan before long, and widely expected to catch up with the United States in around 2050. It has the highest foreign-currency reserve in the world. The transformation, however, has been accompanied by endemic corruption, environmental destruction, a widening income gap, and unraveling social services. The policies of President Hu Jintao and Premier Wen Jiabao have tempered some of these problems by eliminating the agricultural tax, paying more attention to the "weaker communities," and taking measures to curb graft. But there's a growing sense that deeper accommodations must be made: on the one side is a swelling mass of disadvantaged people who bear the brunt of social inequity and want more reform and fairness; on the other is a large body of mid- and high-level bureaucrats and Party elites who are in a mercenary alliance with business interests and resist any structural change. Everyone knows that, in the political realm, something will eventually have to give.

Agitation for political reform has, in recent years, grown more assertive while taking on more varied and artful forms: instead of using the fraught term *ren quan* (人权, human rights), for example, people talk about *fa zhi* (法治, the rule of law) and *wei quan* (维权, defending civil rights) to discuss consumer rights or migrant-labor rights or private-property rights. Each year, there are more cases in which journalists expose corruption, lawyers take up civil-rights suits in court, scholars investigate the "blank spots" of history (the Sino-Japanese War, the great famine of 1959–62, the Cultural Revolution), publishers defy taboos and print "sensitive" books. From time to time, a statement or a petition is signed by a group of people, though they usually take pains to present themselves as an assortment of individuals rather than as an organization. Acts of this nature tend to be sporadic and spontaneous, although—with the rapid expansion of the Internet and international communication—news travels fast, and the task of controlling information becomes more daunting. On the Chinese Internet, the voices of criticism are so diverse that censors face the equivalent of a guerrilla war with a thousand fronts. For every offender who gets caught and punished, a hundred get away. These critics can't be easily located, isolated, and destroyed the way the CDP was.

Meanwhile, globalization has made the government and the leaders more mindful of their own image. The official talk of "peaceful rising" and "building a harmonious society" in recent years reflects a softer approach in both international and domestic politics. On the whole, the political atmosphere in China really has eased, and people are a little less afraid. In private and in public, Chinese discussions of political reform are getting louder.

So Aunt Zhong had a point when she told Jianguo that the situation in China is improving. And not everyone has forgotten the CDP incident. Several of my liberal Chinese friends have told me that, thanks to men like Jianguo, who tested "the baseline" with their lives, others now know exactly how far they can push. As one of them, Cui Weiping, put it, "The officials think of us as moderates because of them. They are the reason we are not in prison. For this alone we are grateful." Cui, a literary and film critic, has translated Havel's essays into Chinese. She writes publicly about the need to build civil society in order to battle totalitarian culture. She respects men like Jianguo but says that "real change will come from small, ignoble places. Social movements, not the elite or lone heroes, are going to make history."

Another prominent liberal figure, Xu Youyu, a philosopher at the Chinese Academy of Social Sciences and a forceful advocate of political reform, told me that he would never make "foolish decisions" such as those made by the CDP founders. "It was stupid in terms of political strategy," he said. Xu, who is well-versed in Western analytical philosophy and liberal theory, emphasizes the importance of "rational analysis" before taking any action. "Perhaps they were eager to set a record—to be the first to openly form an opposition party in Communist China," Xu said. "If that's what motivated them, it's the sort of human weakness I could forgive." Like Jianguo, Xu had been a Red Guard, and he has written a candid and moving memoir about the Cultural Revolution, with soul-searching reflections on his own youthful delusions. He signed a copy for Jianguo and asked me to bring it to him. Not surprisingly, the censor at the prison book desk rejected it.

But Jianguo isn't an educator like Xu. He's a man of action. The CDP founders are all men of action, and history has not been kind to them. I remember something I heard a Chinese CEO once say: "The person who takes one step ahead of others is a leader. The person who takes three steps ahead of others is a martyr." The CDP men are martyrs. I used to console myself with the old Chinese saying "Bu yi chengbai lun yingxiong" (不以成败论英雄, "Do not judge a hero by victory or defeat"). Yet Jianguo also seems a mulish simpleton, a man with a black-and-white vision of politics, oblivious of all shades of gray, not to mention the rainbow of hues that you'd need to paint a semblance of Chinese life today. In other moods, I would think of Confucius's remark about one of his disciples, Zilu: "He has daring, but little else."

Neither attitude seems quite right to me now. I recall a conversation I had with Perry Link, a distinguished China scholar at Princeton University, about Wei Jingsheng. Wei is Jianguo's personal hero, a legendary figure in the Chinese democracy movement. Back in 1978, when he was a twenty-eight-year-old electrician, Wei had the audacity to post essays on the Democracy Wall demanding democratization; Deng Xiaoping, he said, was a dictator. Wei was charged, absurdly, with "leaking state secrets," and sentenced to fifteen years in prison. During his time behind bars, through sickness and periods of solitary confinement, he never backed away from his views. Once he had been released, he immediately resumed his prodemocracy writing and activities, and he was sent back to prison. After serving two years of a fourteen-year sentence, he was freed, ostensibly for "medical reasons," and flown to the United States, where he kept up his personal campaign against the Chinese government. The West must not be fooled by [China's] reforms, he warns, for the Communist Party will never change its true nature. What's certain is that Wei will never change. Over time, many of his early admirers have come to see him as a man with a simplistic, static vision of China and the Chinese Communist Party. In fact, the Party appears to be far more agile and adaptive than Wei Jingsheng.

I told Perry about my ambivalence toward people like my brother and Wei. I admired their courage, their deep sense of justice, but felt uncomfortable with their almost religious sense of self-certainty. "People like Wei Jingsheng are like the North Pole," he told me. "They are frozen, but they define a pole."

Yes, I thought, my brother is frozen, with his unchanging, unchangeable vision of what is to be done. He reduces a vast, complicated tangle of problems to a single point source of evil: the Communist Party. End one-party rule, and the evil is eradicated. Even as he was locked up, he has locked the world out, refusing to listen to anything that disturbs his convictions, closing his eyes to a reality ridden with contradictions, ambiguities, and possibilities. For all this, Perry is right: people like Jianguo define a pole.

And, of course, those who locked him up are on the wrong side of history. Liu Ge, a friend who is a partner at an illustrious Beijing law firm, likes to remind me of this. "All the countries that have succeeded in modernization have a multiparty system, while those sticking to one-party rule are losers," Liu said. "Democracy makes a country win and dictatorship makes a country lose. The rulers today want to make China better, and they have done a lot of things well, but they cannot face their ugly past—how they turned China into a place with a hundred holes and a thousand wounds, the Cultural Revolution, the Great Leap Forward, and so on. So they are not confident enough to take radical critics like your brother."

Gradually, though, I have come to feel a certain degree of impatience with the impulse to see Jianguo mainly through the lens of Chinese politics. I'd rather see my brother not as an integer in the realm of political calculation but as a flawed but admirable human being, with perhaps one striking oddity: his uncompromising insistence on upholding his idealism at any cost. A novelist friend of mine who has listened to me talk about Jianguo over the years once compared him to the creatures she'd seen in the 2005 documentary *March of the Penguins*. "The penguins are silly, laughable creatures—they are fat, they waddle, they fall on their bellies, and they are single-minded," she said. "But when they are in the water they are beautiful! What your brother does politically is absurd, but his idealism and his courage in their purity are beautiful."

Maybe the question of whether Jianguo is a hero or a fool is beside the point. Above and beyond the consequences of his action is the moral meaning of his action. By keeping his promise to himself, he has fulfilled his own vision of a righteous life, his own sense of purpose. During one of my prison visits, I mentioned that a former classmate of Jianguo's, an expert on rural issues, had just won a prestigious official award. "That's good," Jianguo replied. "He helps the reform from within the system. I'm outside the system. There are a lot of big intellectuals who can help reform with their knowledge. I don't have enough systematic education to do that. But people like us have a role to play, too." He smiled at me. "Character is fate. Just remember this: your brother is a simple, old-fashioned, outdated, and stubborn man. Once I make up my mind, I stick to it." In the past few years, he has lost much of his hair, and a recent attack of shingles had left some scabs on his forehead, but his face was as serene as I'd ever seen it.

In early 2007, with a year and a half to go, Jianguo started talking about how many books he'd like to finish reading. "Really, it's not bad here," he assured me. "I'll get out in 2008, and if you are in Beijing then, we'll watch the Olympics together." We spoke about several of our Shanghai cousins, all successful businessmen and lawyers. "I'm very happy they do well in their business," Jianguo said. "But each person has his own goal. To achieve democracy in a country, some people must offer their blood and lives in the struggle. Look at South Korea, or Taiwan: there had been so many crackdowns, so many prisoners. But, wave after wave, individuals rose up. They gave their lives to pave the way to their democracy."

His eyes were intent, his gestures expansive; for a moment, you could tell, he had even forgotten that he was in prison. "China is a huge country," he went on. "We have 1.3 billion people. We ought to have at least a few men who are willing to do this."

Postscript

On June 28, 2008, Jianguo was released after serving the last day of his nine-year jail term. A small group of relatives gathered in his apartment to welcome him home. My daughter brought him flowers. Jianguo choked up when we embraced. It was the first time I saw his tears.

In the ensuing three months, during the Beijing summer Olympics, a team of policemen followed him daily, and a police car was parked in front of his residence at night. The policemen were friendly and polite: they accompanied him on shopping trips, carried heavy bags for him, even bargained for him at stores and helped him install an air conditioner at home. Since they followed him anyway, at my suggestion Jianguo would sometimes ride in the police vehicle when he went out. I did it with him a few times as we went to meet friends at restaurants. In the restaurant, the policemen, usually two on a shift, would take a table at the other side of the room, and eat their meal while keeping an eye on us. Once, when Jianguo visited my apartment and spent an entire afternoon and evening talking, napping, eating, I felt sorry for the young agent standing outside, waiting by the staircase, so I offered him a chair. He declined, politely, even a bit shyly. These were some of the most bizarre experiences I have had in China.

"They called me *dage* [大哥, big brother]," Jianguo told me, "but of course they are just doing their job, and they would ransack my place or arrest me anytime if an order is issued."

Then, one day after the Olympics ended, the police car and the agents vanished. After that, Jianguo moved around freely, except on days deemed "sensitive," such as during a special anniversary or a Party congress. On those days, the policemen would "resume their post," watching and restricting Jianguo's movements. Once in 2009, for reasons not completely clear, they took him to the police station for a twelve-hour "inquiry," and confiscated his computer and mobile phone. But when I asked him what happened at the police station, Jianguo laughed: "Oh, I just gave them a big long talk about my views on politics and democracy, while they kept filling my teacup and also let me take a few breaks." It sounded almost like he enjoyed having the police officers as his captive audience!

Lengthy prison life has seriously weakened Jianguo's health. Despite medical treatments and therapy following his release, he suffers numerous ailments and tires easily. Nevertheless, his passion for political reform and his concern with China's social issues remain undiminished. These days he spends a good part of his energy tracking events on the Internet, posting essays, and communicating with a group of friends and kindred spirits. He was among thousands of signatories for "Charter 08," an influential manifesto that called for democratic reforms and an end to the Communist Party's monopoly on power.

After a slightly shortened version of this essay appeared in the

New Yorker magazine on April 23, 2007, several Chinese versions, translated by enthusiastic readers, promptly appeared on the Chinese Internet and, despite official censors' blockage, circulated widely. I have since received many letters from readers across the world who expressed their admiration for Jianguo's courage and conviction.

Incidentally, on the day of Jianguo's release, as relatives surrounded him and chatted, one of the local policemen standing in the room stepped up to me and asked: "You must be Zha Jianguo's sister Zha Jianying, aren't you?"

I confirmed this.

"Well, I have read your essay about your brother," the young policeman said. Then, probably unable to find suitable words to go on, he simply grinned at me broadly.

Servant of the State

On the afternoon of October 18, 2009, the writer Wang Meng addressed a full house at the Frankfurt International Book Fair. It was the fair's last day, and China, this year's guest of honor, had worked hard to demonstrate its cultural appeal. Earlier on, Xi Jinping, designated to be China's next Communist Party secretary, had flown in to open the China theme hall with German chancellor Angela Merkel. Celebratory events followed. The pianist Lang Lang shared a stage with German artists at the old Frankfurt opera house. There were Peking Opera performances, Chinese folk arts on display, forums on China's growing economic and political might.

But all was not rosy. There had been a glitch weeks earlier. Two Chinese dissident authors were invited to an affiliated event and then disinvited; word spread that the organizers dropped the pair under pressure from the Chinese government. The two showed up anyway, but when they spoke at a forum on "China and the World: Feeling and Reality," the official Chinese delegation walked out of the room. The incident caused a sensation, with German media accusing the forum organizer of being "spineless" and caving in to China's censorship of its writers. The organizer was fired quickly. But after a round of protests, a conciliatory tone settled in. By the time the large delegation of Chinese writers and then later, Wang Meng, arrived in town, calmness was restored.

At seventy-five years old, Wang Meng is perhaps the most famous living writer in China. A short, trim man with black-rimmed glasses and a full head of salt-and-pepper hair, Wang has been a versatile man of letters with a long, prolific literary career. He has published widely in nearly every genre, and some of his work is considered the best literary expressions of that time in China. Having served as the culture minister in the 1980s, Wang is accustomed to ceremony. In Frankfurt, Wang was asked to give an overview on the present state of Chinese literature. "Chinese literature is developing very quickly," Wang told the audience, in the blandly diplomatic language of someone whose job it was to put the best face on things. "So is the readers' taste. Whatever accusations exist, I can only say this: Chinese literature is at its best of times. . . . China has over a hundred literary journals, many writers of serious literature, and over a thousand novels published each year. One can say China is a big literary nation."

He might as well have changed the word *literature* to *blogerature*, for his remarks were greeted by a storm of derision on the Chinese Internet, which has an estimated 70 million bloggers. One blogger compared contemporary Chinese literature to Chinese manufactured goods—large quantity, cheap price, low on added value, no brand. How can Wang call this "the best of times"? Is the old man muddleheaded or trying to be sarcastic?

Other remarks were more extreme. Calling Wang a liar and a toady, a popular young blogger named Li Chengpeng offered his verdict:

In truth, Chinese literature is at the same level as North Korea . . . the majority [of Chinese literary publications] are full of falsity and perversity, with many writers taking money from the state and creating junk and gibberish. As for the over thousand novels each year, there are millions of pirated and covert editions . . . if one can call this a big literary nation, then why not call Sweden a big literary nation since it's the number one seller of patterned toilet papers? . . . Wang Meng's way of thinking is the same as the eminent men in all [Chinese] fields: as long as it's large, plentiful, and junky, everything Chinese . . . is at the best of its time.

Li's essay was entitled "Old But Not Dead Becomes Meng," a nasty word play which turns a famous line by Confucius into an insult on Wang's given name. With a tone inversion, Meng (蒙) happens to mean "to fool" or "to lie." Within days Li's blog post received over 150,000 hits, followed by over 2,000 reader comments. A lot of them assaulted and jeered Wang mercilessly.

For two weeks Wang made no response. When he did, his tone was calm. "What I meant was that [Chinese] writers' living and writing environment is at its best time." He was comparing it with Mao's days, he explained, and he was addressing a foreign audience in Germany. It's pointless to talk about it out of that context, he said.

It occurred to me that Wang's speech could be aimed at a particular foreigner at Frankfurt. Wolfgang Kubin, a professor of Chinese studies at Bonn University, is one of the most distinguished Sinologists in Germany, especially in the study and presentation of contemporary Chinese literature. A tall, serious man with an elegant, melancholy face and white hair smoothly brushed back, Professor Kubin had led the German Sinologists to welcome the visiting Chinese writers, many of whom, including Wang, have been his good friends. But the Chinese were well aware of the fact that Herr Kubin has been one of the most outspoken critics of contemporary Chinese literature. In fact, he made waves in Chinese media when he famously "trashed" Chinese studies in a 2006 interview with *Deutsche Welle*, a German magazine. Using the word "trash" three times during the interview, Kubin offered a resoundingly negative evaluation of Chinese writers since 1949. As he sees it, none is a great writer since most of them write poorly because they have a poor mastery of their mother tongue and are ignorant of foreign languages; their awareness is low and their vistas are limited; they despise themselves and each other. And finally, they have no guts whatsoever. Asked whether he considered Gao Xingjian—the first and, so far, only Chinese winner of the Nobel Prize in Literature—to be a great writer, Kubin's reply was glacial: "Gao Xingjian? Don't joke about this."

This was promptly reported in the Chinese media with head-lines like "Famous German Sinologist Shellacks Chinese Literature as Trash." Interestingly, the reaction was a lively mixture, with a good deal of Chinese cheering and applauding Kubin for firing such cannonballs.

Hence, Wang's Frankfurt speech might very well be a gentle yet direct response to Kubin. However, Wang's statement evidently made no dent on Kubin's opinion, for shortly afterward the German made a blasting encore, this time directed especially at contempo-rary Chinese novelists, pronouncing their work as "of rather me-diocre quality." Interviewed by a magazine, Kubin said that all his Chinese counterparts privately hold the view that the contemporary Chinese novelist is an utter ignoramus, one who "has no literary culture, no mastery of his language, doesn't know a word of English, and hasn't the slightest knowledge of foreign literature." In short, on the world stage Chinese novelists are *"tubaozi* [土包子, hillbillies], as one calls migrants in China who have left the countryside for the big cities."

This time, however, few eyebrows were raised at the Kubin *sturmunddrang*, either because the Chinese have grown jaded or they are too busy with other hot topics of the day to bother. No reac-tion either from the Chinese writers, which prompted at least one blogger to comment: "Chinese writers probably can also claim that Kubin is trash, but they have not done so. That shows a humility that contrasts sharply with Kubin's elitist and dismissive criticism."

And no one has heeded another detail: in the 2006 interview, Ku-bin had trashed the Nobel Prize as well. "You have to write poorly in order to win," opined the professor. "If you write well, you will never win it. Therefore the Nobel Prize in literature is also trash."

In China, Wang has long been speculated to be a Nobel candidate. Reports and rumors have circulated for years about the likelihood of his winning it, and the Chinese media regularly takes him to task on the subject: Has he been nominated? What does he think of this year's winner? What's his view of the prize?

Wang's response has been to cool the Chinese obsession. The Nobel Prize has had an uneven record, he would say, it has selected great writers, but has also left out even greater ones. It tends to provoke irrational reaction and goad people into aggression, as when a red cloth dangles before a bull's eyes. He noted a certain pattern in the Nobel selection. "To show that they are *teliduxing* [特立独行, independent and idiosyncratic], they like to award dissident writers in socialist countries, and leftist writers in Western countries."

It's a sharp insight. When Gao Xingjian won the Nobel Prize in 2000, both the Chinese foreign ministry and the official Chinese Writers Association issued angry protestations, calling it a decision based on politics rather than literary merit. Having lived in Europe for over a decade and become a French citizen, Gao is seen as a dissident in exile. At the breaking of the news, Wang was contacted, but he was away and out of reach. In later interviews, he said his own attitude differed from the official stance. Selected by Northern Europeans, Wang said, the Nobel Prize cannot and should not have any obligation to satisfy Chinese standards. Therefore, to worship, envy, denigrate, or oppose it are all meaningless. Instead of criticizing the Nobel Prize, he said, why don't we try to improve our own literary prizes? Or better yet, try to focus on literature itself and produce better works?

While many Chinese writers bemoaned the selection of Gao, whom they do not consider a great writer, Wang has never criticized him. The two men had been friendly in the 1980s and admired one another's work. Gao wrote rave reviews of Wang's fiction, praising its inventiveness and humor. Wang was enthusiastic when Gao published an introductory book on modernist literature. They both fought the ideological clutch on Chinese writing, and they were detested and attacked by the same apparatchiks. They were trench mates in the 1980s Chinese culture wars.

Another little-known fact has to do with the circumstances of Gao's departure from China. In 1988, a West German organization invited Gao to visit for six months, but the Chinese side raised questions about his eligibility, and the Culture Ministry official in charge of foreign travel approval put the case on hold—until Minister Wang intervened. Wang gave the green light. Gao left China and never returned.

To the young Chinese bloggers today, the 1980s is almost ancient history. They are not likely to be aware of or interested in these happenings in the past. And so in the eyes of many young irreverent radicals on the Internet, Wang seems no different than any other old conservatives defending the Chinese Party and all the writers who sold out to the regime.

Recently, proving that Wang's insight about "the Nobel pattern" goes beyond literature, a Chinese dissident writer was nominated for the Nobel Peace Prize. Liu Xiaobo, a literary professor turned human-rights activist, was sentenced to eleven years in prison in December 2009 on charges of "inciting subversion of state power." Liu's main "crime" was co-authoring "Charter 08," a prodemocracy manifesto that called on the Communist Party to enact political reforms and uphold the constitutional rights of Chinese citizens. The document was first signed by 303 Mainland intellectuals (I was among them) and then by thousands of Chinese around the world. The heavy sentence shocked all of us and outraged the international community. A few months later, several former Nobel laureates nominated Liu: Václav Havel, Desmond Tutu, and the Dalai Lama.

The news made me think of Wang. It is not just because of his remark on "the Nobel pattern" but also because of an essay he wrote many years ago, in the heat of a literary debate, in which he dismissed Liu Xiaobo as a fame-mongering opportunist. The circumstances were different, and Wang was not writing about Liu's political action. Still, the essay was rather famous at the time and has deeply damaged Wang's reputation among liberal Chinese intellectuals. One of them is Zhu Xueqin, a Shanghai historian who has since become a prominent public intellectual. Zhu wrote a caustic essay about Wang at the time, and told me recently that his views haven't changed. After the Frankfurt controversy, Zhu sent me a fresh essay. It commemorated Gu Zhun, a persecuted yet fiercely independent thinker during the Cultural Revolution. But Wang came up toward the end of the essay: condemning present Chinese literature as evading reality, Zhu called Wang's Frankfurt speech a shameless lie.

The essay put me in a melancholy mood: I have known Wang and Zhu for many years, and I am fond of both. But they are definitely not fond of one another. So I e-mailed Zhu to say that my opinion of Wang is different from his. After some hesitation, I also e-mailed Wang to express my chagrin at the recent controversy, and attached Zhu's essay.

Both men replied promptly. Zhu's message read: "I know your opinion about Wang is different and that's why I sent you my piece. It wouldn't be interesting if we had the same views."

Wang's message read: "No problem. Whatever. I don't have time to worry about this sort of thing, and I'm long used to it. Thanks."

Two months later, Liu Xiaobo was sentenced. I couldn't help wondering about Wang's reaction. I e-mailed him again. This time, there was no reply.

I first met Wang Meng in the early 1990s, not long after his departure from the Culture Ministry. Despite his national stature, I sensed a vulnerability about the man, which I speculated had to do with the curious situation he was in then. He was loathed by people at both ends of the Chinese ideological spectrum. He was the only Chinese minister who had refused to visit "the heroic soldiers wounded in crushing counterrevolutionary rioters" on Tiananmen Square. Yet, because he had taken his stand in the meekest possible fashion (he pleaded illness), it earned him little admiration among the rebels. Hard-liners and dissidents alike had a simple question: are you with us or against us? Wang had no simple answer. Shaped by some of the most turbulent decades of twentieth-century political history, he found an abiding principle in an aversion to turbulence.

The courtier was once a rebel. Wang Meng was born in 1934, in Beijing, to parents who had arrived from a rural backwater in Hebei province. When he was three, the Japanese invaded China and oc cupied Beijing, and Wang remembers having to bow to the bayo-neted Japanese guards at the city gates. But the most painful aspect of his childhood was the shadow of poverty and the constant battles between his parents, who were trapped in an unhappy, volatile mar-riage. His father, having studied in Beijing and Japan, became en-amored with all things modern and Western. A college teacher and a dreamy idealist, he was prone to grand speeches yet incompetent in practical matters and office politics. As his career foundered, the large family dependent on him struggled with debt and hunger. As a boy Wang sometimes ate "glue"—boiled flour goo—to crush hunger. There were horrendous instances of domestic violence: in a fight, his widowed aunt would pour a pot of hot green-bean soup onto his father, and his drunken father would pull down his pants to embarrass the women.

Wang was the eldest son and was a brilliant student. Winning essay and debate competitions and enjoying tuition waivers, he was loved by his teachers and everyone in his family. But secretively, the sensitive, precocious boy was reading leftist books and was en-thralled by radical ideas about social revolution. His early leftist in-clinations, he joked later, were revealed in a third-grade poem:

If I were a tiger,
I would devour rich people . . .

Soon, the underground Communist agents recruited him, and he set to work as a middle-school agitator. The work was dangerous but exhilarating, giving him a new sense of purpose in life. He was barely fourteen when the Party accepted him as a member. A year later, the Party took over China.

To this day Wang likes to insist that, for a young person, nothing could be more exciting and beautiful than experiencing a victorious revolution. "From this day on, the Chinese people have stood up!" Mao Zedong declared on the rostrum of Tiananmen Square and the entire nation rejoiced. The purity and innocent euphoria of the first days of the People's Republic was among the dearest of Wang's memories. He was addicted to the passionate rallies, the dancing parades, the comradely meetings, and the songs they sang together—they were far more thrilling than anything he had studied at school! He marveled at how, within a few days, Beijing cleaned away its gigantic garbage dump, a notorious problem in the old capital. The revolution, he believed, also swept away in one great stroke the degenerate old way of life that trapped his parents and kept China backward. His trust in the cause was total: how joyful, how proud it was to be a part of something so wonderfully transformative!

He was assigned to work at a district branch of the Communist Youth League. Here, as a young cadre, he learned political skills that would benefit him all his life. Two things he valued the most: first, being watchful and sensitive to different points of views and personalities; second, focusing on the positive and taking the long view. He was, in a way, grooming himself to become a balanced optimist.

Always drawn to literature, Wang spent a full year working on a novel—a lyrical portrait about a group of radicalized teenagers, budding romance mixing with innocent passion for the revolution—that ended up stuck with editors and rounds of revision. Meanwhile, he wrote a novella that changed his life.

"A Young Man Comes to the Organizational Department" (组织部新来的年轻人) caused an immediate uproar when it was published in 1956. The story, set in a district Party office, depicts an idealistic young cadre much like Wang himself clashing with a range of variously jaded, savvy, and corrupt senior Party officials. Parts of the story are tinted with a mildly melancholy mood and hints of a romantic affair. This portrayal of Party officials as questionable characters, of a reality with shades of gray, was unusual at a time when literature served merely as the Party's propaganda trumpet. Established Party apparatchiks at major newspapers accused Wang of harboring unhealthy skepticism and bourgeois sentiments. Given the temper of the time, Wang's budding career could easily have been destroyed.

But something extraordinary happened: Chairman Mao learned of the controversy and intervened. At a Central Party Committee meeting on propaganda work, Mao praised Wang's novella as a work "against bureaucracy." Mao had always worried about the erosion of revolutionary fervor by "bureaucratization." He invented the notion of "permanent revolution" to fight both this tendency toward ossification as well as any rivals to his power. A master manipulator of populism, Mao liked to support the little guy against the big guy in political battles, especially when the latter is perceived as challenging his own authority. According to some later analysts, by backing Wang, Mao wanted to send a message to Peng Zhen, the powerful and popular mayor of Beijing, whom he suspected of being behind the apparatchiks' attack on Wang. "I don't know Wang Meng," Mao said about the obscure twenty-two-year-old. "He's not my son-in-law, but his critics don't convince me. . . . Bureaucracy doesn't exist in Bejing? I support anti-bureaucracy. Wang Meng has literary talent."

Half a century later, Wang described the experience of listening to the tape recording of Mao's remarks in a high official's office. "Sitting there, I felt bathed in spring wind and spring rain. Meanwhile, I warned myself: don't get carried away, watch your performance, be even more modest and cautious after this good fortune has fallen on you from the sky." Mao's words bestowed not only the highest political protection but also instant fame: attacks on Wang evaporated.

Unfortunately, the wind shifted soon. A few months later, when invited to air their opinions, intellectuals grew more critical about the Party rule. Mao switched quickly to attack mode and launched the "Anti-Rightist Campaign." In the ensuing frenzy, a half million people were denounced and sent to labor camps, Wang among them. He was, after all, too small a chip on the great power chessboard to be worthy of the Chairman's continued attention. Stripped of his Party membership, Wang was ordered to a mountainous farm outside Beijing along with a group of fellow "rightists." There, for the next four years, they did menial labor during the day and "self-criticism meetings" in the evenings.

Later Chinese writing about the Maoist purges has tended to depict innocent victims suffering under cruel leadership. But Wang would describe in mordant, sometimes hilarious, detail how nearly all intellectuals, himself included, enthusiastically participated in the campaigns, attacking not only others but themselves.

Most of the "Rightists" were, like Wang, true believers and Party loyalists, and their ordeal drove many to depression, divorce, and suicide. Wang himself underwent a period of crushing self-doubt. He convinced himself that he deserved this retribution for the privileges he had enjoyed, and tried as hard as he could to redeem himself through hard labor. Carrying rocks and planting trees, he wrote later, improved his health, which had been delicate since childhood.

And he was fortunate to have married on the eve of the storm. Cui Ruifang, a gentle, kind young woman Wang had met through Youth League work and courted with passionate love letters, proved to be a lifelong bedrock of emotional support and a kindred spirit. A year older than Wang, she had great faith in him and his literary talents. He would not have survived without her, Wang wrote later. "I was lucky in two things in my life: love and literary success."

In 1962, in the wake of the Great Leap Forward and the devastating famine that killed over 30 million people, the campaign craze slackened and Wang was allowed to move back to the city. It was a relatively peaceful time. Wang and Cui both got teaching jobs, and, for the first time, they and their two young sons (occasional visits home were permitted during the years of exile), were able to live together. The apartment they were allocated was just one room, but it was full of sun.

Wang, however, was restless. Finding the life of a college teacher staid and confining, he longed for a writing career and literary glory. So far he had published very little, and his fiction was criticized as "too intellectual." But he knew nothing about workers and peasants, deemed to be the only worthy subject for "new literature." A sharp decipherer of ideological winds, he also saw disturbing signs in Party directives. Mao had broken with the Soviet Union and constantly suspected Khrushchev-like traitors within his own Party. The political climate was again becoming fraught.

That fall, Wang applied for a transfer to the Xinjiang Uighur Autonomous Region, a far west region populated mostly by Chinese Muslims. The idea was as bold as it was smart because it killed several birds with one stone: the move would answer the Party's call for writers to "delve deep into the grassroots"; would broaden his urban, intellectual canvas; and would fling him far from the political quake center in case of trouble in the future.

Cui supported the idea, and the transfer was quickly approved. In the winter of 1963, the entire Wang family packed their few belongings and boarded the westbound train. At that time, Urumqi, the Region's capital, was a very long way from Beijing—it would take them five days and four nights to reach it. But, excited by their exotic adventure, the Wangs were in such a merry mood they even brought their goldfish in a glass jar.

"How long do you think we'll be there?" Cui asked as the train pulled out of Beijing.

"A few years," Wang replied confidently. "At the most, five years."

Within a week of their arrival, all the goldfish died—Xinjiang's water turned out to be too cold and hard. The Wangs would spend the next sixteen years on the western frontier.

Xinjiang suited Wang. Thanks to some sympathetic officials, he enjoyed friendly treatment at first. Arrangements were made for him to travel extensively to collect materials for writing. He marveled at the region's spectacular beauty: magnificent snowcapped mountains, rocky desert, towering poplars, and lakes as incandescently blue as the sky. He was charmed by the Uighurs' approach to life—by the way peasant families grew roses even when they didn't have enough to eat; they would sometimes eat roses sweetened with sugar. He fell in love with the *nang* (馕, Muslim-style flatbread) and lamb that dominated the local cuisine, was moved by the passionate, melancholy Uighur songs, and enchanted by the "symphonic music" of their language.

But he soon discovered that he was still a subject of *fengsha* (封杀), the word for an official ban on a person and his work, which literally means "seal off to kill." After getting a travel piece into a local magazine, he found that nobody would print more of his writing, nor was he allowed to attend political meetings, a sign that he was in disgrace. On the other hand, he was not treated as an ordinary exile or an outright "enemy of the people." He still received a cadre's salary, even after he was relocated further west to Yining, a town on the western border. There, he spent six years in a Uighur village, living with a Uighur family, sharing their food and bed. He did farm work and learned to ride horses. Idle in his state of political limbo, he channeled all his intellectual energy into learning Uighur, practicing by reciting the *Little Red Book* in the language. The effort was rare for a Han and won him great affection among the villagers. A daughter was born; Cui and Wang named her Joy of Yining, after the Uighur town where they lived.

In 1966, Mao launched the Cultural Revolution. In Beijing and other big cities, intellectuals and bureaucrats were brutalized. The Red Guards ransacked homes, burned books, and beat up teachers, sometimes torturing and killing them. Unable to bear the humilia-tion, some, like the celebrated novelist Lao She, committed suicide. In Yining, a terrified Wang burned all his personal correspon-dence. But geography mattered. The campaign was defanged and descended into a slapdash farce by the time it reached the remote border town, and Wang was protected by his Uighur friends: they hid him in the village during a violent period. The elderly Uighur peasant who sheltered him consoled him: "Don't worry, Old Wang, three kinds of men are always needed in any country: the king, the courtier, and the poet. Sooner or later you will return to your post as a poet."

Wang knew he could do nothing except lie low and bide his time. He learned to smoke, swim, and drink hard liquor, and entertained himself by playing cards with neighbors and friends. Years went by in aimless gloom. On his fortieth birthday, in 1974, Wang an-nounced to his wife that he could wait no more: he would resume writing on that very day. He spent the next year on *The Scenery on This Side*, a novel about Xinjiang rural life, trying laboriously to toe the Party line. It was pure torment. Eventually he had to abandon the hopeless project.

Finally, in 1976, Mao died and the Cultural Revolution came to an end. Like a blade of grass wilting in a long winter, Wang re-joiced at every sign that spring was returning. Watching familiar faces reappear on TV, he was often moved to tears and thought with sadness about those who did not survive to see this day. Though still uncertain, he wrote and submitted new stories eagerly, taking care that they were not too politically risky.

One afternoon in 1978, Wang was making dumplings at home when he saw his wife rushing home through the rain, waving a copy of *People's Literature* that had just arrived in the post office. "Your story is in it!" she yelled as she came inside. Wang grabbed the copy with his flour-stained hands, and couldn't believe how fast it was happening: he was being published in the most prestigious literary journal in China. Soon he was invited to a writers residence at Beidaihe, the famous seaside sanatorium outside Beijing favored by the party VIPs—a sure sign that he was on his way back to the center. He confessed to being "drunkenly happy" when he received the invitation, and quit smoking at once. He spent six weeks at Beidaihe, swimming in the ocean, trading news, and renewing ties with old literati friends.

Everything was happening at amazing speed. Within a year, Wang regained his Party membership, and his first novel, buried in his drawer for twenty-five years, was published to immediate acclaim. Then came the long-awaited call: an order of transfer from the Beijing Writers Association (BWA). In June 1979, the Wangs boarded the eastbound train. A large throng of Uighur and Han friends came to the station to say good-bye. When the train started moving, Cui buried her face in her hands and wept. Wang held back his tears. "We'll come back again," he comforted her. "We'll definitely come again."

The China Writers Association (CWA), was modeled after the Soviet Union's association, which was in turn modeled after the French institution: it's a state-funded organization that has branches in every province and major city, and that plays multiple roles. It sets up literary awards (thus consecrating and supporting certain types of writing and writers on behalf of the state), runs writers' residencies and conferences, manages relations between the state and the writers, and, for those chosen as *zhuanye zuojia* (专业作家, professional writers), it acts like a full-fledged employer.

As a *zhuanye zuojia* on BWA's payroll, Wang received a monthly salary, subsidized housing, and medical coverage. All he had to do was keep writing and publishing. It was a coveted position. The Wangs were happy and content even though their first allocated housing was a mere nine-square-meter room in a noisy building, with a washroom in the hallway and a loudspeaker blaring outside in the evenings. In the sweltering summer heat he would strip off his shirt and, wearing only a pair of shorts, produce page after page.

Short stories, novellas, and essays poured out of him; nearly all were printed in major magazines.

It was a bittersweet, exciting thaw; after decades of repression, the people's passion for change and hunger for new reading were tremendous. Fiction and reportage in particular were favored genres with a big impact on public discussion. Literary journals thrived. In 1980, *People's Literature* had a circulation of 1.5 million; other major literary magazines enjoyed readership almost as robust. Wang's touching, deftly turned portraits of innocents and true believers struggling to survive in a dark time struck a chord: they received glowing reviews and won a large following. He also showed a taste for narrative adventure, experimenting with modernist techniques such as stream of consciousness, which piqued conservatives and stirred debate. Controversy only added frisson and enhanced his reputation as a versatile chameleon. Propelled to national fame, Wang quickly established himself as a major literary figure.

He was also emerging as a savvy cultural official. A quick-witted speaker with impressive rhetorical skills and political acumen, Wang was elected to the CWA governing board and later served as its executive chairman. He pushed for more liberal policies, but, with a knack for striking a tone of "balance," he enjoyed the backing of numerous senior Party leaders with whom he maintained warm, deferential relationships. As though guided by an innate compass about the middle road, he never veered too much to either side. In 1985, Wang was elected to the Communist Party's Central Committee.

That year, Wang's second novel, *Huodong Bian Renxing* (活动变人形—the title refers to a Japanese toy that changes shape when you play with it), was published. Widely considered his best novel, it was set in 1940s Beijing and was based on Wang's own childhood experiences, painting a compelling, depressing picture of life in "old China." The book depicts two parents trapped in an unhappy marriage and, partly as an outgrowth, their son's mounting belief in revolution. The year after its publication, Wang became China's cultural minister.

• • •

Years later, when an artist friend remarked that Wang was "a nice guy but had no achievements as a minister," he protested: "But I lifted the ban on nightclubs!" He did that, and some more. Wang was a decidedly liberal minister. Suave, fair-minded, and exuding good will, he was a great advocate for cultural diversity and tolerance. He urged greater openness in the arts, launching an annual national art festival. He brought Western artists to perform in China: Luciano Pavarotti and Plácido Domingo came as Minister Wang's honored guests. He helped ethnic writers, protected young authors, supported experimental writing, and moved to ease the tension when ideological battles started to take on a sinister tone. He tried to invigorate state-funded enterprises with some market measures.

Yet the ferment of the late 1980s made such gestures seem pallid. The so-called *wenhua re* (文化热, culture fever) was taking hold. Artists and intellectuals pressed against the permissible. "Emancipating the mind" was a Party slogan at the time, but younger writers and critics took the notion much farther than officialdom ever contemplated. They had little time for Wang's cautious meliorism. The mood belonged to the likes of Liu Xiaobo.

Liu, who was born in 1955 to provincial intellectual parents, lived in Inner Mongolia as a teenager, where his father had been sent as part of Mao's Down to the Countryside movement, and spent his early adulthood doing unskilled labor. With the thaw after Mao's death, he went to college at Jilin and did his doctoral work in literature at Beijing Normal University, where he started teaching in 1984. In the mid-1980s, he created a sensation with scathing critiques of eminent scholars and intellectuals of the previous generation, whose work he dismissed as derivative and mediocre. One of his more mischievous assertions was made during a 1989 interview with a Hong Kong magazine: "In a hundred years of colonialism, Hong Kong has changed to what we see today. With China being so big, of course it would take three hundred years of colonialism

to transform it into the way Hong Kong is today." Delightedly pil-
ing outrage upon outrage, he pronounced Confucius "a mediocre
talent"; called for China to be thoroughly Westernized ("if you want
to live like a human being, you must choose wholesale Western-
ization"); and dismissed Gao Xingjian, who went on to win the
2000 Nobel Prize in Literature, as a rank imitator, calling Gao's
celebrated play *The Bus Stop* a vulgarization of *Waiting for Godot*. For
an iconoclast like Liu, cultural critique and political reform were
part of the same struggle.

But Wang had come a very long way from his naive Communist Youth League days. Decades of ceaseless, futile "revolution"
and living at the bottom and on the fringe of society had killed all
his illusions about grand talks and sweeping changes. He was now
a level-headed pragmatic realist, a believer in gradual, incremental improvements. Part of it, perhaps, was because Wang genuinely
endorsed the then-liberal Party leadership under Hu Yaobang and
Zhao Ziyang. As Shao Yanxiang, a poet who sat on the CWA governing board with Wang, put it to me: "In general we harbored our
best hopes for the leadership then, and cast our role as helpers rather
than subverters." Lanky and soft-spoken, Shao was a few years older
than Wang, and the two men shared a warm friendship born out of
very similar experiences: Shao was also a young leftist student who
joined the Communist Party early, was denounced as a "rightist"
in the 1950s (partly due to an essay he wrote in defense of Wang's
novella, then under attack), and was sent to labor camps; he then
enjoyed a triumphant comeback in the 1980s. His sentiment of great
hope for the nation's bright future under a more enlightened Party
leadership was then widespread. Despite constant zigzagging and
many setbacks, it was what made the 1980s a romantic era in China.

Meanwhile, Wang was keenly aware of the viper's nest of seething
hard-liners and his own limited power in the entrenched, complex
web of Chinese state bureaucracy, and he moved with characteristic
caution. His mission, as he saw it, was no more than "building a
bridge of understanding between the Party and the intellectuals,

particularly the writers." In the edgy, boisterous scene of *wenhua re*, he detected symptoms of a certain "messianic complex," the fantasy that culture and society could be transformed, in one swoop, by collective willpower and action. This had been the lesson of the Chinese Revolution. But now, among some intellectuals and their intoxicated followers, he recognized a similar mind-set. Privately, he was alarmed. A consensus builder through compromises, he did not approve of impatient overreaching.

Prudence, however, is not always a universally admired virtue. In those years Wang visited the West frequently, and in the winter of 1986 he was invited to speak at the International PEN Congress in New York on an assigned topic: "The imagination of writers and the imagination of government." Among the other speakers were Günter Grass and Nadine Gordimer. "Government *has no* imagination," Gordimer declared, drawing loud, appreciative laughter. Wang admired her courage in challenging apartheid in South Africa, but found her speech arrogant and condescending. As for the American writers at the conference, Wang wrote later: "I must say that they showed off their liberty in the same way as showing off their new cars." In his speech Wang said that if the government's imagination strayed away from reality and people's wishes, it would lead to disaster; otherwise, it would win support from the people, including the writers—as with Chinese government's present reform and open-door policy. During the Q&A, an American participant named Judith Shapiro hinted that Wang was censoring the speech of another attending Chinese writer. This was not the case. So another American participant who had lived in China stood up to defend Wang, explaining to the audience that in fact Wang had been playing an important role in helping to liberalize writing and thinking in China. But Wang's speech didn't go over well. The *New York Times* wrote sardonically of his cozy relationship with his government.

On the other side of the ocean, hard-liners in China attacked Wang for "negating the Party's leadership on writers" while speaking abroad. Wang was chastened by the experience: a gulf of mis-understanding on one side, a pack of lurching wolves on the other. Later, when *The Nation* asked him to write about his impressions of America, Wang conveyed his admiration of many things, but also his feeling that, if Americans could know not only what they know and can do, but also what they don't know and what can't be done, then they would be an even more lovely people. As for himself, he had this piece of advice: "While you try hard to defend and explain China to foreigners, you must watch your own back!" Perhaps only those who endured similar backstabbing and political trauma could understand such caution.

At the same time, the political situation in China was growing increasingly tense. In 1987, General Party Secretary Hu Yaobang, the most liberal of the Party leaders, was forced to resign. In the ensuing campaign against "bourgeois liberalization," Wang found himself under attack. He survived, but had a premonition of tougher battles to come.

A lighthearted vision of cultural and political reform and its tra-vails plays out in a story that Wang published in early 1989, "Tough Porridge" (坚硬的稀粥), which won China's top literary prize for short fiction. It's about a large family that has always eaten porridge and pickled vegetables for breakfast. The grandfather, a revered but open-minded patriarch, offers to turn his authority over the menu to others. When the family's retainer of four decades takes charge, she starts skimping on ingredients and, with the money she saves, buying the grandfather ginseng royal jelly for his health. Soon, the trendy teenager is trying an all-Western breakfast, to which some family members secretly add Chinese spices, causing digestive woes. Various other reforms are attempted, including democratic voting. People start eating separately. A great-grandson goes off to work at a joint-venture company. The intellectual son and his wife move abroad. Eventually, though, they all return to the porridge break-fast, so plain and so soothing.

Nobody was in a mood to be soothed when, in mid-April 1989,

Hu Yaobang died and students, grieving and angry, started to demonstrate on Tiananmen Square. For many liberals, it was a stand-up-and-be-counted moment. Liu Xiaobo was at Columbia University at the time; when he learned of the protests, he promptly gave up the fellowship and flew back.

But Wang felt dread, not elation, as the demonstrations grew. At one point, he spent seven hours talking down his twenty-year-old daughter, then accompanied her to her university, and waited outside the campus gate until she persuaded her entire class not to take to the street. While he was abroad with a delegation in Europe and Egypt, the situation rapidly deteriorated. Deeply disturbed by the news and anxious to get home, he forgot his suit in an Italian country hotel and suffered diarrhea in Egypt. On June 4, the 1980s—idealistic, naive, fragile—came to a crashing end as the tanks arrived on Tiananmen Square.

The massacre destroyed the tenuous bond between the Party and the intellectuals, forcing some of the most idealistic Chinese into a more combative stance: some renounced their Party membership and openly broke with the regime; some went into exile or were jailed. Wang distanced himself from the henchmen, but he made no renunciations, no protestations. He kept a low profile and kept his mouth shut. In the eyes of the hardened radicals, he behaved no differently from a host of other cowardly functionaries.

On medical leave, he spent the rest of the gloomy summer in Yantai, a seaside town where Cui underwent a surgery for a ruptured appendix. In the hospital with her, he composed moody, elliptical poems, mourning the passing of an era. Anxious about China's and his own future, he almost went back to smoking. In wistful moments, he recalled a favorite Pushkin poem he used to recite in his Xinjiang days:

> *In melancholy times one needs to stay calm,*
> *And believe that pleasant times will come*
> *The heart forever yearns for the future*

But at the present it is often sad
All is transient
All will be gone
And that which is gone will become endearing in remembrance.

Recently, Wang had gently reminded the leadership that, when he first accepted the ministerial post, he had expressed a wish to be allowed to return to his life as a writer after three years of service. His humble request was permitted without further ado. On September 4, 1989, Yang Shangkun, chairman of the People's Republic of China, officially terminated Wang's ministerial appointment.

In all the years I have known Wang, I mentioned Tiananmen to him just once, reporting a remark I'd heard about his "soft landing." Wang corrected me: "These are the exact words: 'He flipped a 360-degree backward somersault and landed standing on his feet.' " His eyes glinted behind his glasses. We both laughed and let the subject drop without another word.

It wasn't an easy time. His act of disloyalty—a high-ranking official disobeys at a moment of state emergency when the sound of tanks was not yet out of earshot—meant that he was willing to face the consequences. It also meant that the apparatchiks who had always detested Wang's liberal tendencies, envied his popularity, backstabbed him, and attempted to sabotage his career were vindicated now: why, Minister Wang has ejected himself—good riddance!

He was the subject of investigations. Some of his former colleagues, including his vice ministers, distanced themselves from him. Conservative publications denounced him. But there were also quiet, sometimes secretive, friendly gestures. More than one retired high official offered encouraging words in private. *Dushu*, a revered intellectual monthly, asked him to write a column. Wang immediately accepted the offer, telling the editor how grateful he was that they were not abandoning him. He appreciated all the extended hands.

But with him newly vulnerable, hard-liners like He Jingzhi, the post-purge cultural minister, and the head of the CWA, a hack writer named Malaqinfu, pushed the idea that Wang's "Tough Porridge" was actually a veiled attack on Deng Xiaoping, who, ostensibly retired, was still the supreme power at the time.

It's hard to convey how unsettling the charge was. China has a long tradition of *yingshe* (影射, shadow assassination), in which writers use allegory to criticize high officials. In fact, the Cultural Revolution was directly triggered by such suspicions: a historical drama written by a Party intellectual was accused of being an oblique attack on Mao. The charge was absurd, but Mao took it seriously; he ordered the newspapers to denounce the author (who eventually died in custody, having been beaten), and the self-fueling mood of paranoia grew into a frenzied nationwide campaign. So when the accusation began to spread, Wang responded forcefully. He wrote to Jiang Zemin, the Party chairman; he filed a libel lawsuit; and, most devastatingly, he released a fawning, obsequious letter that Malaqinfu had privately written to him when he was a newly appointed cultural minister.

Many liberals cheered Wang at the time. Not Liu Xiaobo. Wang disregarded the laws about privacy, Liu wrote many years later, "because he thinks that you have to be petty to handle a petty guy, to be a hooligan to fight a hooligan, but he doesn't seem to understand that this will make all of us hooligans together." It was a lofty statement of principle, indifferent to the real risk of persecution Wang faced.

"I lived through *fengsha* for more than two decades," Wang told me later. "It's an awful state to be in." This time the *fengsha* was briefer. In the fall of 1991, Wang was allowed to attend a writers' event in Singapore; as a former minister, his foreign travel must be granted from the highest level of leadership. A year later he was appointed to be a member of *Zhengxie* (政协), the political consultation body for the government. He retained his benefits and the perks, which are accorded to all former officials by rank. Wang still had, courtesy of the state, his courtyard house (later a large apart-

ment), a secretary, a car, and a driver at his disposal. The smoothness
with which Wang eased himself out of a political tight spot must
have been irritating to his enemies.

Wang gratefully resumed the life of a full-time writer. He had
been, from day one, a reluctant bureaucrat. Despite a reputation of
being "foxy" and "slippery," he never felt he was temperamentally
suited to be a high official. "I'm a straight man, I don't mince my
words when I talk, and I get excited easily." When faced with the
call of wielding brutal power to crush rivals or enemies, he admitted he was a "weakling." "I simply can't harden myself up to do it,"
he said. Another anxiety was that the job would take too much
time away from writing, which he was certain was his true calling.
So he not only requested a three-year term limit, he also tried to
keep on writing between official functions and while traveling. He
would compose a few pages of fiction in the short interval between
checking into a hotel room and going to a meeting. In this fashion
he managed to publish a steady trickle of short stories and articles
while serving as a minister.

Now a "civilian" again, he would rise early and go to his desk
right after breakfast, composing without interruption until noon.
In the next two decades he worked with joyous industriousness and
produced a vast output: novels, short fiction, essays, criticism, verse,
reviews, lectures, and autobiography. He even translated some John
Cheever stories.

Some of his best nonfiction work came out of this period. Though
his formal education ended after middle school, Wang is a prodi-
gious, discerning reader with a gift for writing the kind of charming essay that combines erudition, analysis, and personal insight. In
the early 1990s he turned his attention to classics and produced two
series of widely admired essays, the first on the eighteenth-century
masterpiece novel *Dream of the Red Chamber* and the other on the
legendary late Tang poet Li Shangyin. Wang took on the famous
texts with such fresh energy and scintillating intelligence that the
pieces were a great pleasure to read. They also contained interesting

insights on Chinese politics. Produced shortly after Tiananmen, it was apparent that Wang was delving into history to reveal deeply encrusted patterns of power and psychology and indirectly commenting on the contemporary. Ruthlessly clear-eyed yet compassionate, these essays reverberate between the past and the present China.

Wang also frequently reviewed the works of contemporary writers. These were broad-minded, judicious, thoughtful appraisals. Though chiefly a realist himself, Wang appreciated experimental writing and went out of his way to promote and help young Chinese modernists. But some of his most widely talked about essays were about high Party officials. One, for instance, was a commemoration of Hu Qiaomu, a Politburo member and propaganda chief with whom Wang had enjoyed a decade-long friendship. In Wang's portrait, Hu comes across as a complex figure—at once an arrogant Party loyalist, a scared man, a persecutor, a protector, a harsh ideologue, and a talented man of aristocratic taste (Hu served as Mao's secretary and composed many of Mao's celebrated speeches and poems). Wang was candid about his own warm feelings, even gratitude, toward Hu, but didn't flinch in his assessment of a man who spent his life as a devoted tool of Party propaganda. Chinese writing on such subjects has been either strident or evasive. Wang's powerful, subtle portrayal was a breakthrough.

China's landscape changed dramatically after 1992, the year Deng Xiaoping pushed for deeper marketization during his famous southern tour. As economic reform and growth accelerated, the Party enforced Deng's "no debate" directive on the political front, muzzling the intellectuals and the media. While the population turned to the absorbing business of making money and accumulating wealth, literary journal circulations declined, as did college enrollments in the humanities fields. Intellectuals and writers, at the center of public discourse in the previous decade, splintered and scrambled to adapt: some built new careers and thrived in the marketplace, others grew anxious and felt lost.

It was a confusing, anxiety-ridden transition, and Wang, re-emerging as a high-profile public figure, got himself in trouble repeatedly for his opinions. In 1994, when a reporter asked about his views of the Chinese Writers Association, Wang said that a system of writers living off the state has many problems. The remarks led to an immediate uproar among the many "professional writers" dependent on CWA stipends. How could Wang say this, they demanded, since he himself enjoyed the full VIP treatment of a former minister? As a matter of fact, ten years earlier, Wang had openly proposed to reform the CWA system by mixing reduced state support with market measures. Few had paid attention then, but the issue was explosive now that the government was cutting subsidies for so many state enterprises.

Wang also got involved in a debate known as "the loss of humanistic spirit" (人文精神失落). A group of Shanghai humanities professors fretted that rising consumerism was eroding social mores. Wang disagreed. He published a series of essays that eloquently defended the cultural diversity, market reform, and an end to China's intolerant traditions in the name of utopia. He championed a hugely popular and controversial young novelist named Wang Shuo, whose "hooligan style" some had condemned as subversive. Throngs of scholars and writers joined in, but the debate was messy and confusing: many terms and ideas were so poorly defined that the discussants often argued with more emotion than clarity.

Then came the fateful battle of words that caused serious damage to Wang's reputation. In 1994, a young Nanjing critic named Wang Binbin published an article, "The Too-Clever Chinese Writer." Many Chinese writers, Wang Binbin contended, had well-developed survival skills but lacked the "bookish" courage to tell the truth when it was dangerous to do so. One of his examples was Wang Meng.

Wang flew into a rage. He fired off two essays right away, and one of them ended with four satirical poems. He rejected the demand for others to "be tragically strong" at all costs and at all times, and suggested that the young critic was attacking famous people, Red Guard–style, mainly in order to make his name. But Wang's contemptuous tone grated.

His gravest miscalculation was his attack on Liu Xiaobo. In a piece entitled "Black Horse and Black Pony" (黑马与黑驹), Wang mocked Wang Binbin (the titular "black pony") as a cheap copy of Liu, the "black horse" from the previous decade. Liu was a brave activist during the 1989 protests, and was put behind bars after the Tiananmen massacre. He spent the 1990s in and out of jail and labor camps. Kept under police surveillance and banned from teaching or publishing in China, he could write only for dissident magazines in Hong Kong or overseas, relegated to a shadowy existence in the marginalized dissident community.

In his essay, Wang mocked Liu ruthlessly:

About ten years ago, a black horse appeared on the literary scene; he struck a majestic posture, as though he commanded the wind and clouds and could easily roll back ten thousand troops; he talked the grand talk of someone who considered himself original and everyone and everything beneath him; he killed in the east and hacked in the west, charging to the left and breaking to the right; he employed strong language to take reason under hostage, and wagged his tongue freely; he aimed especially at those who were famous and eminent to launch his attacks and hurl his curses, as though he was entering a no-man's-land and a treasure chamber; he shouted his solitude while grabbing the megaphone, and he praised death as he invited fame and profits; his self-trumpeting and self-aggrandizement, his yelling and selling, have been mocked in private, but also attracted some eyeballs, and was even cheered on by a few youngsters who have always resented the famous and the eminent but were born too late to get a chance to put the tall paper hats on those heads and parade them at the street rallies.

After this caustic reference to the Cultural Revolution, Wang concluded, "He was a hero for a moment, but where is he now?"

The essay read like a piece he had dashed off quickly, surfing along with lithe dexterity and wit-laced panache, but the superior tone was chilling. How could Wang attack a political prisoner who was unable to speak publicly? And this while Tiananmen remained a big taboo and a deep scar in the national psyche. Many, including Wang Binbin, felt that Wang had sunk to character assassination. Several older writers came to Wang Meng's defense: it's inappropriate, they argued, to demand truth-telling and self-sacrifice in absolute terms. But morally, the battle was already lost.

In Chinese cultural life, it was one of those moments of almost tectonic slippage, in which a fault line becomes a chasm. "Among young people, Wang Meng is finished," a Beijing friend told me. "He really hurt their feelings." In truth, Wang's reputation among liberal intellectuals never fully recovered. The Shanghai scholar Zhu Xueqin tells me that he still finds the assault unforgivable. In Zhu's mind, it was *luojing xiashi* (落井下石, dropping a stone over someone's head after he falls into a well).

I had first met Liu in early 1991, at a small hot-pot meal celebrating his release from prison, and I recall the glee with which he mocked various cultural luminaries. There were raised voices after he told the fashionable young novelist at the table that the eminent critic who'd discovered and championed him was nothing but an ignorant trend-monger. He could be overbearing—even, at times, unbearable. But his critical lance was accompanied by genuine courage and political conviction. His role in Tiananmen wasn't simply that of a cheerleader or provocateur: he tried to negotiate with the army for the students' peaceful withdrawal from the square. And he may be the only Tiananmen leader who published a book exposing the movement's moral failings, not least his own. In the same unsparing spirit that Wang wrote about intellectuals under Mao, Liu detailed the vanity, factionalism, self-aggrandizement, and antagonisms that beset the student activists and their intellectual compadres. He shed a harsh light on himself, analyzing his own complex motives: moral passion, opportunism, a yearning for glory and influence.

I have never discussed "Black Horse and Black Pony" with Liu or Wang. In the larger scheme of things, perhaps it could be shrugged off as merely one misfire. It was only one of many essays Wang dashed off on a series of interlinked debates. Yet the controversies evidently affected him deeply. More than a decade later, he wrote four chapters in a memoir about his arguments at the time. But he did not mention Wang Binbin or Liu Xiaobo by name. He said that back then his main fear was the recurring specter of the Cultural Revolution. On guard against any thinking that might push China back to the "ultra-leftist track," he hastily defended market reforms and commercial trends, warts and all, as important steps forward for the nation. The cry over the "loss of humanistic spirit," he thought, came out of those who felt marginalized in a new era, one that chased after the "material" rather than the "spiritual"—the latter being the traditional terrain of the intellectuals. He also recognized in this cry the specter of the Red Guard and the radical culture they grew up with, which, in his view, fed them with a narcissistic, inflated self-image as elite rebels. But after a century of critical destruction, Wang thought, it was now the time for construction. He was particularly incensed by the suggestion that China's problems should be blamed on the lack of courageous martyrs among its intellectuals and writers, when so many of them had already been persecuted or executed, or had committed suicide. "Why are you so bloodthirsty? What about your own record?" he demanded. You could feel the heat hissing on the pages.

But Wang was also self-critical. He chided himself for rushing into these debates without a measure of sympathy for the other side. Why, he should understand that they are attached to their Red Guard youth just as he is attached to his underground Communist activist youth! He was too presumptuous and smug! He failed to see that the young people were fed up with him and his opinions! He had occupied the stage for too long!

In the end, Wang decided to "let it go": "Some say good, some say bad. It's absolutely normal. Most readers don't care at all about these ink fights."

He quoted Diderot to give himself a boost: "If I am attacked by everyone, I shall feel sad. If I am praised by everyone, I shall be too embarrassed to live on, because it would prove that I am a hypocrite."

Although readers have become increasingly fascinated by his essays, Wang for a long time considered himself primarily a fiction writer. The measure of his writerly achievements, he seemed to think, largely depended on how his fiction work was regarded. So, shortly after he was released from official duties, he embarked on his most ambitious writing project: four interlinked novels he dubbed *The Seasons Series* (季节系列). It was a fictional chronicle of the People's Republic of China, from its birth to the present era of reform, as experienced by his generation of revolutionary intellectuals. For the next decade, even as he traveled frequently and took part in periodical "ink battles," Wang worked diligently on the novels, publishing them one by one until the last one came out in 2000.

The reception was lukewarm. The culture fever of the 1980s had given way to a focus on economic growth and entertainment. The rise of a lively pop culture—one increasingly drawn to the Internet and new media—further dampened public interest in serious fiction. But even among the literary community, *The Seasons Series* received mixed reviews. Critics complained that Wang's narrative style, exuberant and witty at its best, has grown garrulous and showy. His language lacked polish and restraint. Descriptions and monologues were heaps of hyperbolic adjectives and set phrases, a murky torrent.

Once I was with Wang and Cui, she mentioned one of the *Seasons* novels and asked what I thought of it. Fumbling for a response, I said I hadn't read it yet. It would have been more accurate to say I wasn't able to finish it. Wang was quick to change the subject, but I could sense his disappointment. He clearly felt that the true value of these novels had not been understood. Nobody else, he felt, would have written about the Chinese revolutionary experiences with such candor and sympathy.

If you are wondering whether an important literary work has fallen victim to critical trends, here's a sample from *The Season of Carnival* (狂欢的季节), taken from a long passage on Mao:

> He is memory, he is emotion, he is achievements, he is nightmare, he is struggle. . . . For the Chinese who tenaciously live on, he is their light and manto [bread], their hot pepper and grain liquor, their door god, their piperazine citrate and qigong . . .
>
> . . . The old man's Cultural Revolution really made a fine mess . . . with his own hands he destroyed the party he established, the country he established, the faith and the order he established, and then he destroyed the Proletarian Cultural Revolution he launched and led . . .
>
> But after all, in the Chinese revolution and the world revolution, this was a people's carnival, Mao Zedong's poetic rhapsody. . . . It was a carnival of heroism and idealism, the thinking of the avant-garde. It was a carnival of willpower, of concept and language, of history created in search of a little new meaning. . . . Human life is a carnival—an experiment with the carnival, to be more precise. . . . Mao Zedong let the young people liberate themselves to the extreme for a time, got rid of all ropes and rules. It excited all of mankind, the entire world. It was a little cruel. But is all that obedience and rigidity not cruel to life and to youth? The Cultural Revolution was indeed thoroughly thrilling. That's why the Berlin Wall was covered with West German Red Guards' posters, and California's Berkeley established the People's Republic of Berkeley, and the French Culture Minister, the writer Malraux, greatly admired Mao Zedong, and later, many years later, the boxing fans all over the world watched on live television: Tyson tattooed his arm with a portrait of Mao. . . .

Okay, my rendering of the original into English is less than satisfying. Still, what is this? Nuggets of insight? Brilliance and complexity? Or is it a hodgepodge of pop philosophy in a bad novel? Setting aside the overwrought prose, what is the reader to make of the suggestion that the Cultural Revolution was just "a little cruel"?

A Cheng, a leading contemporary Chinese novelist widely admired for his elegant language and laconic style, once told me, "Mao is China's Hitler," and he is far from the only one to think so. In fact, since the death toll under Mao's rule far exceeded Hitler's genocide, it may be argued that Mao was far worse than Hitler. By some accounts, the 30 to 45 million deaths during the 1960–62 famine (mainly caused by Mao's policies) surpassed the total death toll of all famines in Chinese history. "The most intolerable thing about Mao was not his ideal," said A Cheng, "but that he took hostage of an entire population and used the lives of ordinary Chinese people in pursuit of his ideals." Although a lot of data and forthright public criticism of Mao is still forbidden—the Party's legitimacy is still bound up with him—many consider him a cynical despot and his rule the greatest catastrophe in Chinese history.

And then there is the havoc he wrought on Chinese culture and language. Many Chinese intellectuals use the term *Mao wenti* (毛文体, Maospeak) to refer to the kind of official language typified by *People's Daily* editorials and CCP propaganda slogans. They held Mao responsible for violating the elegant, refined Mandarin vernacular with this crude, strident language of the new state, the language of the proletarian dictatorship that is full of hubris and lies. Some contend that, after decades of communist rule, *Mao wenti* has seriously and pervasively contaminated Chinese writing, like a linguistic poison, which partly explains why there has been no great literature since 1949.

It's an argument with consequences. There's a sense in which China's future will be determined by which of the contending interpretations of Mao's legacy prevails. Wang's old friend and former

CWA colleague, the poet Shao Yanxiang, has denounced Mao's policies as "anti-humanity." Shao, who now describes institutions like CWA as a *paichusuo* (派出所, district police station), is among a host of retired reformist intellectuals who lost their faith in the CCP after Tiananmen. In his memoir, *Farewell, Mao Zedong*, he candidly details his early Communist indoctrination and later disillusionment. Books like this or *Mao: The Untold Story* by Jung Chang and Jon Halliday are usually published in Hong Kong and banned in the Mainland. But they often get uploaded or excerpted on the Internet (for those who know how to "climb over the Great Firewall" to read) or smuggled in privately, and thus enjoy a limited stealth circulation in the Mainland.

But Wang was not impressed by Chang and Halliday's book. Nor does he agree with Shao's judgment. "Blaming China's problems on Mao is too simplistic," Wang told me. "As a politician, Mao's good deeds and bad deeds were both determined by China's history and culture. He was a political and literary genius. You know his poetry and calligraphy. And I think he did two great things. The first was leaving Hong Kong alone in 1949, even though at that time he could have taken it over with a brigade. The second was breaking with the Soviet Union. So he left a window open to the West and got China out of the big socialist family. But you want to talk about Mao's cruelties? Well, if you recall all the tortures that happened at the Chinese courts, all those slow-cutting executions in the past dynasties, he certainly had plenty of predecessors! But this is not yet the time for a real discussion about Mao."

Other critics have their explanations for Wang's ambivalence toward Mao. "Mao had once helped Wang," Zhu Xueqin says. "It's very human that Wang feels grateful; I fully understand that. Still, after looking at Mao's good side and the bad side, one ultimately should reject Mao. Wang can't take that final step. Why? He's too clever, too calculating."

Others think the explanation is generational. "This is a common phenomenon among Wang's generation of educated Chinese," Xie

Youshun, a noted young literary critic from Fujian, told me. "They tend to be hard on their own biological fathers, but absolutely devoted to their spiritual father figures. Wang is not talking out of political expediency, since denouncing Mao is quite fashionable among intellectuals these days. This is true loyalty."

Xu Zidong, a professor of modern Chinese literature at Hong Kong's Lingnan University, thinks Wang's generation has been brainwashed. "It's difficult for our generation to understand their loyalty and faith in the Communist Party," he said to me. Xu has written a penetrating paper on Wang's second novel, *Huodong Bian Renxing* (活动变人形), and concludes that the novel is partly devised to justify the necessity of the Chinese revolution.

Once, when Wang was being interviewed on television, the host asked him whether he had been "brainwashed" by Communist ideology. Wang chortled: "Brainwashing? Do you think anyone can take out my brain and give it a wash?" He went on explaining how he *chose* to embrace revolution and Communism. It was a choice of free will; there was no coercion. Then he cited a line from a famous poem by the poet Bei Dao: *I do not believe!* "Well," Wang said, his face solemn on the screen, his voice rising slightly. "I can say this about my generation: *We believe!*"

Bei Dao is the Allen Ginsburg of my generation of Chinese who, born in the decade straddling the 1950s and 1960s, grew up in the Cultural Revolution. The themes of his early poetry—alienation, skepticism, personal salvation through romantic love—struck all the keynotes of our journey from being Mao's little red children to bitterly disillusioned adults. We are the generation that embraced the values of liberal democracy when China opened up to the West in the 1980s, and lost our hope again when the government rolled out the tanks in 1989. We have, out of all these experiences, a profound distrust of the Communist Party. Some of us consider the entire communist revolution a tragic mistake in modern Chinese history. And yet, as we journey on from our radical, disillusioned youthful years to the more matured age of our lives, and as China's

reforms and development enter a more complicated phase, our perspectives on the Chinese Revolution, and on our parents, are also
going through revisions. In the 1980s, I had many heated arguments with my father about his faith. The son of a wealthy landlord
turned Communist guerrilla fighter and later persecuted academic
intellectual, his life story was not very different from Wang's. Yet
watching Wang defending his generation's dignity and their choice
to believe, I was both fascinated and touched. In Wang's avowal, I
recognized my father, who, until his death, was willing to revise but
not renounce his faith. I was also touched because Wang is one of
the few Chinese writers who has taken personal responsibility for
his youthful zealotry. There was unsparing honesty and courage in
such writing. Yet why does he feel so compelled to reaffirm a faith
that has brought so much destruction and delusion?

One afternoon in late 2009, I had tea with Wang in Beijing's Sanlian Café, where he had just autographed copies of his new book on
Lao Zi. Dressed in dark slacks and a black jacket with a mandarin
collar, Wang looked both alert and relaxed. In the course of our
chat, I asked about the persistent criticism that he is an apologist for
the Chinese government. "Churchill once said, 'I support democracy not because it is so good, but because it would be worse without
it,'" Wang replied, smiling. "My view on the Chinese Communist
Party is the same: I support it not because it's that good, but because
it would be worse without it. I once told a foreign friend: You are a
very capable man, but if you have to govern China, it won't last more
than three days before the country falls into chaos and you lose your
own head. And if *I* had to take the job? Since I dipped my foot in
Chinese politics a little and I have some understanding of it, I might
last two weeks. After that, China would fall into chaos, and I'd lose
my head too. So, I'm not talking about the legitimacy of the Chinese revolution. I'm talking about its inevitability. Let me tell you
about my recent visit to Beichuan"—the center of the devastating
2008 Sichuan earthquake. "I stood there looking at the sight of the

ruins—it's absolutely terrifying, just awe-striking! Experts tell me: a great earthquake like that is caused by an interlinked assortment of underground movements that have been happening for a thousand years. That's why when it finally erupts, it must shake heaven and earth." He took a sip of tea and looked at me closely. "You see what I mean? It's the same with the Chinese Revolution."

This image he conjured up, of a great, inevitable eruption with terrifying consequences, suddenly reminded me of an earlier conversation at Wang's home. I had pestered Wang then with a similar question: "If the Communists hadn't won, isn't it possible that we Chinese would have suffered less in a different path toward modernization?"

Wang had answered: "Egalitarian leftist trends had been pent up for several thousand years in China until the Opium War gave it a shove. It erupted with the 1911 Revolution, which toppled the imperial system, but it had not reached a climax. It had to go on, driving toward a climax. China has a long tradition of violent dynastic changes. And what are the two things that excite young people the most? Sex and revolution!"

But, I pointed out, despite the revolution's immense human cost, plenty of the social and moral ills—corruption and inequality—of old China persist.

"Yes, they still do, don't they?" he said, frowning. And then he sighed. "Jianying, what happened, happened a long time ago. I'm not interested in these 'what if' questions." With a look of weariness, he ended my probing and turned to other topics.

These conversations reminded me of a story Wang published in the 1980s, "Hard Times to Meet" (相见时难). The protagonist, Wong, seemingly an authorial alter ego, meets with an old friend, a Chinese woman who lives in the United States. Preoccupied by the horrors of the Chinese Revolution, she insists on having a "deeper discussion" with Wong. Wong mentally rehearses his response: "Those who are terrified by the horrors, please go away. History will not stop its forward march for fear of paying a price. . . . You may feel depressed. You have the right to feel depressed. But I have no right to feel depressed, because I am a master of present China." And yet Wong is made so uneasy by the prospect of this conversation that he goes on a trip to avoid her.

"I am a master of present China": that's not something Wang ever said to me. But there was no avoiding the pride, and responsibility, he felt in belonging to the elite of this new China. And then there is the panorama, the long view. Que será, será. The Communist revolution and its victory, the great famine, the Cultural Revolution, the cult of Mao, and the Red Guard's mania . . . the revolution's roaring, soaring fire has swallowed up tens of millions of lives, including its own loyal children, in the course of reaching its climax. But all of these are as interconnected and inevitable as the terrifying, awe-inspiring eruptions of Mother Earth. Tragic, yes, but also somehow magnificent. In this ancient land haunted by an aggregation of ghostly forces and suppressed underground murmurs, it was all part of the great cost we Chinese must pay for our nation's progress to modernity.

Wang was, in a way, putting to good use the two invaluable skills he had acquired in his Youth League days: he was taking the big picture, the long view; and he was balancing his perspectives. That's why, surveying it all from a higher plain, Wang could describe the mistakes of the revolution as "a few staggering footprints in a specific time frame."

What's more important, the revolutionary climax is over, the destructive passions are dissipated, and the Party has turned to a constructive path. So why not be positive and look ahead? As the protagonist in one of his famous short stories, "Salute from a Bolshevik"(布礼), put it sentimentally: "The dear mother may beat her child, but the child will never resent his mother, for the mother's anger will fade and she will hold her child and cry over it."

This is probably how Wang salvaged and kept his faith on a delicate yet firm balance. If he can no longer be an innocent true believer in communism, he can now be a wise true believer in the inevitable progress of history. It also means he can remain an incorrigible optimist. "You can be a real optimist only after you have tasted real bitterness and suffered real pain," Wang likes to say. "For joy will come after you have drained all your tears [泪尽则喜]."

Wang's attitude toward writing is also bathed in a wide-ranging optimism. "A writer should not be a judge of the world," he said in an interview. "He should be an interested, passionate lover of the world. Some writers like to curse the world. I try my best to avoid this type of people, for they affect my appetite and health. The world is rich. Creators of literature should not be narrow-sighted."

Wang often invokes the image of the sea, his favorite symbol for both the world and the best of writing. Here is a phenomenon that inspires awe and worship: its grandeur, its murky force, its violent poetry and great calm, its perpetual energy and all-encompassing capacity, its eternal mystery. In the past thirty years Wang has been spending nearly every summer at Beidaihe, in a seaside hotel owned by the CWA, writing in the morning, swimming in the afternoon. He takes great pride in swimming in the ocean—a feat his father yearned to accomplish but never did, a hobby that has taken on an existential meaning for the son. "Dream of the Sea" (海之梦), one of his most lyrical stories, is set by the sea.

But such a broad view of literature as a loving panoramic mirror of the universe can also be a weakness. Wang has proved himself to be a literary decathlete, a prolific all-around man of letters, but he may also have dissipated his energy by going to so many places and covering so much. Being good at so many things can make good art, but can it make great art?

A friend from Hebei once said to me, "Wang Meng is like a typical Hebei cook. He likes to put everything into the pot—garlic, potato, meat—and mix them all up. But it doesn't mean what comes out is great cuisine."

Xie Youshun told me that he finds Wang's writing very broad but not very deep. "He has covered too wide a range, tried a lot of techniques, but hasn't dug deeply into the human nature. His work is more concerned with human standing in social relations, less with the individual self. He is not interested in interrogating his own soul. He learned from Western modernist fiction at a superficial level, but avoided the painful and ignominious aspects of the self-probing. So in the end his work lacks that intense power of the great literature which touches the depth of your soul." In other words, Wang is not a Dostoevsky or a Tolstoy, nor is he a writer like Joyce or Woolf, who would take a style (like stream of consciousness) to an extreme and exhaust its possibilities as an art form.

But Sun Ganlu, a leading figure in China's modernist fiction scene, ranks Wang as one of the very best writers in contemporary China. "Some writers are stylists, like sculptors who can carve with precision and refinement. They are very good at small, short works. But they are not majestic. Wang writes like a great river gushing a thousand miles with gusto." Sun said in the 1980s he wasn't impressed by Wang's writing, but now he appreciated it much more. He finds Wang's language appealing because it has a special texture and warmth. "It has a young Bolshevik's passion, certain petit bourgeois sentiments, tinges of modernism, and the deep feelings of a man seasoned through so many historical changes. It's a rich body of work where you can find all the important themes of modern China: enlightenment, revolution, reform, tradition, modernity, democracy. His writing is a step-by-step reflection of our times."

If Wang wins the Nobel Prize in Literature one day, Sun said, it would be a fine choice. "Not everything he's written is great, but he has the weight."

Wang keeps on producing at a furious speed. Since finishing the *Seasons Series*, he has put out another novel, dozens of short stories, a book about his "philosophy of life," a three-volume memoir, and about ten books of criticism, lectures, interviews, and essays. Roughly a book and a half per year.

And he travels a great deal, spending one third of every year on visits abroad and domestic. He gives public lectures. He attends literary events. In the past few years, he has also become a frequent talk-show guest on Chinese television. Sometimes I happened to be a guest on one of these talk shows. Every time he showed up at the studio we would end up taping four or five episodes at one shot. With cameras rolling and lights flooding, we would discuss different topics for two to three hours, with hardly a break. Once, to set a date for our next studio taping, Wang text-messaged me his schedule. I couldn't believe my eyes: that month Wang was going on six trips, including Australia and Macao!

Many people are amazed by Wang's energy and productivity; some are slightly puzzled. "He is a polymath, but why is he writing so much?" a literary critic wondered to me. When I told him about the "Hebei cook," he shook his head. "The question isn't why he likes to mix so many things in the pot. The question is: why is he always in the kitchen? It makes you wonder whether he is trying to run away from something."

Wang jokes about his "writing too much" as an overcompensation syndrome from the two decades of *fengsha*, but he is clearly proud of his productivity and his ability to cover the distances. In the Confucian literati tradition, travel is as important as reading in one's quest for true knowledge. It is how one gets to know the real world and real people. But even with the best of intentions and most earnest striving, can someone like Wang, constantly surrounded by VIP privileges and media lights, still retain any authentic access to his surroundings?

In the summer of 2009, I joined Wang and a group of writers on a trip across Xinjiang. The nine-day program was sponsored by the China Writers Association and hosted by its local branches in Xinjiang; it was partly to commemorate Wang's writing about Xinjiang and partly for *caifeng*: giving the writers an opportunity to gather fresh material from the grassroots. Wang has written a lot about Xinjiang. The essays are infused with a deep gratefulness and affection for the region where exile had turned into a blessing. His stories about Uighur life, a series of Chekhov-like tales written in simple language and realist style, are among the best and most moving of his fiction works. Without any narrative indulgence, these works show a real attentiveness to details of ordinary life; the moody beauty of nature, gentle comedy; and black humor amidst disaster. Reading them, you could feel Wang's genuine respect for a culture and a people. Given his cosseted existence, I wondered what remained of such connections.

This was my first CWA event and an eye-opener. From arrival to departure, we were looked after. We stayed at four-star hotels, enjoyed sumptuous meals with endless rounds of liquor, listened to speeches by local officials, watched folk performances, attended regional literary festivals. All was prearranged, and local officials and guides accompanied us everywhere: the daily banquets, the sightseeing tours, the shopping trips. There was no free time to roam the streets or meet people on our own. Toward the end of the program, in Kashgar, a couple of writers and I decided to skip another banquet and venture out on our own to a Uighur neighborhood. Two hours later, an anxious local guide found us and gave us a stern warning not to do it again. "You could be lost," she said, "and get stabbed in a back alley!" But whenever I asked questions about Han-Uighur conflicts, our hosts looked away and changed the subject.

We got more protection than ordinary tourists. When our group traveled from one town to another, police cars came to lead the way for our fleet of vans. I asked one of the local hosts whether this was due to ethnic tension in Xinjiang. No, he answered, it was due to the presence of two minister-ranked officials traveling among us: Tie Ning, the CWA chairwoman, and Wang Meng. This is standard treatment of high officials, he said. When traveling by air, Wang and Tie always fly business class and board the plane from the VIP lane.

When we reached Bayandai, the Uighur village where Wang used to live in the 1970s, a mob of paparazzi descended on him and followed him every step of the way. An elderly man came up and buried his face in Wang's shoulders and started sobbing. He was a former village head who knew Wang from thirty years earlier, and the two men embraced for a long time. Soon Wang was chatting in Uighur with elderly villagers he knew from the old days. On the whole, though, the scene was nearly surreal, with the forest of TV cameras and their glaring lights and a large crowd of onlookers. Another feast waited for us, but Wang barely warmed his seat before he was asked to write some calligraphy for the village. He left the table. The entire entourage took off shortly afterward, leaving the villagers gaping at the cars and vans departing in a storm of dust.

One day, a member of our group happened to overhear Wang laughing and talking in Uighur with the chairman of the Xinjiang regional government, and remarked that Wang sounded like "a different Wang Meng." The Uigur official replied, "Oh, that's the real Wang Meng, the one from Bayandai!" Later, Wang related this exchange to a largely Uighur audience who packed a conference hall to hear him. He talked about how, at certain times in China, you just can't be your real self even if you want to. As he spoke, he grew emotional and started chopping the air with his hand. "That's right: that Uighur-speaking Wang Meng is the real Wang Meng! And the real Wang Meng will always belong to Bayandai, to Xinjiang!" He was almost shouting. The applause of the Uighur audiences was long and hard.

It's obvious that the Uighurs loved and eagerly adopted Wang. Despite the fame and status he had acquired, there was genuineness and spontaneity in the way Uighurs interacted with him: they grabbed him, hugged him, cried, laughed, and involved him in rapid Uighur dialogues. And Wang never hid his delight in such moments. One day, in a plaza near Kashgar, a Uighur lad danced up to Wang during a kitschy "folk" ceremony, followed by a whole troupe of singers and dancers dressed in colorful costumes. Wang instinctively burst into a dance himself, swinging his arms and body and tapping his feet in perfect rhythm, Uighur-style. The lad beamed as though he'd just won the lottery. The crowd cheered wildly. A staged routine had been transformed into an occasion of real merriment.

But such moments were rare among the daily procession of vacuous speeches and pomp. I often wondered how Wang really felt about the extravagance and artificiality of our *caifeng* tour.

On July 5, just hours after we departed from Xinjiang, reality intruded. Bloody riots broke out in the region's capital, triggered by a brawl in southern China in which two Uighurs were slain. By the end of the riots, nearly two hundred people were dead and almost two thousand injured, most of them Han. As ethnic tension escalated, the government placed the region under heavy military patrol and shut down the Internet. Wang kept mute on the subject.

In October, all Chinese media celebrated the sixtieth anniversary of the founding of the People's Republic of China. Wang was a guest in several talk-show segments that month. During one, he described his deep personal bond with the Uighurs, telling a few well-worn stories from his Xinjiang years—like the one about the time he and a Uighur friend sat by the highway and drank a whole bottle of liquor from a shared bicycle bell cup. He sounded warm, self-deprecating, a little nostalgic. The message was unmistaken: ethnic harmony and Han-Uighur friendship is totally possible. But he said nothing about the present. The state media wouldn't allow any critical discussion of the government's ethnic policies, anyway. So the riots went unmentioned.

Wang's pragmatism brought to mind what he had said to me once when his spirits were low. "China is pitiful—any leader who talks about democracy loses his power," he told me. "With per-capita GDP still so low, the country is a paper tiger. The slightest stir of wind and grass makes the government nervous." Then, he had said wistfully, "If only China gets to develop in peace for another twenty years, then the situation will be different. But now?" He sighed. "Well, at least it seems we won't go back to the Maoist age."

•   •   •

If the great accommodator allowed himself dreams of social transformation, I had noticed that devotees of social transformation had been growing less averse to accommodation. The year before our tea at the Sanlian Café, I'd been at a welcome-back dinner that Liu Xiaobo hosted for my brother, Jianguo, who had just served a nine-year term in prison for his pro-democracy activism. For a few months, policemen, two on a shift, followed Jianguo wherever he went. Jianguo, undeterred, talked headily about plans for mobilizing China's dissidents. Liu tamped down Jianguo's enthusiasm, and later asked me to caution my brother about his exaggerated expectations. He used a classical formula: "*Buyao yilan zhongshan xiao!*" (不要一览众山小!, "Don't stand on top of a mountain and think that everything is beneath you!") Recalling Wang's earlier portrait of the cocky black horse, I couldn't help smiling.

Liu, once a firebrand who equated moderation with capitulation and politeness with servility, had matured. Even as he solicited signatures for Charter 08, he was gracious toward those who declined to sign. A Shanghai professor told me that after he decided not to sign—he didn't want to jeopardize a scholarship fund for young Chinese scholars that he was setting up—Liu made a point of telling him that he fully understood and respected his decision, that it was important to be able to continue to do one's best work in one's own field. In the years just before the Chinese state decided it could not tolerate him living as a free man, Liu sought a relationship with the state that was no longer simply combative. The world wouldn't have it so.

Supine acquiescence or intransigent opposition—are those really the choices? Wang's relationship with the Chinese state is ultimately at the center of his work and life. It is also at the center of the controversies about him. Unlike many Chinese liberal intellectuals, who now stress their independent spirit and distance from the state, Wang never tries to separate himself from it. Describing his return from Xinjiang to Beijing, Wang admitted that he "felt moved as soon as I entered the Great Hall of the People," the location for

China's highest state functions. And he continued: "The People's Republic of China has never been an object outside of me. When the water you drink, the food you eat, everything comes from the 'state,' even your shit needs to be handled by the government's hygiene department, how can you really boast about your distance?"

With his warmth and wit, his optimism, his professed faith in (and gentle criticisms of) the Party, Wang humanizes the state. That's why people who rebel against the state and want to break with the system dislike him, and why others like him. Indeed, his own character and long career—the resilience and adaptive skills, the energy and ceaseless activities, the high productivity—are almost a parable of the Chinese state. How can you beat a phenomenon that makes an amazing comeback from a great catastrophe and keeps on going, expanding and reinventing itself?

Jin Zhong, editor of *Open* magazine, a Hong Kong monthly that is vociferously critical of the Chinese Communist Party, sees Wang as influential but dangerous. Wang reminds him of Zhou Enlai, Mao's loyal, obedient premier. "Zhou was a beloved, popular figure among Chinese people because he had a humane and charming personality. But he never challenged Mao, and ultimately he was in the service of great evil." In Jin's opinion, men like Wang are the foundation of China's authoritarian system and would only make it last longer.

Another harsh remark was made by Zhang Er, a Chinese poet who now resides in the United States. "China is still a culture of master and servants: one person rules from the top and all others are subservient. Wang is just an outstanding servant."

The Chinese word for "servant" is usually *puren* (仆人), as in "public servant" (*gongpu*, 公仆). But the word she used, *nucai* (奴才), can be translated as "servant" or "slave material." She chose the pejorative term carefully, because she regards Wang as a familiar specimen—a contemporary example of a long Chinese tradition in which the best and brightest of the country willingly and loyally served the imperial court.

Other liberals take a gentler view. One tells me, "Wang understands China deeply. He knows it could only change gradually, little by little. To rush the process is dangerous. If you look at his whole career as a writer and an official, he comes out as a mainstream moderate. What he embodies is *Zhongyong Zhidao* [中庸之道], the middle way." He was using a Confucian term, alluding to a tradition in which a true gentleman is one who avoids extremes, takes a careful, reasonable measure of all things under heaven, and arrives at an ideal balance.

There is even a sense in which Wang and Liu Xiaobo, seeming opposites, have been participants in a common cause. Liu, after his radical anti-Communist youth, matured into a seasoned, moderate champion of nonviolent political reform: he continued to be critical of the government, but gave it credit for economic reforms and for those instances where it displayed greater tolerance. "I have no enemy and no hatred," Liu stated at his trial. In an article published last February, he wrote that political reform "should be gradual, peaceful, orderly and controllable," that "orderly and controllable social change is better than one which is chaotic and out of control," and that "the order of a bad government is better than the chaos of anarchy." Wang—often from within the palace gates—has been a nimble and persistent advocate of liberalization and tolerance, having battled against the hard-liners throughout his official and literary career. The fact that the two men have, in different ways, both moved toward the center surely says a great deal about where China is today.

Zhongyong zhidao: Wang's sensibilities and talents are, in fact, continuous with the Confucian tradition. If, broadly speaking, Western culture emphasizes liberty, innovation, and the individual, then the Confucian culture emphasizes benevolent rule, refinement, and social harmony. There's some irony in the way that Confucianism—for all the radical attempts of the past century to sweep China's "feudal tradition" into the dustbin of history—has returned with vengeance. The trend is visible in popular TV lectures on *The Analects*, in bestselling books about Confucianism and Taoism; in the vogue of reading classics among schoolchildren and adults. It's in the new government slogan of "building a harmonious society," in Premier Wen Jiabao's penchant for peppering his speeches with classical quotations, in the state-funded establishment of Confucius Institutes abroad. So much of the contemporary culture of the state—the bureaucracy, the power hierarchy, the theatricality and sonorous rhetoric—represent a return to an old imperial tradition. As an anthropologist friend observed to me: "You can almost see the present Chinese bureaucracy and the Communist Party as an extension of the Qing dynasty!" And Wang, like many of the protagonists in his fiction, really does evoke the image of the good official from the Confucian literati tradition: someone loyal to the emperor and the state, compassionate toward the people, diligent in his duties, devoted not to changing the system but making it work better.

Western individualism and democracy, on the other hand, will be a contradiction—a problem for Wang, ultimately. Writing about his many visits to America, Wang noted the intense self-regard and the loneliness of American life, the solitary individual who lives in a big house or on a ranch in the middle of nowhere. The Chinese, he observed, are not fit for such a way of life. He admits that he finds solitude unbearable and gets homesick easily. "China has all kinds of problems," he once said to me, "but it doesn't have loneliness and boredom, because Chinese life is always *renao*!" *Renao* (热闹) means, literally, hot and noisy.

Yet loyalty to Chinese culture has not prevented Wang from promoting cosmopolitanism. In an interview after winning the gold medal in the 2004 Athens Olympics, the hurdler Liu Xiang exclaimed: "This proves the yellow race can also be number one!" Wang pointed out that such words were petty, in bad form, even racist. His criticism set off a barrage of flaming retorts from Liu Xiang's fans. In China, Liu Xiang is a huge icon just like Yao Ming. But Wang is not afraid of criticizing their prickly nationalistic pride.

Wang apparently has an insatiable appetite for foreign travels, and his travel writing is full of an almost childlike delight in the multiplicity of the world: beautiful Africans, Italian pastas, evening bell in Cambridge, and rodeo in Texas—all are noted with admiration and intelligence. He has been tirelessly exhorting the Chinese to be more broad-minded, more openhearted, to learn from others, including Western democracies. To him, the ability to enjoy and learn from others is critical in keeping your own culture vital and rich.

Of course, for Wang, every ship must have an anchor, and all journeys must lead home. Confucius himself was an indefatigable traveler and a humble learner, and every Chinese is familiar with the famous lines from *The Analects*: "Among every three persons I meet on the way, one must be a teacher for me" (三人行必有我师). Yet in the end, what Confucius cared more than anything else in his life was using one's knowledge to serve the country, to provide useful ideas for the state, whether through an official career, or by teaching and writing. It is in this sense that Wang is a descendant of a long and enduring Chinese tradition, and like all who devote their lives to serving a great center of power and culture, his legacy—his achievements and compromises—will be assessed accordingly.

Postscript

On October 8, 2010, Liu Xiaobo was awarded the Nobel Peace Prize while serving his eleven-year sentence in a prison in Liaoning Province. Chinese foreign ministry called the decision of the Nobel Prize Committee a "blasphemy," and the state media blocked all coverage of the news. Many Chinese citizens nonetheless learned about the prize via the Internet and celebrated.

Two weeks earlier, in September, Wang gave a talk at Harvard's Asia Center. Before he arrived, he lamented to me how little dialogue there had been, in the post-1989 era, between Chinese and American writers—less, he said, than between Chinese and American military officials. He carefully prepared his talk in English, in the hopes of speaking across a chasm. Toward the end of his remarks, departing from prepared script, he recalled his childhood deprivations, the humiliating memory of the Japanese occupation, and his youthful involvement in the Chinese revolution. He retold a conversation he had when his grandson turned fourteen, the age Wang joined the Communist Party. When he criticized the boy for spending too much time on computer games, the boy replied, "Poor Grandpa, I understand you. I'm sure you had no toys when you were a kid. If you had a childhood without toys, what else could you do except join the revolution?" As the audience laughed appreciatively, Wang continued, "I think perhaps he is right. Times are different; the world has changed. So has China. I can't imagine that my grandson's generation will copy my path in life. But I firmly believe that all governments in the world have an obligation to provide sufficient toys and good books for the children and young people; otherwise, the young people have the right to join a revolution, to overthrow that useless government." The audience applauded loudly. But Wang was not finished.

"I have mentioned the past repeatedly," he said, "which reminds me of Barbra Streisand's song in the 'The Way We Were.' " He repeated some of the famous lyrics: "*If we had the chance to do it all again, tell me, would we? Could we?*" And then he continued, soberly: "I'd like to tell you, if I had the chance to do it all again, I would and I could as I did. Meanwhile, I still hope I can be your faithful and trustworthy friend, forever."

Epilogue

Predicting China's future is an impossible yet sometimes tempting task. So far, experts' records have not proven to be much better than that of fortune tellers. The efforts remind me of what a friend told me about the 2010 Microsoft convention in Seattle. The two designated major themes at the convention, he informed me, were "Cloud Computing" and "China." Well, perhaps trying to figure out a country like China is much like computing in the clouds! But I, too, have occasionally succumbed to this temptation. In the opening section of *China Pop*, my 1995 book on China's cultural transition after Tiananmen, I wrote:

After a century of tumultuous wars and revolution at great human cost, China appears to have finally turned to the path of 和平演变 (*heping yanbian*), "peaceful evolution." In her long struggle for modernity, this is a profoundly important shift. For the more optimistic champions of gradualist reform, Tiananmen may represent the tragic last gasp of the radical, revolutionary approach to changing China. The current path requires its own human toll and a good deal of compromise and deferment. Yet many believe that, in the long run, this way of change will bring more substantial gains at a lower cost of human sacrifice.

At present, the slow transformation from "communism, Chinese style" to "market economy, socialist style" remains fluid, shifting, its future uncertain. China will probably remain a 四不像 (*sibuxiang*) for a long time, a bizarre, hybrid animal neither horse nor donkey, neither here nor there.

Fifteen years on—it seems to have gone by in a flash!—I can still stand by these statements, but the landscape has altered enough to warrant some additional remarks. As I write these words in fall 2010, China has just surpassed Japan to become the second-largest economy in the world, after overtaking Germany as the largest exporter and the United States as the biggest automobile market; hence its actions have an increasing impact in the international arena. In both political and academic circles around the world, people wonder and fret about the implications of China's reemergence as a global power. Is it going to be a responsible, benign great power that might someday offer an alternative, attractive set of cultural values? Or is it going to be a selfish, menacing great power that will accelerate the depletion of natural resources and challenge world peace?

With some reduction and exaggeration, I think analysts about China loosely fall into two schools.

The Cassandras. People in this school generally find present-day China unappealing and its future alarming. Even if they are impressed by the speed of China's economic ascent, they do not see that rise as a necessarily positive phenomenon. They are convinced that, under China's authoritarian regime, unchecked power does not balance efficiency with fairness or advance inclusive reform but instead creates payoffs largely for the political elite themselves. The official class is hopelessly corrupt and recalcitrant in its resistance against any real, meaningful democratic changes. Economic inequality, an abusive justice system, intolerance of dissent, environmental deprivation, shallow consumerism, and the periodic flaring up of an uptight nationalism all point to a future China that, at best, would be a gross, strident new Asian empire and, at worst, a fascist military state or a big collapsed mess in the wake of an inevitable implosion.

The Cheerleaders. People in this school find today's China remarkable and its future inspiring. Awed by the transformation of the past three decades and recalling China's glorious imperial past, they foresee a renaissance of Chinese civilization that, combined with the country's size and economic might, will turn China into a new cultural mecca over time. They talk admiringly about the "Chinese model of development" where the state plays a strong, decisive role, cutting red tape and supporting enterprises to achieve amazing results. For veteran critics of capitalism and Western hegemony and those uncomfortable about a world where America is the sole superpower, the prospect of a "G2" world where U.S.-China relations will be the dominant bilateral relationship is a welcome phenomenon on the way to a multipolar, more balanced international order that is more sensitive to the stories of developing nations.

Both of these views contain some truth, and yet I cannot fully embrace either one. The Cassandras I respect and often admire; many of my good Chinese friends are severe critics of the Chinese government and Chinese character and are pessimistic about China's future. I consider their criticisms and misgivings extremely valuable and helpful in alerting everyone to the pitfalls and the potential disaster—in fact, their loud protests are partly why their predictions will probably not come true. Personally, however, I just don't see a great doomsday ahead for China. On the other hand, I'm skeptical of all the rosy, romantic interpretations about China and its unique mission for humanity's future. China may be number one in foreign-exchange reserves, but, in per-capita terms, it is still a developing country lagging behind the majority of the world. And it certainly hasn't sorted out the conundrum of its own conflicting values. What exactly is this "harmonious society with a socialist market run by one Party only?" A riddle? Or a symptom of a schizophrenic muddle? In my opinion, at this point and for a long time to come, China's biggest enemy, biggest concern, and biggest project will still be China itself—amounting to more than one-fifth of humanity!

Nevertheless, after three decades of extensive reform and explosive growth, China has entered a different stage of development and is facing a different set of problems. While I don't believe that anyone can really predict its future, I do see a number of fundamentals as crucial in shaping its trajectory.

1. The economic reform since 1978 has put China on a high-speed track of relatively peaceful change. Despite all its flaws and problems, it has mainly been a success story. The period will go down in Chinese history as an age of great industrialization and urbanization. It has lifted hundreds of millions of people from poverty, improved the living standard of the majority of Chinese, produced a sizable emerging urban middle class, laid the foundation of a modern infrastructure, and turned China into the largest manufacturing center in the world. While the pace of growth is likely to slow down at some point, the great process of urbanization and development will continue for decades to come, spreading to the vast, still-poor interior and western regions, dominating the Chinese imagination, and channeling a great deal of national energy through it.

2. The Communist Party has survived numerous crises, remains firmly in power, and is gradually changing. Thanks to reform achievements, it has regained a level of legitimacy both domestically and internationally. It is no longer a Party of utopian ideology but a Party of assorted material interests and a pragmatic agenda. Though not openly admitting its past mistakes, it is acutely aware of the trust deficit as well as the legitimacy issue. It is corrupt. It is paranoïd. It jealously holds on to its power and ruthlessly crushes any challenger. But it is also resourceful and resilient. Up to a point, it is adaptive and responsive to the circumstances and the times. However,

breakthrough change—from a Party that rules by the threat
of violence, coercion, and lies to a Party that accepts general
elections and the rule of law—is extremely difficult and will
probably take generations to accomplish.

3. Totalitarian culture—top-down rule; primacy of the collective
over the individual; a sophisticated, self-serving mammoth
bureaucracy; a subservient, fatalistic attitude toward officials
and politics; lack of public spirit—has existed in China for
two thousand years and has formed certain deeply ingrained
mind-sets and habits. Though profoundly challenged by the
values of Western modernity, it still endures as the most tenacious obstacle in China's path toward true democracy. The
emergence of a civil rights movement in recent years, gathering a swelling rank of people from all walks of life, offers a ray
of hope but faces a long, tough road ahead.

4. Through its economy and via its huge Internet and myriad
circulations and exchanges, China is now deeply, irretriev-
ably connected with the rest of the world. A growing sense
of interdependency compels mutual accommodation. While
the world is coming to terms with China (including making occasionally disturbing gestures of appeasement), China
is also more than ever influenced by and concerned with the
ideas and the ways of the world. Joining the WTO and hosting an Olympics are just two major events to indicate China's desire to be a respectable global citizen. Inside China,
the growing personal freedom and social tolerance, the more
diversified and cosmopolitan strands of culture, the more assertive demands for human dignity and individual rights, the
lively, spirited battle against censorship all have to do with the
fact that China has become a more porous and open society
through its increased connections with the outside world.

Keeping these fundamentals in mind, I tend to cast myself as a
cautious optimist when contemplating China's future. The nation

has paid a very steep tuition to learn the cost of ignorant radical excess during the mad epoch of Maoism. Secular pragmatism and respect for knowledge, major traits of the Chinese attitude toward life in the Confucian tradition, have enjoyed a comeback since then. There is an excessive focus on money-making and materialistic success in present Chinese life, but this is understandable given the long history of poverty and the current vacuum of spiritual belief. However, common sense and decency, moderation and restraint—other aspects of Confucian and Taoist virtues—are also being discussed more and more. Calls for social justice and political reform are getting more insistent. Protests against forced land and housing evacuations, environmentally hazardous projects, police abuse, and state media censorship erupt more frequently, as do workers' demands for higher wages. Among policy-makers and the media, green economy, sustainable development, the need for a more humane labor and migration policy, the importance of indigenous innovation, and soft power have gained new currency in the public discourse. The younger generation, schooled on nationalism and weighed down by an intense, high-pressure education system and an increasingly competitive job market, is also showing signs of renewed interest in culture, historical memory, and social activism.

I'd also like to state my reservations about and disagreement with some of the prevailing arguments in the current Western press about how China is doing and where it should be going. In the wake of the world economic crisis, many praised the Chinese government's able response through a massive stimulus package, and then pushed China to raise its currency value and encourage domestic consumption. Reality is far more complex. The large stimulus package was indeed effective immediately, as reflected in GDP growth figures, but it went heavily into supporting state enterprises, infrastructure projects, housing, and stocks speculation, which has dubious long-term implications: it strengthens an already powerful state at the expense of small- and medium-sized private enterprises; it drives up housing prices, exacerbating inequality and risking a bubble; it builds more roads, railways, and airports so that the same low-wage production model can keep going and reach the interior and western regions. I am disturbed by and critical of the first two happenings, though I find the third one both logical and justifiable. People sometime forget the simple fact that there are several Vietnams in China's vast interior, figuratively speaking, that are still poor and waiting for that road and opportunity. Shifting away from export-oriented low-wage production, upgrading its economy, improving social services, and boosting domestic spending are the right and inevitable direction, but it won't and can't happen quickly due to China's huge population, complex state politics, warped yet hard-to-reform education system, and long cultural tradition that has never emphasized science, technology, or even originality. The situation is far more entangled and difficult than Paul Krugman et al. have made it out to be in the press. Raising the yuan quickly will solve it all? I don't think so. It won't solve America's job and trade imbalance problems, which is clearly Krugman's primary concern; nor will it solve China's inequality and development problems. Even though China is nowhere near Japan in 1987 when Tokyo bowed to U.S. pressure and let the yen appreciate quickly (by 50 percent), some Chinese have taken note of the two-decade Japanese recession that followed afterward. The moral of the story? Gradual, incremental adjustment rather than drastic change is the wiser and probably fairer way to go.

On a related issue, I'd caution against premature reading of recent Chinese strikes for higher wages as a powerful major development toward democracy. So far there has been only one major strike (in a Japanese-run auto factory) that revolved around wages and succeeded. I signed an open petition in support of the strikers but, after logging on to their Web site, I was appalled by all the ugly violent sloganeering posters harking back to Maoist times. Another major worker incident had to do with suicides in a Taiwanese plant (a big Apple supplier), and wages were raised only after the Chinese press and commenters on the Internet started a passionate public campaign. Other incidents of labor unrest have often revolved around corrupt deals government officials and bosses cut at state plants that sell out workers' interests and were often violent, sometimes resulting in bosses being beaten to death. Official rubber-stamp unions have always existed, but independent unions are still strictly forbidden. Wide alliances among workers and thoughtful leadership connecting labor concerns with larger democratic issues have yet to emerge.

Though proud of the country's recent economic ascent, many Chinese elites are keenly aware of the two big questions their nation faces these days: the question of democracy and the question of creativity. The next great transition, from compliant subjects to true citizens, from Made in China to Created in China, will be even harder to achieve than what's been accomplished thus far. It needs a good deal of bold yet careful rethinking about existing political institutions, economic structures, educational philosophy, and cultural conventions. It needs patient consensus building, complicated negotiations, and difficult reforms. It needs vision, resolve, talent, and some luck. It takes courage. It takes time. But everyone understands that only when China solves these critical problems can one then talk about a true cultural renaissance.

Over thirty years ago, the poet Bei Dao wrote: "我不相信!" ("I do not believe!"). More than twenty years ago, the rock singer Cui Jian sang: "我一无所有" ("I have nothing to my name"). These were two of the most famous lines from two of the most celebrated Chinese pop culture icons. They were disillusioned, angry, and sad declarations of an entire generation standing on the ruins of a passionate revolutionary era. After decades of hard work and fast growth, most Chinese today will no longer declare, "I have nothing to my name." Indeed, some Chinese have a lot to their names—China can boast more millionaires than France now and is widely reported to be second only to the United States in the number of dollar billionaires. But what about "believe"? Do the Chinese dare to believe again, and in something besides money?

These days the Chinese pop culture scene is awash with new voices and new images. Sensibilities have changed. Parody and laughter thrive. Entertainment reigns: a thousand TV shows bloom; singing contests and karaoke bars proliferate. An estimated 70 million bloggers have turned the Internet into a crowded space of opinion silos and populist outbursts. Serious probing and artful protest are also alive and kicking, though they must operate with a delicate balance: if their voices do not get drowned out by the deluge of amusement and catch wider attention, then they are carefully watched and must be watchful in turn. The line is blurry and constantly shifting. But prison, staged trials, or the lonely road of exile are always there, awaiting the last hardheaded troublemakers standing. The situation causes confusion, fear, and paralysis: George Orwell stays relevant, but Aldous Huxley has joined him in the Middle Kingdom. The new CCTV building in Beijing stands over this fantastic, irony-charged scene as a giant symbol: an ultra-futuristic, transparent piece of architecture designed by Rem Koolhaas to house the ultra-conservative, opaque headquarters of Chinese state media. The bizarre, potent blend—a Brave New World patrolled by Big Brother—could kill all hopes in the bosoms of warm-blooded idealists, for it seems to mean the worst of all possibilities.

Yet life defies theories. In the face of cheerful indifference, jaded apathy, fearful compromise, cynical swagger, and pure evil, acts of noble courage and idealism—or just common decency—continue to rear their head and surge forward, sometimes when you least expect it. I see it every day in China among civil rights lawyers and NGO workers, investigative journalists and scholars, young bloggers and retired Party officials, wealthy entrepreneurs and small businessmen, student volunteers and lone artists. Some of them are famous public figures; others are ordinary citizens and anonymous individuals. I have written a few of them into this book, but mostly I like to keep them cradled around my heart as lights that sparkle and inspire in moments of soul-eroding pessimism. To me, their existence means that the dream of a future China as not merely a nation of plenty, a nation of strength, but also a nation of grace, is alive and well.

"Never doubt that a small group of thoughtful, committed citizens can change the world," the cultural anthropologist Margaret Mead once wrote. "Indeed, it is the only thing that ever has."

Well, if they can change the world, I'd like to believe that they can change China.

Acknowledgments

Once again, I must thank André Schiffrin, my editor and publisher at the New Press. Ever since publishing *China Pop*, my first book in English, he has urged me to do a sequel, but only nudged me in the gentlest possible manner and waited with seemingly endless patience and unswerving belief. André's steadfast support over the years and his many judicious comments and helpful suggestions on the manuscript are deeply appreciated.

Thanks to Henry Finder, whose brilliance has always dazzled me and who helped me revise and adapt three chapters from this book for the *New Yorker*. Henry is the most laconic and the most amazing editor that I have the good luck to meet and to work with. It has been a great pleasure.

Thanks to Molly Friedrich, my agent, who has a knack for lighting up a day instantly, whose exuberance, candor, insight, and humor have always accompanied her suggestions and advices. Many thanks, Molly, for all your support.

I want to thank the Guggenheim Foundation for a fellowship awarded in 2003 when I moved back to Beijing that helped me get started on this book. Acknowledgment is also due to the India China Institute at the New School: my job, as the China representative for the institute since 2004, has offered me invaluable opportunities to work, travel, and interact with scholars, journalists, and civil society groups in India, China, and the United States. It has been an enriching, sometimes eye-opening experience, and I have benefited intellectually from the many conversations I had with ICI fellows or the ICI-sponsored events in the course of writing this book. To Bob Kerrey, Arjun Appadurai, Paul Goldberger, Tim Marshall, Ashok Gurung, Grace Hou, Anita Deshmukh, Suzanne Dvells, and Nina L. Khrushcheva, all at The New School, for friendly support and encouraging comments on my writing.

I am of course deeply indebted to everyone I have interviewed or talked with in China for this book. Some of their names and their words appear in the book; others, for various reasons, don't. But I am grateful to all those who have informed, debated, argued, and discussed with me on the topics and the characters explored and depicted in this book.

I want to thank Emmett McTigue for reading many draft chapters and offering detailed, useful feedback and for his distinctive perspective, friendship, and enthusiasm about these essays. Appreciation also goes to Leo Carey, who made many good suggestions and helped me revise the chapter "The Barefoot Capitalist."

Thanks to the New Press team for all their assistance with the copyediting and production of the book, especially Jyothi Natarajan and Sarah Fan, whose patient coordination, meticulous attention to detail, and smart professionalism made the process as smooth as it was pleasant. To Hai Zhang and Kaushal Man Shrestha for their helpful feedback on the book cover design.

Finally and as always, I must thank Benjamin Lee, my husband, for his affection and humor; for his tough, discerning comments; for those stimulating, meandering, fun, and helpful discussions over long drinks or long walks after he read a draft; for the "hammer, boost, and light at the end of the tunnel" approach. After all these years, it is still a ball.

This book is dedicated to Siri, who may actually read it someday.

6/11 mc